# Juji Gatame Encyclopedia

## By Steve Scott

TURTLE PRESS          WASHINGTON, DC

To contact the author or to order additional copies of this book:

    Turtle Press
    500 North Washington Street #1545
    Rockville, MD 20849
    800-778-8785
    www.TurtlePress.com

ISBN 978-1-938585-01-2
LCCN 2012018982
Printed in the United States of America

**Warning-Disclaimer**

This book is designed to provide information on the martial arts. It is not the purpose of this book to reprint all the information that is otherwise available to the author, publisher, printer or distributors, but instead to compliment, amplify and supplement other texts. You are urged to read all available material, learn as much as you wish about the subjects covered in this book and tailor the information to your individual needs. Anyone practicing the skills presented in this book should be physically healthy enough to do so and have permission from a licensed physician before participating.

Every effort has been made to make this book as complete and accurate as possible. However, there may be mistakes, both typographical and in content. Therefore, this text should be used only as a general guide and not as the ultimate source of information on the subjects presented here in this book on any topic, skill or subject. The purpose of this book is to provide information and entertain. The techniques and skills presented in this book are dangerous. The author and publishers strongly recommend that anyone practicing these skills and techniques do so under the guidance of a competent, qualified instructor and be physically and mentally capable of practicing them. The author, publisher, printer and distributors shall neither have liability nor responsibility to any person or entity with respect to loss or damages caused, or alleged to have been caused, directly or indirectly, by the information contained in this book. If you do not wish to be bound by the above, you may return this book to the publisher for a full refund.

**Library of Congress Cataloging-in-Publication Data**

Scott, Steve, 1952-
Juji gatame encyclopedia / by Steve Scott.
    p. cm.
ISBN 978-1-938585-01-2
1. Hand-to-hand fighting, Oriental. 2. Arm wrestling. 3. Martial arts--Holding. 4. Mixed martial arts. I. Title.
GV1112.S4524 2012
796.815--dc23
                2012018982

# CONTENTS

The many variations of this application and how this very fundamental movement can be used in so many variations.

*One of the most popular applications of Juji Gatame and its many functional variations.*

**Defense and Escapes**..............................**392**
*The skills and tactics of defending against, and escaping*
*from, Juji Gatame are examined.*

# FOREWORD

When I was a young athlete, two-time Olympian Pat Burris gave me this advice, "Always go for the armlock, because even if the referee doesn't give you the win and makes you stand up again, for the rest of the match, you're fighting an opponent with one working arm. And, if you can't beat a one-armed opponent, you really suck."  I took Pat's advice to heart, as anyone knows who saw me on television winning the Pan American Games. I aggressively attacked my opponent with Juji Gatame, but the referee did not stop the match and made us get back up after groundfighting. Just as Pat predicted, an injured arm hampered my opponent and I won the match. I won quite a few other matches as well, and Juji Gatame was one of my main weapons.

Enough about me (and Pat); what about Steve's book? It is, pure and simple, everything you need to know about armbars and Juji Gatame in particular. The section on exercises specifically designed to build muscle strength used in armlocks is just brilliant. Not only is it a good, safe way to teach beginners some skills, it's also good for any athlete who was ever injured—and all top athletes are injured at some point—to have something they can do to build strength when they are not cleared for grappling.

My favorite part of the book, though, is the drills. To get good at armlocks, you need to do tens of thousands of repetitions. Think about it for a moment, when you are trying a technique that has the potential to dislocate an opponent's arm, you are fighting a motivated individual. Often, there is just one second to catch that arm. And to be able to capitalize on that one second you need to have drilled and drilled so it is almost an instinctive reflex. Let's be honest, though, repetitions can get boring and no amount of yelling "no pain, no gain" from a coach can change that fact. Having a huge variety of drills and exercises, as shown in this book, allows athletes to train from different angles, at different speeds and for different situations. Also, anyone reading this book will benefit from the photos showing the techniques from a variety of angles.

I have known Steve and Becky Scott for many years and count them as friends of mine. Steve is one of the most innovative coaches I know. He's been there and done that and he knows what he is talking about.

AnnMaria DeMars
World Judo Champion
Pan American Games Judo Champion
U.S. National Champion in both Judo and Sambo

# INTRODUCTION

This book concerns itself with one subject and one subject only: Juji Gatame, the Cross-body Armlock. For those who may not be familiar with the subject, Juji Gatame is an armlock used in a variety of fighting sports and martial arts. Basically, the attacker controls and then stretches his opponent's arm out straight, applying pressure as he does it. Actually, it is quite simple in its concept, but complex in its execution.

There may be those who question why so many pages are devoted to the simple act of stretching an opponent's arm. But if you delve into this book, you'll see that the simplicity of this armlock lends itself to a versatility not seen in many other fighting skills or techniques. Maybe Juji Gatame is simple in it concept, but it is multifaceted in its applications, and as you study this book, you will see that there are many applications. Juji Gatame is one of the most versatile and functional techniques in any form of sport combat (or real combat, for that matter).

This book presents a comprehensive, systematic and realistic study of Juji Gatame. Everything presented on the following pages works. The skills featured in this book have proven themselves in every fighting sport used on the planet. There is no fluff or filler material designed to look impressive and to sell books. The skills shown on these pages have been used (and continue to be used) by athletes at all levels of competition in every combat sport that allows joint locks within the structure of its rules. Some techniques and applications may look similar, and there are indeed subtle differences in some of the set ups, entries, breakdowns, rolls, turns and applications presented in the chapters of this book.

While Juji Gatame has proven to be a workhorse in the arsenal of many athletes in a variety of combat sports for many years, there hasn't been (to this author's knowledge) an attempt to produce a book to examine, analyze, catalogue and systematically present this armlock to a large audience. Hopefully, this book will offer a comprehensive and thought-provoking examination of Juji Gatame that can be used as a reliable reference for years to come.

Juji Gatame is the most popular armlock in the world and there are a lot of good reasons why. It is simplicity in motion and because of this, can be adapted in an almost infinite number of ways. Basically, you stretch your opponent's arm over your hips and make him give up; and from this almost humble start, there are limitless ways to make this armlock work in real-world situations.

Over the course of my personal career in judo, sambo, jujitsu and submission grappling, I became fascinated with Juji Gatame. Everyone has a "tokui waza" or favorite technique and Juji Gatame is certainly my favorite technique. Because of this fascination, it's been my approach to methodically study and teach Juji Gatame from a functional perspective. My concern hasn't been in the aesthetics of this armlock; I don't care what a technique looks like as long as it works and works with a high ratio of success. This book offers this functional approach to the study and practice of Juji Gatame, breaking the armlock down into its core components and methodically building it back up, integrating the many factors that make this armlock so versatile, adaptable and successful. Every attempt has been made to examine Juji Gatame from as many different perspectives as possible on the pages of this book. The many set ups, rolls, turns, breakdowns and entry forms used to secure and apply Juji Gatame are dissected, analyzed and examined so that they can be used in real-world situations under the stress of competition and against a resisting and fit opponent. This book also examines a variety of combinations, transitions (from throws or takedowns), defenses and escapes as well as some specific drills that can be useful in developing Juji Gatame. This book also presents a variety of practical and effective traps and levers to control and pry an opponent's arm free and secure the armlock. We will also delve into the tactical applications of Juji Gatame as well as the positions and control methods used to make this armlock work for you and work for with a high ratio of success. Hopefully, this pragmatic approach will offer you, as the reader, a clear picture of how to make this great armlock work for you. Juji Gatame is one of those skills that can be molded to fit the needs of the person doing it and its effectiveness comes from its versatility. I like it because any grappler or fighter in any weight class, man or woman, can make Juji Gatame work and work on a regular basis with a high ratio of success.

As with all techniques, structured, disciplined, consistent and focused training is the key to developing top-level skill. Repetitive drill training on the techniques presented in this book, making sure that the skill is done functionally and correctly, will lead to success. Simply learning a move and practicing it a few times won't build or develop the skills necessary to use it against skilled, resisting, fit and motivated opponents. Disciplined, structured training is necessary for success. Train hard and train smart and it will pay huge benefits for you.

The complete name for the armlock that is the subject of this book is Udehishigi Juji Gatame, or the "arm breaking cross lock." It's an apt name for this effective armlock, but it's also too long and cumbersome for most people. As a result, over the course of its development, the name has been shortened to Juji Gatame, but whatever you call it, the important thing is that this armlock works and works well.

No book or one source of information can offer a complete presentation of any subject, especially an armlock that is as versatile as Juji Gatame. The skills and information presented on these pages reflect my approach to coaching and performing Juji Gatame and I make no claim that everything you need to know about this armlock is contained in this book. In reality however, a lot of practical information is presented in this book and I hope that you can use the information presented on these pages to enhance your study and appreciation of Juji Gatame. Use this book along with the other books that I have written, as well as other books, DVDs and additional sources of information by other authors to supplement your study of Juji Gatame.

My sincere thanks are extended to the many people who helped in the development and production of this book. As with my other books, my wife Becky offered excellent technical advice as well as serving as an objective editor during the writing phase. The athletes and coaches at the Welcome Mat Judo-Jujitsu Club and the Shingitai Jujitsu Association not only patiently posed for many photographs but offered invaluable help in the technical direction taken in this book. Special thanks also go to Turtle Press and Cynthia Kim, who again provided professional excellence in the editing and publication of this book. The photographs in this book are the result of some talented and skilled professionals. My sincere thanks go to Jake Pursley, Terry Smemo, Sharon Vandenberg, Jorge Garcia, Mark Lozano, Victoria Thomas, Rachel Rittman, Holly Weddington and Bill West for the excellent photography they provided for this book.

I have been fortunate to have some good coaches through the years, and the Juji Gatame "bug" bit me long before I met Neil Adams. But the brief time spent training with Neil gave me a wider view and appreciation of what Juji Gatame was and how it could be used as a major weapon at all levels of competition. Neil's influence on my personal appreciation of Juji Gatame has been profound; and as a result, the athletes who have trained with me and used this versatile armlock with success have benefited from his influence. My sincere thanks are extended to Neil.

I hope, as a coach and author, that you can use the skills and techniques presented in this book to enhance your success in the world's most popular and effective armlock, Juji Gatame. Beating an opponent by stretching his arm and making him tap out is an "up close and personal" way of winning. No fighter or athlete with any pride in his soul wants to ever give up to an opponent and I always tell my athletes that if you make your opponent submit to you, he will never forgive you and never forget you. With that being said, let's use this book to take a look at how to make opponents never forgive or forget you.

I hope you enjoy this book. Best wishes, keep training and keep learning.

Steve Scott

## ▰▰▰ TECHNICAL TIP ▰▰▰

**This book is for athletes and coaches in every combat sport or area of personal combat. The act of trapping, stretching and locking an opponent's arm is not restricted to only one discipline of fighting or grappling. A good technique is a good technique, no matter who does it or in what sport or context it is done. Many techniques or positions shown in this book can be done with or without a judogi or jujitsugi. A majority of the photos show the athletes demonstrating the skills in a judogi. In other photos, the sequence of action shows athletes who are not wearing a judogi or jujitsugi. (Most of the photos in this book were taken during actual workouts at Welcome Mat.) My belief is that the core, basic and fundamental technical skills of Juji Gatame should be sound enough so that it does not matter what combat sport it is done in or what type of clothing is worn. There are, however, some specific techniques or variations that require a judogi or jujitsugi, and when this is the situation, it will be clearly presented as such.**

*The photographs used in this book were taken at various AAU freestyle judo competitions as well as during workouts at the Welcome Mat Judo-Jujitsu Club. I wish to thank all the athletes and coaches who patiently allowed themselves to be photographed during their valuable training time. Their skills and expertise added much to the content of this book.*
*Steve Scott*

# USING THIS BOOK

As stated in the Introduction, this book is about one subject and one subject only: Juji Gatame. There's a lot to be said about Juji Gatame and the goal of this book is to examine, dissect, analyze and synthesize this armlock from as many applications, positions and functional situations as possible. No claim is being made that every variation or application of Juji Gatame will be seen on these pages, but there are a lot of ways to do Juji Gatame presented in this book and every attempt has been made to offer the most comprehensive and exhaustive work on this subject in print. The purpose of this book is to serve as a reliable, accurate and realistic source of information and instruction on the subject of Juji Gatame and make as complete an analysis as possible of why and how this armlock works. It is hoped that you, as the reader, will refer to this book time and again for many years to come. It is also hoped that this book stimulates thought by anyone who reads it and this thought is transferred into the action of new and practical applications of this great armlock.

This is the first book, of which this author is aware, that attempts to systematically present Juji Gatame as a singular subject and analyze its many applications into functional, real-world terms. From quite a few years of study and analysis, four specific and unique applications of Juji Gatame have been identified and are presented in this book. They are: 1) Spinning Juji Gatame, 2) Back Roll Juji Gatame, 3) Head Roll Juji Gatame and 4) Hip Roll Juji Gatame. These four, distinctive applications of the armlock are analyzed and examined methodically and then applied in realistic and functional ways that are useful for any combat sport or method of fighting.

Some may wonder why a single book is devoted to the specific subject of Juji Gatame. Why not? Like any skill or interest of any subject there are those who find an affinity for the subject and want to explore it as thoroughly as possible. This is the case in this instance. I was bitten by the Juji Gatame "bug" many years ago and was (and continue to be) impressed by the versatility and reliability of this technique. No matter what combat sport it is used in, Juji Gatame time and again, has proved to be one of the mainstays of successful, effective and practical groundfighting. An athlete who has the reputation of stretching arms is feared, and if not feared, certainly respected by his or her peers. This book is for those of you have been bitten by the Juji Gatame "bug" as well as for everyone else who may want a reliable reference and source of information on the subject. Juji Gatame may, indeed, be only one armlock, but it has

an infinite number of applications limited only by the imagination and creativity of the people doing it.

This book will examine as many functional ways of controlling an opponent and then applying Juji Gatame as possible. As said before, not every variation or application of Juji Gatame is presented in this book, but an honest attempt has been made to systematically and methodically catalogue and examine as many ways to do this armlock as possible.

## TECHNICAL TIP

**Many variations of Juji Gatame will be presented in this book. Some may be similar to the point they look alike to an inexperienced or untrained eye or even at first glance to an experienced coach or athlete. Every application and variation is different from the others and in some cases, the variations are subtle, but every application of Juji Gatame is practical, effective and most of all functional.**

# JUJI GATAME: THE WORLD'S MOST POPULAR ARMLOCK

## "THE PURPOSE OF FIGHTING IS TO WIN." GEORGE MASON

## SOME BACKGROUND AND HISTORY ABOUT JUJI GATAME

There are, fundamentally, two core ways of "locking" an arm. You either bend it over a fulcrum to cause pain or you straighten and stretch it over a fulcrum to cause pain. Juji Gatame is one of four primary armlocks that attack the elbow joint (as well as shoulder joint). There will be more on the four primary armlocks later in this chapter.

Juji Gatame, the cross-body armlock, has been the most consistently used joint lock for many years in a variety of combat sports and in many different applications of self-defense. Whether it's judo, sambo, jujitsu, submission grappling, BJJ, MMA or anything else, athletes and coaches use and respect this armlock. Historically, Juji Gatame was not widely popular until the sambo grapplers of the former Soviet Union began their innovations with armlocks and groundfighting in general. Other European judo athletes and coaches watched and learned what the Soviets were doing and quickly began an intense development of Juji Gatame as an offensive weapon.

When the Soviets burst onto the international judo scene in 1962 at the European Judo Union Championships and inelegantly took their opponents to the mat and made them submit with armlocks and other submission techniques not previously seen, the world of judo (and ultimately, the world of combat sports) changed forever. This was the first exposure to sambo seen by athletes and coaches of Western nations and the world at large. Sambo, the Soviet hybrid grappling sport, took a decidedly utilitarian approach to all phases of sport combat, and in this case, to armlocks. Up to that point in history, no major judo champion on the international level had really developed his groundfighting skills to the point that Juji Gatame was a primary method of winning matches. Traditionally, judo has showed preference to throwing techniques over groundfighting techniques. Catch-as-Can Wrestling, the historical forerunner (along with judo) to some of today's submission grappling, used its version of what we now call Juji Gatame based on early Celtic and Breton forms of European wrestling. After some exposure to Japanese professional wrestlers who were former judo athletes in the early 1900s, several variations of the cross-body armlock were seen in professional wrestling in North America, South America and Europe. But no one was doing flying armlock attacks or well-practiced rolls, breakdowns or entries to Juji Gatame until the Soviet sambo wrestlers appeared on the scene. The Japanese invented Juji Gatame, but it was the Soviets who developed it and showed the world that this armlock is a viable technical skill in world-class competition.

The Soviet sambo/judo men competed in the 1964 Olympics in Tokyo and won four bronze medals proving that this no-nonsense form of grappling called sambo was on the international scene to stay. These sambo men were less interested in what the judo world thought of them than they were in winning matches. Judo was in the initial stages of becoming an international sport in the 1960s. It was making the transition from being a martial "art" to more of a martial "sport." Athletes were more interested in results than the aesthetics of a particular technique. The concept that a technique should be performed based on its function more than the aesthetic quality was quickly becoming the standard in European (and eventually international) judo circles. Soviet athletes were winning on a regular basis in international judo tournaments with their variations of Juji Gatame, and in several cases, against established Japanese judo champions. However, it can not be emphasized enough, that had it not been for the sound fundamentals initially developed by Kodokan Judo, Juji Gatame would not have gained the technical soundness or complexity (and resulting dominance) it has in the world of combat sports.

This author's personal appreciation for Juji Gatame took place initially in 1976 after getting involved in the sport of sambo. Having been involved in judo and jujitsu since 1965, I wanted to try something new and my

coach Ken Regennitter suggested that I try the rough and tumble grappling sport called sambo. I enjoyed groundfighting and took to submission techniques in particular. Ken had seen sambo before and knew that it placed emphasis on armlocks and leglocks and he thought it might be something that I would enjoy. He was right. Sambo was in its infancy in the United States in those years but I was determined to find someone who could teach me. Keep in mind that there was no such thing as the Internet at that time where someone could learn or research new skills. Often, learning more about sambo (and specifically Juji Gatame) was the result of finding someone who would actually get on the mat with you and personally teach you the fundamentals. This was certainly my experience, as I was fortunate enough to meet the Scotsman Maurice Allen in 1976 through our mutual friend Dr. Ivan Olsen. Maurice was the World Sambo Champion in 1975 and was the first person to expose me to how Juji Gatame could be used as an effective and functional weapon. Later, sometime in the late 1980s, I was fortunate enough to meet Neil Adams, the 1981 World Judo Champion from Great Britain, who was (and continues to be) well known and respected for his ability at Juji Gatame. (Neil won his World Championship with Juji Gatame over his Japanese opponent.) Over the next several years, I was able to spend (all too brief) time learning Juji Gatame from Neil. Eventually, several of us made the trip from the United States to Neil's dojo in Coventry, England to spend a few weeks training with him. I was amazed at the fluidity and versatility of Neil's approach to Juji Gatame and the brief period of time spent with Neil gave me a real appreciation for the effectiveness of this armlock, even against elite-level opposition. For the record, Neil informed me that Alexander Iatskevich, the world-class judo/sambo man from the Soviet Union, heavily influenced him in his thinking, training and development of Juji Gatame. Iatskevich, like Adams, certainly deserves a good share of the credit for exposing many people all over the world (this author included) to the functional effectiveness of Juji Gatame. Of course, there have been many other exponents of Juji Gatame who have added tremendously to its development, but the people previously mentioned are the ones who motivated me in my personal journey.

For reasons that still cannot be explained, the study, research and practice of Juji Gatame became a significant interest of mine. Most likely, at least from my perspective, Juji Gatame represents the functional, gritty, no-nonsense and utilitarian approach that I identify with. There are a lot of other people with this approach, and more than likely, if you are reading this book, you are one of them. Over the years, as a coach, it's been my goal to have my athletes use Juji Gatame as a primary offensive weapon and I hope what is presented on these pages will convince you to do the same.

Let's explore more about Juji Gatame on the pages to come.

## ▆▆▆▆ TECHNICAL TIP ▆▆▆▆

**The Japanese initially developed the basic form of Juji Gatame, as we now know it (with early drawings and descriptions dating to the late 1700s and early 1800s), although it has also been used in some other cultural grappling and fighting styles in one form or another in other parts of the world through the centuries. As mentioned earlier, the exponents of Kodokan Judo, starting in 1882, established the framework and fundamental principles for (what we now call) Juji Gatame. However, it was the Soviets and their sambo that showed the world (starting in the 1960s) how effective and versatile Juji Gatame could be. Also, the name of this technique is interesting, and some history about the name gives us some insight as to the original intent and purpose of this armlock. Juji Gatame has been known by other names through the history of Japanese jujitsu, judo as well as other forms of grappling, martial arts and combat sports. In the early years of Kodokan Judo, this armlock was called "Jumonji Gatame." The word Jumonji is translated to mean "cross" or referring to something laying sideways to something else and Gatame refers to locking or holding something in place. In his masterwork THE CANON OF JUDO, Kyuzo Mifune referred to this armlock as "Jumonji Gatame Ude Kujiki" which translates to "Cross Lock Arm Wrenching Skill." Eventually, the Kodokan Judo Institute named this armlock "Udehishigi Juji Gatame" which means "Arm Breaking Cross Lock." It is apparent that the people who invented this armlock intended it to be a technique that could, and did, break people's arms. The combat effectiveness of this skill was reflected in how the Japanese jujitsu and judo masters developed Juji Gatame in the way they did, and why they named it what they did.**

## THE FOUR PRIMARY ARMLOCKS

When it comes to self-defense or fighting on the battlefield, any joint locking technique that causes compliance, pain, injury or death is encouraged and allowed. Joint locks are dangerous and they are dangerous because they are effective. But when it comes to fighting as a sport, rules have to be in place to insure the safety of the combatants. This is certainly the case when it comes to armlocks. Since the advent of the concept of "sport" and sport as it applies to fighting, wrestling or grappling, four primary forms of locking an opponent's arm have been consistently used in almost every part of the world. As combat sports developed and evolved through the nineteenth century, then on to the twentieth century, and now into the twenty-first century, almost every form of sport combat has been adapted so that the elbow is the primary target for joint locks against the arm. Wristlocks have proven to be too dangerous for sport fighting. The wrist joint is far too fragile and in the early days of submission wrestling, jujitsu and judo when wristlocks were allowed in contests, too many wrists were broken (and broken too easily). The joints in the hands have often been off-limits to combat sports as well. The thumb and fingers are comparatively small and easy to break, as are the bones in the hand itself. The shoulder joint, while not a small joint, is a weak one; and while not the primary target of Juji Gatame and other joint locks, is often a secondary victim of an elbow lock. However, again for safety concerns, the shoulder isn't the primary target of a joint lock, at least when it comes to the sporting aspect of fighting.

However, the elbow joint is a hinge joint, and as such, has proven to be able to withstand more abuse than the other joints of the hand, arm and shoulder because of its size and function. And because of this, the elbow joint has become the principle target of those who are so inclined to stretch, pull, bend, crank or wrench an arm of an opponent in a combat sport. (If you are reading this book, you are most likely one of those people so inclined to stretch, bend or crank someone else's arm.)

There are four primary ways of locking an opponent's elbow that are universally used in almost every form of submission grappling or sport combat. I have come to refer to these as the "primary armlocks." One of these four primary armlocks (Juji Gatame) is the subject of this book. Three of these four primary armlocks attack the arm by straightening it and one attacks the arm by bending it at the elbow joint. Juji Gatame is one of the three primary armlocks that straighten the opponent's arm and is unique in that it is the only one where the attacker places his opponent's elbow joint against his pubic bone, taking the elbow out of its normal range of motion and "barring" it as the attacker crosses one, or both, legs over his opponent to assert more control of his opponent's body.

Following is a brief description of the four primary armlocks.

## PRIMARY ARMLOCK: JUJI GATAME (CROSS-BODY ARMLOCK)

This armlock is unique in that it is the only one where the attacker crosses one, or both, legs over the head and torso of his opponent.

## PRIMARY ARMLOCK: UDE GATAME (ARM LOCK, ALSO CALLED THE "STRAIGHT ARMLOCK")

This photo shows one of the many variations of this armlock. Pretty much any armlock where the attacker straightens or "bars" the opponent's arm falls under the category of Ude Gatame.

## PRIMARY ARMLOCK: WAKI GATAME (ARMPIT LOCK)

The distinctive feature of this armlock is that the attacker straightens his opponent's arm with the attacker using the side of his body at the ribcage under his arm as the fulcrum. It is a powerful and effective armlock.

## PRIMARY ARMLOCK: UDE GARAMI (ARM ENTANGLEMENT OR BENT ARMLOCK)

There are two basic applications of this armlock; one with the defender's arm bent in an upward direction (as shown here) and the other with the defender's arm bent downward. This is the only primary armlock where the attacker bends his opponent's arm to cause pain in the elbow joint.

Maybe someone else will devote an entire book to each one of these primary armlocks, but for now, we will concern ourselves with Juji Gatame.

# LEARNING, PRACTICING AND DRILL TRAINING FOR JUJI GATAME

## "THE FIRST TIME IS COGNITION. THE SECOND TIME IS RECOGNITION." MARSHALL MCLUHAN

## TEACHING, LEARNING AND TRAINING FOR JUJI GATAME

Juji Gatame is a core skill for all combat sports. The study of this armlock teaches fundamental skills that go beyond simply stretching an opponent's arm. It is a useful, reliable tool with a high ratio of success used in all combat sports and can be used by both male and female athletes in all weight classes.

Juji Gatame is also a fighting skill. The intention, and ultimately the intent, of learning how to fight is different than learning any other sport or activity. Sports (and life in general) can be stressful enough, but the stress that is present in a real fight or a fight in a sporting context is much greater. How a person trains, practices or learns directly affects how he or she will perform under pressure. People sometimes say that they will "rise to the occasion" under a stressful situation. That's not true. You don't ever rise to the occasion. You rise to your level of training. The better you prepare in your training, the better you will do under stress.

There's a lot of stress in any form of fighting. Whether it's a combat sport or real combat, stress is always present. Only a person who is a sociopath or a person who is totally oblivious or naïve to the situation will not feel stress in a fight. The better we train in a realistic, functional manner, the better prepared we will be for the real thing.

Fundamental, core skills are vital as a basis of all training and skill learning and the serious, realistic study and practice of these fundamental skills in functional and efficient applications prepares an athlete or student for the real world of fighting, either in sport combat or in real combat. Effective practice produces effective results.

A major key to success is structured, disciplined and effective training. Train hard, but be sure to train smart. Simply showing up to the dojo or gym and rolling with the other guys may be fun but if that's all you do, you are not getting the most out of your training time. I'm not trying to sell books, but my books CONDITIONING FOR COMBAT SPORTS (along with John Saylor), TAP OUT TEXTBOOK and WINNING ON THE MAT offer some useful and realistic advice on how to get the most out of your training time. But the main point here is that drill training and working on technical skills of new (and already-learned) moves and techniques, along with structured free practice (call it what you want: randori, rolling, going live or any other term used in your sport) gets the best results. Structured training also keeps injuries in training to a minimum and focuses the athletes and coaches on the ultimate goals they have, both immediate goals and long-term goals.

In the next few pages, some exercises and drills will be presented that are useful in training for Juji Gatame. These are simply a few exercises that can be done, so make it a point to search for as many good, effective ways as possible to train. Training time is limited; we all have lives to lead, so getting the most out of the time you are on the mat or in the gym is vital to your success.

### TECHNICAL TIP

**A major key to success is structured, disciplined, consistent and effective training; that means effective and constant drill training is essential for making Juji Gatame an effective weapon in your arsenal of skills.**

## COACHES: TEACH JUJI GATAME AS A CORE SKILL

When I started my judo career in 1965, the contest rules of judo only permitted black belts to perform Juji Gatame. There is an old, and true, adage that people tend to learn and practice what the rules of the sport allow. What is not allowed in the rulebook is often neglected in terms of learning, coaching and practicing. This was certainly true for armlocks when I was young and starting out, and in some cases, it still is. Armlocks were considered "dangerous" even though there were few injuries resulting from them in either competition

or practice. As a result, few people learned armlocks and even fewer still were skilled enough to use them in competitive situations. Even when a person achieved his or her black belt, scant attention was paid to the study and practice of armlocks. When my personal learning progressed into the study of jujitsu and eventually sambo, the awareness of armlocks (as well as other submission techniques such a leglocks) opened up to me. As the world of combat sports has expanded and evolved in the intervening years since my first involvement in 1965, armlocks have gained the recognition they merit for their effectiveness and versatility.

As a coach, I teach Juji Gatame as a core skill. My belief is that novices should "learn from the ground up" and Juji Gatame is usually the first thing a new person learns in my club. As the novice learns the safety of breakfalls in preparation for throws and takedowns, he or she is also immediately introduced to Spinning Juji Gatame. The spinning application of Juji Gatame not only teaches the actual armlock, it also teaches fundamental skills of groundfighting such as learning how to move from the hips and buttocks, the shrimping or curling movements necessary for good groundfighting, learning spatial awareness, learning how to use the opponent's (and one's own) body or training uniform as handles to manipulate and control the opponent, and a variety of other skills that are examined later in this book in the chapter on Core Skills. The underlying premise of Juji Gatame is to force an opponent to surrender to you. Learning Juji Gatame as one of the first things a novice does teaches that person the aggressive, hardcore and serious approach and attitude that is necessary for the real world of combat sports or the real world of self-defense.

## ARMLOCK SAFETY

The old saying, "When in doubt, tap out" applies to the study of Juji Gatame, or any submission technique for that matter. Especially in training, don't make the mistake of being macho and refusing to submit when you are caught in an armlock or other submission technique. In many combat sports, tapping an opponent or verbally submitting (either by a recognized word or phrase or simply by yelling out) is the safety valve that separates injury from non-injury. A good idea is to tap your opponent or partner and not the mat when submitting. In a busy practice room or gymnasium, you may not be able to hear your opponent tap out as quickly as you feel him tap out. But, in a fight or match, make sure the referee also sees your opponent tap out or hears your opponent verbally surrender. Remember, in a sport combat fight, it doesn't count unless the referee says so.

There is also an old saying, "He didn't tap, so it went snap." This implies that the athlete who has the armlock applied on him (or her) has the responsibility to submit and signal surrender before his arm is injured. Injured pride takes a lot less time to heal than an injured elbow.

A mature attitude is required when practicing and using armlocks or any form of submission techniques. One has to be physically, mentally and emotionally mature enough to practice armlocks and those who are not are wasting your valuable time on the mat. Take care of yourself and take care of your training partners.

## TEACHING ARMLOCKS TO YOUNG PEOPLE

Armlocks are safe for young people who are mature enough to understand that injury could result from poor attentiveness, horseplay or not taking a mature attitude in their study, practice and application. But then, that can also be said for throwing and takedown techniques, as well as most any aspect of judo, jujitsu, sambo, grappling or wrestling. My approach is to introduce Juji Gatame to students who are physically mature enough, as well as mentally and emotionally mature enough, at about 11 or 12 years of age (or at about the onset of puberty), making sure that they learn the correct fundamentals (same as an adult would learn) in a structured and controlled training atmosphere.

Neil Adams once told me, "Judo is an adult activity that we allow children to do." Neil is right and that advice applies to a variety of other combat sports as well. This is certainly the case when teaching young people Juji Gatame.

## DRILLS AND EXERCISES FOR JUJI GATAME

It's a good idea to be specific when warming up for any training session. Do warm up exercises that relate, both directly and indirectly in some cases, to what you plan to do in practice. There are a lot of good exercises and drills you can do to enhance your ability at Juji Gatame and some of them are presented on the next few pages.

# WARM-UP EXERCISES

## ROLLING EXERCISE

An important physical skill is to be able to stay round. This exercise is not only a good warm-up, it teaches how to stay round and keep rolling when doing Juji Gatame.

Sit on the mat with knees wide as shown and grab your feet.

The grappler rolls to one side (in this photo, to the athlete's right), continuing to hold onto the feet as shown.

The athlete continues to roll to his right and across his back as shown.

The athlete rolls across his back and over toward his left.

Roll back to the sitting position and proceed to roll the other direction. Do this as a timed drill (about 30-45 seconds) or roll 5 times each direction as a good initial warm-up.

## SHOULDER WARM-UP

The shoulders take a lot of abuse when practicing Juji Gatame and this exercise helps warm the shoulder area as extend the range of motion in the joint to prevent injuries.

The athlete rolls onto his left shoulder as he extends his left arm as shown.

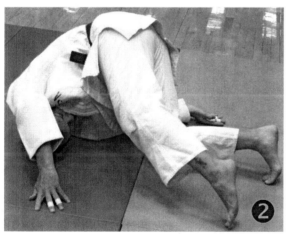

The athlete repeats the exercise on his right shoulder as shown.

## HEAD POSTING: KNEELING

Posting on the top of your head is an important skill when doing Juji Gatame. There are many positions and applications of Juji Gatame where you will have to balance yourself on the top of your head. A good warm-up is to kneel as shown here, rocking forward, backward and to each side with your head.

## HEAD POSTING: ROCKING BACK AND FORTH

As shown here, kneel and use your hands and arms to support yourself as you rock back and forth on the top of your head to both warm up and strengthen the muscles of the neck and shoulders.

## HEAD POSTING: TRIPOD POSITION

Get on the top of your head as shown in this photo and rock back and forth as well as side-to-side gradually and slowly. Don't rock back and forth fast to avoid neck injury. You can do this drill by using your hands for support as shown or without using your hands for support on the mat, allowing the neck and head to take the full force of your weight.

## HEAD POSTING: BALANCE ON HEAD

While this exercise may not be done at every workout as a warm-up, it's still a good one to help strengthen the neck and supporting muscles of the neck and head.

## HEAD POST DRILL WITH PARTNER

The top grappler controls his partner from the top position as shown here. This exercise is a good one to develop the muscles necessary to post on the head and control an opponent from this position. It is also a good drill to teach how to post and balance on the head and maintain control of an opponent.

The bottom grappler will move in different directions with the top grappler moving and adjusting his position as necessary to stay on the top of his head.

## GRANBY ROLL OR SHOULDER ROLL

Many applications of Juji Gatame require that you roll easily. This exercise is excellent for this purpose.

Start by kneeling and placing the top of your head on the mat much like you do in the head posting exercise.

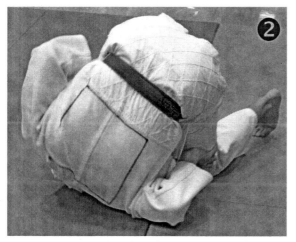

Roll over your left shoulder (high up on the shoulder) as shown here.

Keep rolling across the top of your shoulders as shown here.

Finish the exercise by rolling over onto your head as shown here. Repeat this exercise by doing this roll in the other direction.

## SHRIMP DRILL

Shrimping or curling the body and turning onto the hips is one of the most often-used movements when doing Juji Gatame, especially when doing Spinning Juji Gatame. Do this exercise every workout as part of your warm-up. A good drill is to shrimp from one side of the mat to the other.

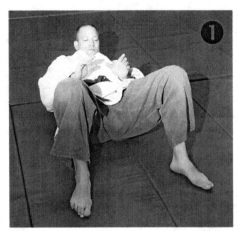

What many people call "shrimping" is the action of curling the body, shifting or moving to the hip and side and using the feet to move. Start by lying on your back as shown here.

Shift your body so that it is curled up as shown here.

Push against the mat with your feet as shown here. Doing this causes you to scoot back.

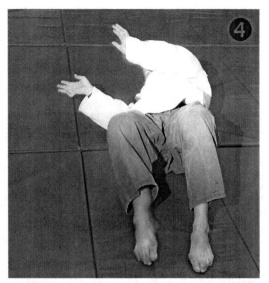

Quickly roll over to the other side of your body.

Curl up as shown here.

Push against the mat with your feet, extending your body. This shrimping action is an important skill in all groundfighting, and especially useful when doing Juji Gatame.

## LEG PRESS LEVER EXERCISE

This exercise is good for both athletes, with the top grappler developing the muscles necessary to lever his opponent's arms free and the bottom grappler using his muscles to keep his arm from being pulled apart.

There are three ways to perform this drill. 1) Decide whom the drill is for. If the drill is for the top grappler, his job is to pry his partner's arms free. The bottom grappler will offer varying degrees of resistance. 2) If you decide the drill is for the bottom grappler, the top grappler will offer varying degrees of resistance in pulling the bottom man's hands and arms apart. The bottom grappler's job is to keep his arms and hands clamped together to develop the muscles necessary to keep them from getting pulled apart when in this position. 3) Both athletes can go 100%, with the top grappler attempting to pull the bottom grappler's hands and arms apart, and the bottom grappler attempting to keep his hands and arms clamped together.

The top grappler has his partner in the leg press. The bottom grappler grabs his arms together. The top grappler uses his arms to grab his partner's arms.

The top grappler pulls back, using both the strength of his arms and the weight of his body. The bottom grappler keeps his hands grasped together.

The top grappler pulls and rolls backward as shown with the bottom grappler continuing to hold his hands together tightly.

## ARM DEFENSE EXERCISE FOR BOTTOM ATHLETE IN LEG PRESS

This is a good strength exercise for the bottom grappler if he gets caught in the leg press and gets his arms extended as shown here. The top grappler holds the bottom grappler's arm as shown to start the drill.

The top grappler offers varying amounts of resistance with the bottom grappler pulling his extended right arm in toward his body as shown.

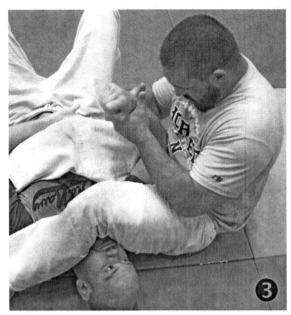

The bottom grappler has pulled his right arm in completing the exercise. Do this is sets of 5 to 10 repetitions per arm for each athlete.

## LEG PRESS BALL GRAB

This is a fun drill and is a good workout as well. The bottom grappler holds tightly to a basketball (or for a tougher workout, a medicine ball) as shown. The top grappler holds his partner in the leg press position and tries to steal the ball away from the bottom grappler. This teaches the top grappler to aggressively pursue getting his opponent's arm to lever it and apply Juji Gatame. This exercise is also good a good defensive drill for the bottom grappler as it teaches him how to keep his arms from being pulled apart and having Juji Gatame applied against him.

## LEG PRESS SCOOT EXERCISE

This is a useful exercise to develop the muscles in the legs and hips necessary for pressing an opponent to the mat in the leg press. The top grappler does not use his hands to grab his partner in this drill at all and makes sure to squeeze his knees together, trapping his partners arms and shoulders as shown.

The top grappler can also scoot forward, driving into his partner and moving him forward.

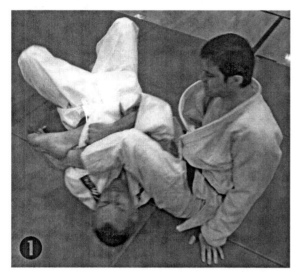

The top grappler holds his partner with a leg press using only his legs as shown.

The top grappler moves his partner back to the original starting point to finish the drill. This drill can be done as a timed drill, going anywhere from 20 to 40 seconds in duration.

The top grappler scoots backward holding his partner tightly with his legs. The bottom grappler can offer varying degrees of resistance from absolutely no resistance to strong resistance.

## LEG PRESS CIRCLE SCOOT EXERCISE

This is a variation of the leg press scoot drill with the top grappler moving his partner in a circle instead of moving him in a straight line. This photo shows the starting position of the exercise.

The top grappler moves to his left, using only his legs to control his partner and moving his partner along with him.

The top grappler continues to move around in a circle, making sure to use only his legs to control his partner.

The top grappler moves around in a full circle to the left and then repeat the drill by moving in a full circle to the right.

## LEG PRESS ROCKING EXERCISE

This is a good drill to train on how to control the bottom grappler with your legs. Sometimes, when holding an opponent in the leg press, you will need to use your legs to rock him toward his shoulders or toward his hips to maintain control or lever his arm free. This exercise is excellent for developing the physical strength and skills necessary to do this. The top grappler does not use his hands and traps his partner's arms and shoulders with his legs as shown here.

The top grappler rolls to his left hip and toward his partner's head, rocking the bottom grappler onto his head and shoulders.

The top grappler rolls to his right hip and toward his partner's legs and hip, making sure to keep his legs pinched together and pulling his partner's head and shoulder up off the mat as shown.

The top grappler rocks back to his starting position to finish. This drill can be done for time, doing as many good "rocking" movements as possible in the specified time limit.

## LEG PRESS HEAD CONTROL EXERCISE

This drill is good for the top grappler to learn how to use his leg to control the bottom grappler, preventing him from coming off the mat. The starting position is shown here. The top grappler makes sure to not use his hands and arms, and only use his legs and feet in this drill.

The bottom grappler sits up, coming off the mat as shown. As he does this, the top grappler uses his left leg (the leg over the bottom grappler's head) to hook the bottom grappler's head as shown. Look at how the top grappler hooks hard with his left leg. The top grappler uses this leg hook on his partner's head to drive him back to the mat.

When the top grappler pushes his partner back to the mat they start the drill over. Do 10 repetitions on each side, then switch and let the bottom grappler do the exercise.

## LEG PRESS STRENGTH EXERCISE

This is a good exercise for groundfighting in general, but can be used for Juji Gatame training as well. The bottom grappler is on his back with both of his feet wedged in the top grappler's hips. The bottom grappler is holding onto his partner with his hands and arms. This is a good strength exercise for the legs.

The bottom grappler uses his legs to press his partner up as shown. Do 10 repetitions and then switch places to allow the other athlete to do the exercise.

## LEG LIFT STRENGTH EXERCISE

This is a good exercise for developing leg strength. The bottom grappler places his legs on the inner thighs of his partner as shown.

The bottom grappler uses his legs to press his partner up as shown. Do 10 repetitions and then switch places to allow the other athlete to perform the exercise.

## PICK-UP EXERCISE (ALSO CALLED "GOOD MORNINGS")

This is a good defensive drill and exercise for picking up an opponent who is attempting a Juji Gatame on you. If you have ever done "Good Mornings" in the weight room, this is similar. This drill strengthens the muscles used by the top grappler when picking up an opponent who is attempting Juji Gatame off the mat.

The top grappler squats above his partner who is lying on the mat. The top grappler grabs his partner's lapels as shown.

The top grappler pulls and swings his partner up as shown.

The top grappler lowers his partner to the mat with control as shown. This is a great exercise to develop the strength to pull an opponent off the mat if you are defending against a Juji Gatame attack.

# DRILLS TO IMPROVE SKILL IN JUJI GATAME

You can invent or create a drill for any situation that actually comes up in a match or fight. Time spent on drill training is time well spent. Presented here are a few drills that I use often in the training of my athletes. These are repetitive drills that can be performed with total cooperation or varying levels of resistance by the defender. In judo, we call these drills "uchikomi" which means repetitive training. Structured drill training on specific skills is essential for success in any form of sport combat. Drills can also be used for training for fitness as well as for training in the tactics of a match or fight.

## TECHNICAL TIP

**Drill training is structured training. A coach must not allow the athletes in a drill training session to horse around or deviate from the drill being performed. Simply showing up and going live, rolling or doing randori full blast for an hour or so is fun once in a while, but it doesn't develop elite-level athletes with elite-level skills. Structured, disciplined training is vital to success in any combat sport. I recommend devoting at least one half of every one of your workouts to drill training. For more on this subject, I recommend my book WINNING ON THE MAT, published by Turtle Press.**

## SPINNING JUJI DRILL:
### GROUNDFIGHTING UCHIKOMI

This drill develops a lot more than just Juji Gatame. It teaches and refines the many skills, movements and reactions necessary for good groundfighting. This drill can be done in varying levels of resistance, but I recommend

that this drill be done with total cooperation on the part of both athletes to better develop instinctive movement. Generally, I run this drill by having one athlete do 5 repetitions each, doing as many sets of 5 repetitions as possible (but still doing good skills) in a specified time period, usually about 3 minutes. At the end of 3 minutes, each athlete does quite a few good, skillful repetitions of Juji Gatame. In my club, this drill is done every practice, often immediately after some warm-ups at the start of the workout. An enjoyable variation of this drill is to have the coach time 30 seconds, with each athlete doing as many good, skillful Juji Gatames as possible in that 30-second period of time. The top grappler keeps count of how many his partner does. The idea is to get as many good, full Juji Gatames as possible. This is a repetitive drill to develop the many skills of Juji Gatame (specifically) and groundfighting in general and not a drill where the athletes go live or randori.

IMPORTANT: You can take any entry or application for Juji Gatame and drill on it with groundfighting uchikomi. In my club, in addition to the Spinning Juji Drill, my athletes often do 3 sets of 5 repetitions each of Head Roll Juji Gatame, Back Roll Juji Gatame or Hip Roll Juji Gatame to instill instinctive reaction and behavior for those specific set-ups for Juji Gatame.

## TECHNICAL TIP

**Uchikomi is repetitive drill training and is a great method of developing the instinctive behavior that is required when an athlete is in a real-world situation in a fight or match. Efficient practice produces effective results. What is sometimes called "groundfighting uchikomi" is any repetitive drill that athletes can perform every workout. Perform a lot of repetitions with your training partner or partners, all the while developing the kinesthetic awareness that leads to instinctive behavior (or the "feel" of doing the skill) that enables you to perform the skill under the pressure of a real fight or match.**

**You can also take any skill or technique and invent a drill to improve it or invent drills that simulate actual situations that take place in a match to ensure that you are as well prepared as possible for anything that might happen in an actual fight or match. Remember, this is drill training, so don't let your drill training workout regress to rolling around and going live or into a randori session. Stay focused, stay structured and stay disciplined in your training.**

## JUJI GATAME SHRIMPING DRILL

This is a good repetition drill to develop the skills necessary for Spinning Juji Gatame. Each athlete should perform a specified number of repetitions, spinning from one side to the other. Often, the athletes in my club do 2 sets of 10 repetitions on each side as a good warm-up before doing the Spinning Juji Gatame drill that was presented prior to this.

The attacker spins back to the starting position.

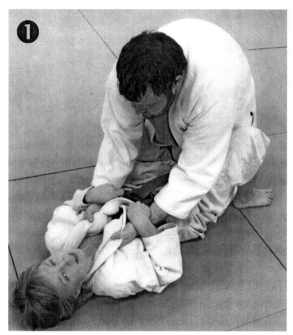

The attacker (on bottom) is lying on her back ready to start the drill.

The attacker spins over onto her right hip and side, placing her left leg and foot over her partner's head and placing her right leg across her partner's left side.

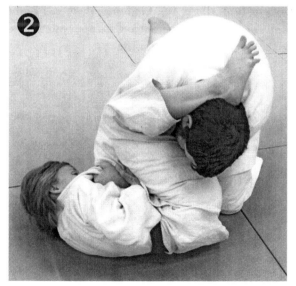

The attacker spins onto her left hip and side, curling up into a compact ball and swinging her right leg over his partner's head and neck. She also places her left leg across her partner's right side.

The attacker finishes the drill by returning to the starting position.

## LEG PRESS HOLD DRILL

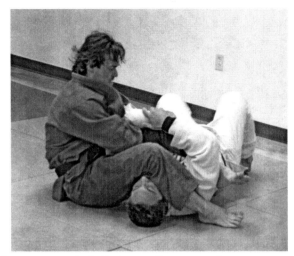

This is a good drill that offers a good warm-up and also teaches the top grappler how to "ride" or control his opponent in the leg press position. The top grappler maintains his leg press position with the bottom grappler moving around, only offering enough resistance to make the top grappler work to control him.

## LEG PRESS "GET THE JUJI" DRILL

This drill is for the grappler on top who has his partner in the leg press position. The top grappler attempts to lever, pry, pull or wrench his partner's (on bottom) arm loose and secure Juji Gatame. A variation of this is to allow the top grappler to switch to another position such as a pin, straddle or mount. If he chooses, he can then again attempt to secure Juji Gatame. This drill can be done in varying degrees of resistance and 30 seconds is the recommend time allowed.

## LEG PRESS "ESCAPE FROM JUJI" DRILL

This drill is for the bottom grappler who is actively trying to escape. The top athlete's job is to hold his partner in the leg press position for the specified period of time or until the bottom man escapes. The top grappler offers varying degrees of resistance. I recommend doing this in timed drills for 30 seconds.

IMPORTANT: Not a lot of people actually practice defensive or escape skills on a regular basis. Working on defensive skills often isn't an interesting as working on offensive skills, but it is a necessary aspect of all forms of sport combat. This is a good drill to develop the defensive and escape skills necessary to keep an opponent from doing Juji Gatame. Make it a point to drill on a variety of defensive and escape situations that actually take place in a fight or match.

## SHOULDER SQUAT AND STRETCH DRILL

The goal in this drill is to have the top grappler hold his shoulder squat or shoulder sit position for as long as possible while his partner on bottom offers varying degrees of resistance. This drill teaches the top grappler to control his opponent and develop a "feel" as to when to roll back and apply the Juji Gatame.

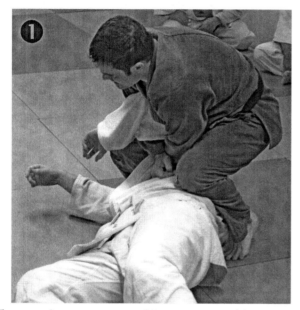

The attacker squats over his partner, making sure to trap his partner's arm tightly to his chest. The attacker will move as necessary to maintain control over his partner as his partner moves about the mat, simulating a resisting opponent.

### TECHNICAL TIP

**The two most effective drills, and ones that should be done at every workout, are the Spinning Juji Gatame drill and the Spin and Stretch drill. Make sure to follow through on each repetition and apply the armlock. When doing this, the attacker doesn't have to apply painful pressure, but instead simply stretch the arm, making sure to secure it correctly and tightly. There's no need to make your training partner tap out on every repetition. Remember, it's his turn next!**

Eventually, the top grappler will sense that he is controlling his partner effectively enough to roll back and apply Juji Gatame. As he does this, the attacker closes all space between his body and his partner's body and starts to roll back to apply the Juji Gatame.

The attacker finishes the drill by rolling back and securing Juji Gatame.

## SPIN AND STRETCH DRILL

This is an excellent drill to develop the skills necessary to follow through from a throw or takedown to Juji Gatame. Being able to transition from a standing situation to a ground situation with control over an opponent is a vital skill. This drill simulates the attacker throwing his partner to the mat and then immediately applying Juji Gatame in a smooth transition. (Without having to actually slam your opponent a lot of times, saving on the wear and tear on a training partner's body.)

The attacker is standing with his partner on both knees as shown.

The attacker places his right foot with his heel on the side of his partner's right knee. Look at how the attacker steps across his partner with his right leg and will spin his partner to his right and onto the mat.

The attacker spins his partner to the mat simulating a throw. This drill is good in the sense that neither athlete has to take a lot of throws to work on the transition from a throw to Juji Gatame. This is also a good drill for when an opponent is on one or both knees and you wish to take him to the mat to apply Juji Gatame.

The attacker spins his partner to the mat as shown.

The attacker immediately squats low in a shoulder sit position and applies a Back Roll Juji Gatame as shown.

The attacker rolls back to finish the Juji Gatame.

**IMPORTANT:** This is one of the best drills that can be used in any combat sport to develop the immediate and instantaneous transition from a throw to Juji Gatame. Knowing what to do after you throw your opponent, and knowing how to do it quickly, efficiently and effectively will win matches for you.

## KEEP ROLLING DRILL

There is an ironclad rule about Juji Gatame: Never let go of your opponent's arm unless you absolutely have to! An attacker won't always get his or her opponent to tap out on the first try at Juji Gatame. The defender may roll out, move in an unexpected way or escape, so the attacker must keep rolling, turning or breaking his opponent down until the defender submits or, if he refuses to submit, is injured by the armlock.

This drill is directed toward the attacker to teach him how to keep control of the defender's arm and to keep rolling the defender and eventually securing Juji Gatame. But this drill is also a good drill for the defender as it teaches him how to react and roll to defend and escape Juji Gatame. This drill is often done best with both athletes cooperating and the defender offering no resistance. But, if the drill is also done for the defender, the athletes can agree to apply varying levels of resistance as they wish.

The bottom grappler shrimps or rolls up onto his right knee and hip as shown. The attacker uses his arms to trap his partner's right arm tightly to his body as he rolls over onto his right hip and side.

The defender sits up onto his knees and the attacker uses the momentum of his partner sitting upright to roll over his right side. The attacker makes it a point to have his partner's right arm trapped to his chest as he starts to roll the defender.

The attacker can use any entry, roll or breakdown for Juji Gatame he chooses to start the drill. In this photo, the attacker is doing a Spinning Juji Gatame to start the drill.

The attacker rolls over to his left and onto his front as shown making sure to keep his legs hooked tightly and controlling the defender throughout the roll.

The attacker has rolled his partner over onto his side and has the bottom grappler in the leg press position.

The attacker continues to roll, gaining more momentum as the roll continues. As he rolls, the attacker uses both of his arms to continue to trap the defender's right arm to the attacker's chest, with the attacker constantly prying and levering the defender's right arm free. Look at how the attacker continues to roll over onto his left hip and side.

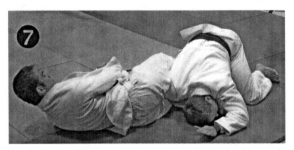

The attacker rolls through and onto his left side and hip and finishes the drill with this variation of Juji Gatame where the attacker is lying on his left side, but the athletes can keep the drill going as long as they wish. The attacker will continue to control his partner and roll him as long as the defender keeps rolling to simulate what can happen against a resisting opponent in a real fight or match. This drill is ideal to develop the skills necessary to secure Juji Gatame on the second, third or even fourth try.

An effective warm-up is one that relates to what you will actually be doing during your workout. Don't just show up, do a few light stretches and start working out. Take the time to warm your muscles (that's why it's called a "warm-up") and perform a variety of exercises and drills that will enhance your training. An effective warm-up is an integral part of a productive workout.

By doing a lot of drill training, you will develop the ability to instinctively execute and perform Juji Gatame under the stress of a real fight or match. Remember the old saying, "You never rise to the occasion, you rise to your level of training."

The next chapter covers the core skills of Juji Gatame. Juji Gatame is effective because it is mechanically sound and can be adapted to fit the requirements of any athlete in any combat sport. Let's get to it.

# THE CORE SKILLS OF JUJI GATAME

**"SMALL THINGS MAKE BIG THINGS HAPPEN. PAY ATTENTION TO THE DETAILS."**
**JOHN WOODEN**

Juji Gatame appears simple, and in essence, it is. Pulling on an opponent's arm is a simple act…if he lets you. When you are facing an opponent who is fit, skilled, motivated and aggressive, it's not so simple anymore.

The core principles and skills of Juji Gatame are examined closely in this chapter. These core, underlying and primary skills are broken down, carefully examined and then put back together again to give as complete of a study as possible in an effort to see why and how Juji Gatame works. If you better understand why something works, you will know how to make it work when you need it to work.

Before we examine Juji Gatame, it is important to remember that this book is, fundamentally, about fighting and close personal combat, whether it's in a sporting context or in another context such as law enforcement defensive tactics, a military situation or a self-defense situation. Effective groundfighting is aggressive, relentless and fast-paced; all of which requires superb physical fitness and an aggressive mindset. Control your opponent's position, break him down and secure a winning technique such as Juji Gatame, all the while making it increasingly uncomfortable for him. As I have said in some of my other books, when it comes to the subject of combat sports (no matter which combat sport it is), it's a fight, not a game.

## THE ANATOMY OF JUJI GATAME: WHY AND HOW IT WORKS

Anytime an athlete crosses one or both of his legs over his opponent's head and torso and uses his crotch, pubic bone or hips as the fulcrum to extend, straighten or stretch his opponent's arm, that is Juji Gatame. The actual application of Juji Gatame is, at its core, the basic application of using a lever and a fulcrum. Think of the opponent's extended arm as the lever and the attacker's pubic bone and crotch as the fulcrum. The more effectively one athlete uses these basic principles, the better he or she will be at doing Juji Gatame. The intriguing part is how to get an opponent in a vulnerable position to be able to apply the principles of the lever and the fulcrum on a consistent basis with a high ratio of success. The part on how to achieve this is what makes up the rest of this book.

## STRETCHING THE OPPONENT'S ARM: A VIEW OF JUJI GATAME FROM ABOVE.

The key point in any armlock (or joint lock of any kind) is to take the joint that is being attacked out of its natural range of motion. Use your crotch and hips as the Fulcrum and use your opponent's arm as the lever: The attacker is stretching his opponent's arm using his pelvic bone and crotch as the fulcrum point for his opponent's elbow. The opponent's elbow is bent against its natural range of motion and "barred." This is why armlocks that stretch and bend the opponent's arm against a fixed point at the elbow are often called "armbars." As shown in this photo, the attacker is using his crotch as the fulcrum to stretch and straighten his opponent's arm. Look at how the defender's entire arm is compromised, creating pain in the shoulder and making his entire arm weaker and less able to defend or escape. Not only does Juji Gatame lock the elbow joint, it causes pain in the shoulder, stretches the opponent's biceps and triceps and stretches the tendons and ligaments in the shoulder joint as well as in the elbow joint. The important thing

is to stretch your opponent's arm and extend the back of his elbow across a part of your body (usually your crotch or hips) that serves as a fulcrum.

## STRETCHING THE OPPONENT'S ARM: TWO VIEWS OF JUJI GATAME FROM THE SIDE.

This photo shows how the defender's elbow is positioned at the attacker's pubic bone as it is being stretched. As the attacker pulls on the extended arm, he arches his hips in an effort to create more upward pressure at the pivot point of the fulcrum. The attacker holds the extended arm as close as possible to the end of the arm near the hand. The attacker pulls the extended arm toward his head and as he does this, bends his head forward (and off the mat). This combination of actions allows the attacker to not only pull on the extended arm but the arm is also pulled slightly downward at the wrist as it is being pulled.

This photo from the side shows how the attacker uses both the weight and strength of his legs (as well as his hips) to control the head and body of the defender by pressing downward (in this case toward the mat). Another key feature in stretching an opponent's arm is the close proximity of the attacker's hips, thighs and buttocks to the defender's shoulder (in this photo, the defender's right shoulder). There should be as little space as possible between the attacker's hips and the upper body of the defender, especially at the shoulder to ensure a firm, compact and secure grip. This closeness of body space between the attacker's hips and buttocks and the defender's shoulder, upper body and head ensures that the elbow of the stretched, extended arm that is being attacked is situated at, or slightly above, the attacker's pubic bone creating an effective fulcrum.

## ▮▮▮▮ TECHNICAL TIP ▮▮▮▮

**Juji Gatame is more than simply an elbow lock. It causes pain in the entire shoulder and arm of your opponent. Not only are the joints of the elbow and shoulder compromised beyond their normal range of motion to a significant degree, all the muscles in the opponent's arm are stretched beyond their normal range of motion and function as well. This also includes stress on the tendons and ligaments of the arm and shoulder.**

## STRETCHING THE OPPONENT'S ARM: POSITION OF DEFENDER'S EXTENDED ELBOW AND ARM.

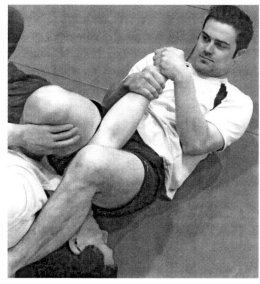

In order to create pain in his opponent's elbow (as well as the rest of his arm), the attacker must force the joint out of its normal range of motion. The defender's arm is the lever and his elbow is the pivot point that has primary contact with the attacker's fulcrum (his pubic bone or hips). Remember, however, that the defender's

arm isn't simply a fixed rod or solid object. It's a human arm with a hinge joint (the elbow) located in the middle of it. When extending and stretching the defender's arm, the attacker must make sure that the elbow is pointing downward and the inside of the elbow joint is pointing upward and trapped on the attacker's pubic bone creating the pivot point of the fulcrum. Often, coaches will tell athletes that the thumb of the extended arm of the defender must be pointed upward or that the palm must be facing the ceiling. These are good ways to get someone to make sure that the elbow of the extended arm is situated in a downward position and placed on the attacker's pubic bone, crotch or hips so that he can use the arm not only as a lever but also to take the elbow joint out of its normal range of motion, thus causing pain in the joint. If the defender's palm is facing upward toward the ceiling, then his elbow is usually situated in the most advantageous position to straighten it further and take the joint out of its normal range of motion. My best advice when straightening and stretching an opponent's arm in Juji Gatame is to make sure that the defender's arm is as straight as possible and that you pull as hard as possible. If you get overly concerned with having his thumb up, his thumb down or the position of his hands and fingers, your opponent will have already rolled his arm over and pulled it away, escaping the armlock.

## STRETCHING THE OPPONENT'S ARM: THE ATTACKER ARCHES HIS HIPS

To take the elbow joint out of its natural range of motion, as much force as possible must be applied at the direct point of contact between the elbow and the pubic bone that serves as the fulcrum. To multiply and maximize as much force as possible, the attacker must add a counter-movement that drives into the elbow, extending it further out of its normal range of motion.

Arching the hips creates this counter-movement. Look at how the attacker is arching his hips as he applies Juji Gatame in this photo. The defender's arm is stretched as far as it will go and the elbow is being pulled out of its normal range of motion, creating pan and producing the tap out.

## STRETCHING THE OPPONENT'S ARM: ATTACKER'S HEAD OFF THE MAT AND LOOKS AT HIS OPPONENT AS HE ARCHES

This same photo shows how the attacker's head must be off the mat and bent forward, looking at or to his opponent (with his shoulders and upper body making contact on the mat) as he arches. If the attacker's head is placed in this way, the attacker's hips can thrust forward more forcibly and the body can arch more effectively and create more torque. If the attacker rolls his head back allowing it to rest on the mat or looks upward toward the ceiling or away form his opponent, the body will not be able to arch as well as if he looks at his opponent as he arches his hips. It's simply a matter of body mechanics and applying the most efficient method of the use of a lever and fulcrum as possible; with the additional factor of having a lever that has a hinge joint in its middle. Remember, pull your opponent's arm hard and arch your hips.

## STRETCHING THE OPPONENT'S ARM-THE BASIC GRIP: GRAB OPPONENT'S ARM LIKE A BASEBALL BAT.

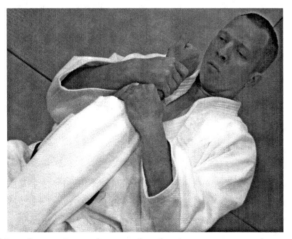

This close view shows the basic way to grab your opponent's arm. Look at how the attacker is using both of his hands to grab near the defender's hand on his wrist. This ensures a strong pull on the lever (the defender's arm) over the attacker's fulcrum (the attacker's public bone and crotch). The higher up the attacker grabs toward the defender's wrist and hand, the less resistance the defender has to pull his arm free, roll it over or extract it in any way. The attacker will be better able to stretch the arm that is levered over his pubic bone (the fulcrum). It's recommended that this grip be the initial way of grabbing and controlling the defender's arm when an athlete first learns Juji Gatame, however this is an excellent method of grabbing an opponent's arm when doing Juji Gatame and is used at all levels of competition. Using the hands in this way, the attacker makes sure that he has both hands on his opponent's arm (the attacker's two hands and arms are usually stronger than his opponent's one arm; especially if the arm is extended) and that they are placed near the defender's wrist, assuring the attacker of a more efficient lever to secure the Juji Gatame. **IMPORTANT:** The "baseball bat" grip is the basic grip when learning and practicing Juji Gatame. Other grips and methods of trapping and stretching the defender's arm will be examined in the next few pages as well as later in this book in the chapter on Levers.

## STRETCHING THE OPPONENT'S ARM: PULL OPPONENT'S FIST TO YOUR HEAD

This same photo shows that by pulling the defender's arm in the direction of the attacker's head, face or chin, the arm is more fully extended. I often tell my athletes to pull an opponent's fist to their chin. This way, I know that the attacker's head is bent forward and looking at the defender's arm and body, making sure that the attacker's head is off the mat allowing for a better arching of the hips when applying the armlock and that the defender's arm is being pulled and stretched as hard as possible.

## KEY POINTS WHEN APPLYING JUJI GATAME

Let's analyze Juji Gatame further by looking at some other key points used in most every effective application of this armlock.

## KEY POINT: THE ATTACKER'S KNEES AND LEGS TRAP THE DEFENDER'S ARM-SQUEEZE KNEES TOGETHER.

The attacker must squeeze or pinch his knees and legs together tightly to trap the defender's extended arm (as well as the defender's shoulder). Don't give your opponent any "wiggle room" to extract his arm that you have worked so hard to stretch out! By squeezing your knees together, you also squeeze your inner thighs together, trapping your opponent's arm even more tightly between your legs. Doing this, you trap your opponent's arm more tightly in place and do not allow him the chance to roll or turn his hand and arm over to extract his elbow free from the pivot point of your pubic bone.

## KEY POINT: THE ATTACKER'S BUTTOCKS, HIPS, LEGS AND CROTCH ARE AS CLOSE AS POSIBLE TO THE DEFENDER'S UPPER BODY AND HEAD. ATTACKER TRAPS THE DEFENDER'S HEAD WITH HIS LEG.

The attacker's crotch is situated as close to his opponent's (in this photo) left shoulder as possible. The defender's left arm has been pulled in as close as possible by the attacker to his pubic bone and crotch area. The attacker's

right hip and buttocks is jammed as close as possible to the defender's shoulder, neck and head as shown here. The attacker uses his right leg and foot to draw or pull in and hook the defender's head, controlling it much like a nutcracker clamps onto the nut before cracking it.

## KEY POINT: HOOK AND CONTROL OPPONENT'S HEAD WITH YOUR LEG.

Look at how the attacker hooks his right leg over the defender's head to control him in this leg press position. The defender is attempting to bridge and turn into the attacker to escape from his compromised position. The old saying "where the head goes, the body follows" is certainly true in this case as the defender is forcefully using his right leg to hook and control the defender, preventing him from escaping by driving his head down to the mat.

The attacker uses his leg to hook the defender's head and neck as he rolls him over to apply Juji Gatame. Look at how the attacker's right foot is positioned with the toes pointed, enabling the attacker to have more power in his hooking action. This aggressive and forceful hooking action of the leg controls the defender's head and upper body as the attacker rolls him over.

The attacker is using his left leg, instep and foot to push on his opponent's head as he rolls him over with this head roll Juji Gatame. The attacker manipulates and controls the defender's head in almost every application of Juji Gatame.

Using the legs for head control can come in any position as shown here. The attacker is using his right leg and foot to hook and control his opponent's head preventing him from gaining an upright posture to escape the Juji Gatame attack. The attacker is also using his left leg to hook over the defender's head. By hooking and pulling the defender's head down with his legs and feet, the attacker prevents his opponent from gaining an upright and stable body position and pulls the defender down into his Juji Gatame.

**TECHNICAL TIP**

Where the head goes, the body follows. This is certainly true when applying Juji Gatame. Use your feet and legs to manipulate and control your opponent's head for maximum control over him.

## KEY POINT: THE ATTACKER GETS HIS LEG OVER DEFENDER'S HEAD AS QUICKLY AS POSSIBLE FOR BETTER CONTROL.

In some cases, especially after the attacker does a Head Roll application of Juji Gatame, the attacker may not have his leg hooked over the defender's head to control it as the roll is completed. This photo shows an example how the attacker may not have his leg completely controlling his opponent at the end of a roll, turn or breakdown.

The defender will often attempt to sit up onto his buttocks or shrimp into the attacker to escape the armlock, and as he does this, he may attempt to lift his head off of the mat or turn it in such a way that he can initiate his escape.

The attacker immediately uses his right leg to hook over the defender's head.

The attacker presses the defender's head down to the mat with his right leg and establishes a strong leg press position to apply Juji Gatame. Keeping in mind what has been said before, "where the head goes, the body will follow," it is essential for the attacker to place his leg over his opponent's head as quickly as is feasible to maintain control and establish further control of the situation.

## KEY POINT: THE ANCHOR FOOT

The anchor foot is the foot that hooks, manipulates, controls and "anchors" an opponent's hip, leg, arm or any body part to limit its movement and is the leg or foot that does not control the opponent's head. The anchor foot or leg works in unison, but often independently, from, the leg and foot that hooks and controls an opponent's head and neck. The anchor foot is often used in controlling an opponent when using a head roll Juji Gatame or a hip roll Juji Gatame and is sometimes used in the back roll Juji Gatame. The anchor foot also provides the attacker a stable point to hook onto as he rolls or spins his opponent into Juji Gatame. Following are some photos showing how the anchor foot is applied and used to secure Juji Gatame in a variety of positions and situations.

## ANCHOR FOOT FOR HEAD ROLL JUJI GATAME

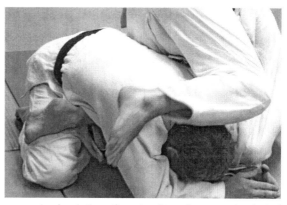

The attacker's anchor foot in this photo is the left foot that is hooked and "anchored" on the defender's right upper leg and hip area. This anchor foot controls the defender's hips and lower extremities and keeps the defender from freely moving or escaping.

This photo and the two that follow show how the attacker anchors his foot to control his opponent and give himself stability when applying the Head Roll Juji Gatame. The attacker is standing behind his opponent in a standing ride position. The bottom man is on all fours in a defensive position.

The attacker initiates his roll into Juji Gatame by using his right leg and foot to hook onto the defender's left upper leg and hip as shown. This is the anchor foot that isolates and controls the defender's movement.

The anchor foot not only prevents the defender from escaping, it is also used by the attacker to stabilize his body when rolling or turning the defender into Juji Gatame as shown here.

## ANCHOR FOOT FOR SPINNING JUJI GATAME ATTACKS

The attacker wedges his left foot into his opponent's right hip in this photo showing how to use an anchor

foot when applying Juji Gatame from the back or in a spinning application. This is a good example of how the attacker uses the anchor foot to provide a stable point in which he can more easily swing or otherwise place his other leg over his opponent's head to control it and apply Juji Gatame.

## ANCHOR FOOT TO ANY PART OF LEG, HIP OR BODY

This photo shows how the attacker anchors his right foot to his opponent's lower leg, and as a result controls his opponent's entire leg and hip area.

## ANCHOR FOOT FOR BACK ROLL JUJI GATAME

The attacker is sitting behind his opponent and controls him with a seated rodeo ride as shown here. In this photo, the attacker is using his hands to grab his opponent's lapels and pulls the defender close to the attacker's chest for maximum control of the defender's upper body. Look at how the attacker is using both of his legs and feet to manipulate the defender's legs, controlling them.

The attacker initiates his Juji Gatame from this position by shifting his left leg across the defender's hips and anchors his left foot on the defender's right upper leg and hip as shown in this photo. Using the left foot to anchor the defender's right hip (and lower body) allows the attacker to effectively control the defender as he starts his attack with Juji Gatame. This anchor foot also locks the attacker's left foot and leg onto the defender, giving the attacker a stable base to attack from. As the attacker does this, he shifts his body to his left side to give himself more room to stabilize his position and quickly swing his right leg over his opponent to apply the Juji Gatame.

The attacker quickly rolls to his left hip and side allowing him room to swing his right leg over his opponent's head to apply the Juji Gatame.

## KEY POINT: ATTACKER ACCORDIONS (SQUEEZES) OPPONENT'S SHOULDERS TOGETHER WITH HIS LEGS AND FEET.

The attacker is using his leg press position to control his opponent and as he does, he uses his legs and feet to hook and manipulate the defender's arms and shoulders so they are weak. Look at how the attacker is using his legs to draw in the defender's right arm and shoulder and squeeze the defender's arms and shoulders close together. This weakens the defender's arms and shoulders by crunching them close together. If the defender were able to "square" his shoulders he would be better able to push off the mat with his shoulders and either pull his arm free or initiate an escape. By squeezing the defender's arms and shoulders together in this way, the attacker is better able to lever the defender's arm free to apply Juji Gatame.

## KEY POINT: EVERYTHING IS A HANDLE.

The above photo also shows how everything and anything can be used as handle to control your opponent. The attacker is using his right hand to grab his left lapel, effectively trapping his opponent's left arm. The attacker, in the process of squeezing his opponent's arms and shoulders together, is using his feet to hook and manipulate the defender's right shoulder, arm and elbow for control. Not only can any body part or any part of the uniform be used as a handle, you can use your hands, arms, legs, feet or any part of your body to grab, manipulate or control your opponent.

## KEY POINT: ATTACKER USES HIS LEGS TO MANIPULATE AND CONTROL OPPONENT.

## KEY POINT: THE ROLL OR TURN CREATES MOMENTUM AND THE BALLISTIC EFFECT OF JUJI GATAME.

In addition to using a leg to accordion or squeeze the defender's shoulders together, the attacker can use either, or both, legs and feet to manipulate his opponent's arms, shoulders, head, hips or pretty much any part of his opponent's body. This photo shows the attacker using his legs and feet to trap the defender's arms as he accordions the defender's shoulders together. The attacker is using his legs and feet to manipulate the defender's arms toward his head, making the shoulder area and arms weaker and more vulnerable to being pulled apart so the Juji Gatame can be applied.

When the attacker rolls, turns or breaks his opponent down, the attacker gains momentum and an increased ballistic effect in applying Juji Gatame. This photo shows how the attacker sets his opponent up by trapping his arm in preparation for rolling back to apply the Juji Gatame. As will be pointed out in the following pages, rolling an opponent (especially if the attacker can roll or turn his opponent quickly with a fast mat tempo), the attacker exerts both control and power as he applies the armlock during the course of the rolling action. The momentum of the rolling action also closes the space between the attacker's crotch, pubic bone and hip area and the defender's upper body, shoulder and arm (that is being attacked). It doesn't matter how or in which direction the attacker rolls or turns. The strength of the attacker's hips as he rolls or turns his opponent, along with the trapping of the defender's arm between the attacker's legs, creates tremendous torque and power that is directly applied on the joint that is being attacked (the elbow or shoulder).

This shows how the attacker is using his left leg and knee to push the defender's head and upper body forward. The attacker uses his right leg placed across the defender's torso to trap his opponent to the mat as he uses his left leg and knee to manipulate the defender's head and upper body. The attacker also uses his left forearm and hand to push and control the defender's head with the intention of quickly placing his left leg over the defender's head to apply Juji Gatame.

As the attacker rolls (in this case, the attacker rolls backward; but the attacker can roll or turn in any direction that is most effective for the situation), he traps his opponent's arm in tighter to his chest and torso pinning or hugging the defender's arm so that it is attacked to the attacker's body. Doing this allows the attacker to use the entire weight of his body (which has been increased because of the momentum built up in the rolling action) to exert far more pressure on the elbow and shoulder joints to cause more pain. An important element for the attacker to perform is at the immediate conclusion of his rolling or turning action, the attacker applies more pressure on the elbow joint by arching his hips. This twofold action of rolling to create momentum and the sudden stopping action of the attacker arching his hips against the elbow joint by the pubic bone creates the ballistic effect that makes the armlock work.

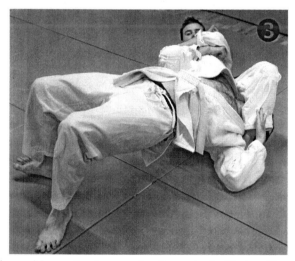

The sudden pain that results from the ballistic effect of the attacker arching his hips as he rolls onto his back causes the defender to come off of the mat in an arch or bridge. This arch by the defender is a natural reaction in an effort to reduce the stress and pain that the attacker is applying on the defender's entire arm, and especially on the defender's elbow joint and shoulder joint.

## KEY POINT: WHEN APPLYING JUJI GATAME, SIT UP AND ROLL BACK.

**IMPORTANT:** This may seem repetitive from the previous key point, but this is a subtle, yet important aspect of exerting as much control over an opponent as possible. In keeping with the core skill of rolling or turning an opponent to create momentum, the attacker will almost always finish his rolling action by positioning his crotch and pubic bone as close as possible to his opponent's arm and shoulder (that is being controlled and attacked). The attacker wants to ensure that his hips, legs and crotch are as close as possible to his opponent's near shoulder (of the arm that is being attacked), leaving little or no space to ensure that his pubic bone is a strong fulcrum. Doing this leaves little or no room for the defender to pull his arm free, turn or shrimp into the attacker or otherwise escape from the armlock.

This photo shows the attacker is rolling the defender over onto his back.

As he rolls the defender over onto his back, the attacker makes sure to finish sitting up as shown here. Doing this places the attacker's upper leg and hip right (in this photo) tightly against the left shoulder and head of the defender, giving the defender little room to pull his arm free or turn in to start an escape. Look at how the attacker's right leg is hooked over the defender's head and neck for more control. The attacker makes sure to trap the defender's left arm to his chest and torso for control of the arm.

The attacker rolls back, arches his hips and stretches the defender's arm to secure the Juji Gatame.

## KEY POINT: USE THE WEIGHT OF YOUR BODY TO ROLL BACK AND STRETCH OPPONENT'S ARM.

After trapping the defender's arm, the attacker holds the arm tightly to his chest and torso and rolls back (as well as arches with his hips) using the weight of his body to pull and straighten the defender's arm. Rather than use only the strength of his arms, the attacker uses his entire body weight to extend the defender's arm. The defender may be physically stronger than the attacker. A strong opponent who is on his back and defending against Juji Gatame may be able to actually bend and curl his extended arm back in and, by sheer strength, pull his arm free and escape the armlock.

## KEY POINT: CONTROL THE ROLL: KEEP ROLLING; NEVER LET GO OF OPPONENT'S ARM.

Keep trying to secure the armlock. You may not get your opponent on the first try, but you will get him.

Don't give up on your Juji Gatame. If at first you don't succeed, try, try again. You may not always get your opponent on the first attempt, roll or turn. In that case, don't let go of his arm and keep rolling. You may have to roll or turn into a different direction or you may have to move into a completely different way, but the important thing to remember is to never let go of his arm (unless you have been put into a compromised situation) and keep trying to stretch his arm. This photo shows the attacker doing a Spinning Juji Gatame and rolling his opponent over onto his back.

The attacker has rolled his opponent over and is controlling him with a leg press position.

The defender mounts a good defense and manages to sit on his hip and attempts to pull his arm free. The attacker uses the momentum of his opponent as he sits up and starts to roll over to his right side. Look at how the attacker does not let go of his opponent's arm that he has trapped to his chest.

The attacker continues to roll to his right and over onto his front side as he continually pulls on his opponent's arm. The attacker "stays round" and uses the defender's momentum to secure more control over him.

The attacker has rolled over and is situated on his left side as he continues to stretch the defender's trapped right arm.

The attacker has rolled through and onto his left hip and side as he stretches his opponent's arm to get the tap out. The attacker's initial intention was to roll his opponent onto his back and into a leg press position to apply his Juji Gatame. But the defender's defensive skills forced the attacker to "go to plan B" and continue to roll the defender over until he was able to stretch his arm and secure Juji Gatame.

### ▌ TECHNICAL TIP ▐

**"Mat tempo" is how fast or slow the athletes move around on the mat. A successful Juji Gatame often results from a fast tempo on the mat. Groundfighting is not always slow. Sometimes it is, but many submission techniques result from a flurry of fast (and controlled) movement by the attacker. With practice and a lot of experience, a good grappler can vary and control the tempo or pace of the action on the mat.**

## KEY POINT: STAY ROUND.

While this may sound strange to some people, if the attacker stays as round and curled up as possible when working for his Juji Gatame, he will often have a better chance of securing it. This series of photos shows several things. One important things it shows is something that was previously mentioned and that is for the attacker to keep trapping his opponent's arm and "control the roll" by continuing to try to roll or turn his opponent into his Juji Gatame. This photo shows the defender using a good defensive move by using his left hand and arm to push down on the attacker. The defender has managed to get to his knees in a stable position and is able to "posture up" and get a fairly upright body position. He also is working on pulling his right arm free and he has used his left arm to shuck off the attacker's left leg and foot from over his head and is pushing down on the attacker's left leg to control it. The defender has also managed to stack the attacker high up on his shoulders. At this point, it appears as though the defender may escape this Juji Gatame.

Another thing this series of photos shows is that the attacker is "staying round." By curling up and being as round as possible with his body, the attacker increases his mobility and ability to roll in almost any direction. By being able to roll in any direction, the attacker can not only react to his opponent's body movement, but he can also better control his own body movement and the movement of his opponent. The attacker (on bottom) has now rolled over to his right shoulder enough to trap and pull the defender's right arm closer to the attacker's chest. The attacker has also closed the space between his body and the attacker's body and has hooked his left foot and leg over the defender's head again, controlling it.

By staying round, the attacker has rolled across his shoulders and in the process, prevented the defender from standing up to escape. Another thing this photo sequence shows is how the attacker has used his legs by squeezing them together at the knees to better trap his opponent's right arm to the attacker's chest. As he has done this, the attacker has pulled the defender's right arm enough so that the defender's right arm is now levered with the elbow joint directly on the attacker's pubic bone, creating the fulcrum. The attacker arches his hips into the action of the armlock and gets the tap out.

## KEY POINT: ATTACKER USES HIS HANDS AND ARMS TOGETHER OR INDEPENDENTLY.

The following photo on page 54 also shows how the attacker is using his left hand and arm to trap his opponent's right arm and is using his right hand to grab the defender's uniform for more control. Each hand has a specific function and the effective use of them will give more and better control of an opponent. This will also be mentioned later in an analysis of how to finish Juji Gatame.

## KEY POINT: MAKE IT UNCOMFORTABLE FOR YOUR OPPONENT.

The defender is on his back and in a bad way, and the attacker is there to make sure that it doesn't get any better for him. If your opponent is placed in an uncomfortable or painful situation, he is far more likely to comply with what you want him to do. Don't cheat or do something that will permanently injure an opponent, but combat sports are rough. You can sap an opponent physically, mentally and emotionally if you grind him into the mat.

## KEY POINT: ATTACK OPPONENT'S WEAK POINTS, ESPECIALLY THE SHOULDERS.

In keeping with the idea that the attacker should make it as uncomfortable as possible for his opponent, it is important to remember that the shoulder is one of the weakest joints in the body and is certainly a target when applying Juji Gatame. When levering an opponent's arm free to straighten it, make it a point to roll toward the defender's head area, thus applying a great amount of pressure against the shoulder joint.

## KEY POINT: BE MOBILE AND WILLING TO CHANGE POSITIONS AS NECESSARY.

Groundfighting is a fluid, transitional series of positions and situations. Be willing to move or switch from one position to another as necessary to control your opponent. The photo below shows how the attacker is moving from a pinning situation and transitioning to Juji Gatame. Change position as necessary to initiate and maintain as much control over an opponent as possible at all times.

## KEY POINT: USE HANDS, ARMS, FEET AND LEGS TO STABILIZE POSITION.

This photo also shows how the attacker is using his left hand to "post" or support himself for stability as he moves form one position to another. The attacker is also using his left foot to stabilize him as he uses his right foot to push off the mat in the process of moving from one position to another. Use any part of the body to stabilize your position.

## KEY POINT: POST ON HEAD FOR STABILITY.

The attacker must post on the top of his head, not on

the side of his head or on his shoulder. By posting on the very top of his head, the attacker has more mobility to move in any direction. Not only that, the strength of the neck and muscles in the neck area provide a good, stable base. The attacker can roll in any direction when he posts on the top of his head and is not limited in the direction he may have to roll. If he posts on his shoulder or the side of his head, the attacker is limited to rolling in only one direction. This photo shows how the attacker is initiating a head roll Juji Gatame and posting on the top of his head and using his left hand to post onto the mat for added stability.

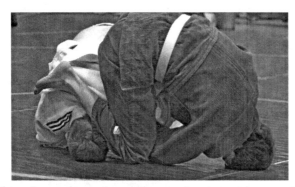

This photo shows how the attacker is posting on his head, providing a stable base so he can apply his head roll Juji Gatame. By posting on the top of his head as shown here, the attacker has a full field of vision and can better control the situation.

## KEY POINT: SCRAMBLING FOR THE ARMLOCK.

A "scramble" takes place when neither grappler has the advantage. Anyone with any experience knows that a scramble can take place in any and all combination of situations or positions that occur in groundfighting. This photo shows how the top grappler is working to

control his opponent's wrist while sitting on his head while the bottom grappler scrambles to turn in to get to a stable base.

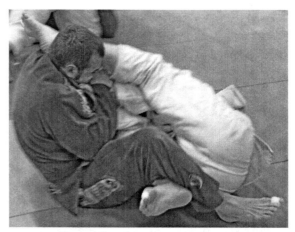

When in a scramble, think as logically as possible and always look to improve your position. You may not be able to pull off the cool armlock that you had in mind initially, so you have to do what you can to get to another position in order to either get out of trouble or move to a position of better control, even if it's temporary control. This photo shows a tough scramble where neither grappler has the advantage.

### TECHNICAL TIP

A scramble is a neutral situation. Neither athlete has the advantage. Always try to control the position and avoid a scramble situation unless you are in trouble and the best you can do to get out of trouble is to get into a scramble.

## APPLYING JUJI GATAME: THE BASIC POSITIONS FOR FINISHING JUJI GATAME

To get a better appreciation for the effectiveness of Juji Gatame, let's look at how we want things to end. What follows are the finishing positions that have an opponent vulnerable and under the attacker's control. After that, we can examine the positions that are useful for starting the process of controlling an opponent and getting him into that vulnerable finishing position.

The important thing is to stretch your opponent's arm and make him give up. It doesn't matter if he's on his back or if you are on your back or if you and he are lying belly-down on the mat or even if one or both of you are on your knees. In other words, Juji Gatame can be applied from just about any position you and your opponent may be in; the important thing is to stretch his arm and make him give up. However, the basic position to finish an opponent off is when he is flat on his back with both of the attacker's legs controlling his body. This is where the "juji" or "cross" comes into the name of the technique. But, as said earlier, a defender doesn't have to be flat on his back for an effective Juji Gatame to be applied. We will look at the two basic finish positions first, and then examine some of the other common (and not so common) positions that take place.

## THE TWO MOST COMMON FINISHING POSITIONS

Presented here are the two basic positions used when doing Juji Gatame. Following that is an explanation of some other common finishing positions used for Juji Gatame in many combat sports. Then, point-by-point, we will analyze the various components that make Juji Gatame work.

### BASIC FINISH POSITION: ONE LEG OVER THE OPPONENT'S HEAD AND THE OTHER LEG JAMMED IN THE OPPONENT'S SIDE.

This is the "classic" finishing position that is considered the most basic. While "basic," this finish position is used often and with effective results. The attacker's right (in this photo) leg is placed over the defender's head and neck and traps the defender's head. The attacker's left leg is bent at the knee and his shin and foot are jammed in the side and back of the defender's body near the armpit area, shoulder blade, the upper back at the latissimus dorsi, lower back or even at the hip. However, the closer the attacker's bent knee is jammed in the area

of the defender's armpit, the better. Also, look at how the attacker's knees are as close together as possible so the he had more control over the defender's extended

### ▆▆ TECHNICAL TIP ▆▆

**The attacker's legs and knees trap the defender's arm. The attacker must squeeze or pinch his knees and legs together tightly to trap the defender's extended arm (as well as the defender's shoulder). Don't give your opponent any "wiggle room" to extract his arm that you have worked so hard to stretch out! By squeezing your knees together, you trap your opponent's arm more tightly in place and do not allow him the chance to roll or turn his hand and arm over to extract his elbow free from the pivot point of your pubic bone. While emphasis is being made on squeezing the knees together, the attacker must make sure that his inner thighs are also used to trap his opponent's arm.**

This photo shows how the attacker's left leg is bent at the knee with his shin and foot jammed in the side of his opponent's body as he applies his Juji Gatame. Don't be mistaken that this position with the knee jammed in the side of the defender is a weak one. This is a strong and effective use of the legs to control the defender.

This photo shows how the attacker's right leg is placed over the defender's head, controlling it. The attacker makes sure that his right heel (in this photo) is jammed in the neck of his opponent. The attacker draws, or pulls, his right heel tightly into his opponent's neck, which in turn, moves the defender's head close to the attacker's upper leg and hip as shown. Doing this provides control over the defender's head, preventing him from sitting up and limiting his ability to turn his head or use his head to bridge in an effort to escape.

## FUNCTIONAL FINISH POSITION:
### ONE LEG OVER THE OPPONENT'S HEAD AND ONE LEG OVER THE OPPONENT'S TORSO

This is a common "belly up" application of Juji Gatame. The attacker's left leg (in this photo) is placed over the defender's head to control it. The attacker's right leg is placed over and across the defender's torso at the chest, stomach or hip area to control the lower part of the body. You can clearly see why Juji Gatame gets it name from this finish position.

With one leg placed over the defender's torso and the other leg placed over his head, the attacker is able to

"accordion" the defender's shoulders, squeezing them together and making his upper body weaker as a result. Crunching or squeezing the shoulders together also pulls in the defender's arms in together. A good analogy is when you bench press in the weight room. Do you bench press with your shoulders squared and flat on the bench or do you bench press with your shoulders drawn or crunched together and your arms squeezed together on the bench? Naturally, you want your shoulders square and flat so you have a solid, stable base and you can use your arms to push or press the weight off of your chest. With the attacker using his legs and feet to draw, accordion or crunch the defender's shoulders and arms together, he is better able to lever (or pry) the defender's arm free to stretch the arm and apply Juji Gatame. Sometimes, the attacker will hook his feet or ankles together as shown in this photo and sometimes he will use his feet to hook under the defender's far shoulder to control it. Either way works and it's a matter of preference and opportunity if you hook your feet or ankles together to control your opponent's shoulders.

Finishing in this position with one leg over the opponent's head and one leg over his torso is often a matter of opportunity. Some set-ups, turns, rolls, breakdowns and applications of Juji Gatame will have the attacker finish in this position and some may not. Some athletes and coaches believe that having the leg placed over the torso offers more control over the defender, and this may be the case in some situations. However, after many years of observation at all levels of sport combat, I believe both finishing positions with the defender "belly up" are equally strong and should be used as the opportunity presents itself.

## OTHER FINISHING POSITIONS

As mentioned before, neither the attacker or the defender have to end up in the classic "belly up" position with both athletes on their backs in the leg press position to finish Juji Gatame. It can happen from just about any position as the following photos show. These photos show some common finish positions that take place. In all situations, the attacker wants to exert as much control over his opponent as possible with one, or both, legs crossed over the defender's head and neck. This allows the attacker to use the strength of his legs to hook, manipulate, push, pull, or in any way control his opponent, allowing him to stretch the arm to secure the Juji Gatame.

## BELLY DOWN APPLICATION OF JUJI GATAME

A common application of Juji Gatame is the "belly down" position as shown here.

## APPLYING JUJI GATAME WHEN LYING ON YOUR SIDE

This application is fairly common and takes place when the attacker controls his opponent and the defender doesn't completely turn over onto his back or onto his front.

## APPLYING JUJI GATAME WHEN ATTACKER IS SCISSORING OPPONENT'S TORSO WITH LEGS

The attacker may not always have secure control over the defender's head and in this case, the attacker hooks his feet together to control the defender's body. As long as the attacker is able to have a good fulcrum with his pubic bone, he can stretch his opponent's arm.

## APPLYING JUJI GATAME WITH TRIANGLE CONTROL ON OPPONENT'S EXTENDED ARM

Sometimes, the attacker will use his legs to "triangle" the extended arm of the defender.

## "DOUBLE TROUBLE" OR APPLYING JUJI GATAME WITH A SANKAKU (TRIANGLE CHOKE)

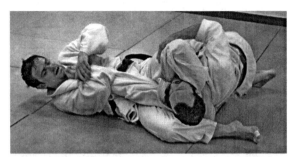

"Double Trouble" takes place with the attacker has his opponent in both a choke and an armlock, or in a pin and an armlock (or even a leglock and an armlock). This photo shows the attacker using the Triangle Choke as he applies Juji Gatame. With the attacker applying both a choke and an armlock, the defender is in double trouble.

## APPLYING JUJI GATAME WITH ONE LEG OVER OPPONENT'S SHOULDER AND THE OTHER LEG OVER HIS TORSO

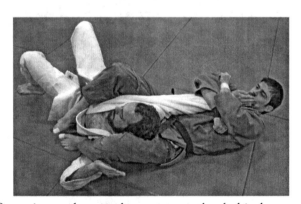

Sometimes, the attacker may not hook his leg over his opponent's head but instead hook his leg over his shoulder as shown here. While not the most common applications of Juji Gatame, it works.

## APPLYING JUJI GATAME WITH FOOT AND LEG SCISSORS OF OPPONENT'S HEAD

In some circumstances, the attacker may exert control over his opponent's head as shown here. This isolates and controls the defender's head and can be used to apply Juji Gatame.

## APPLYING JUJI GATAME WITH FEET TUCKED UNDER OPPONENT'S HEAD AND TORSO

While this is not an ideal way to finish a Juji Gatame, it may happen. If at all possible, the attacker should immediately place his leg over the defender's head, but sometimes that may not be possible.

### TECHNICAL TIP

Don't let go of your opponent's arm unless you absolutely have to. Stick with it and don't let him escape. If your opponent loosens your control or somehow manages to roll or move out of your first attempt at Juji Gatame, don't let go and keep trying to improve your position. Not all successful Juji Gatame attacks are done on the initial roll or set-up; you may have to roll your opponent a different direction to get it on the second or even third try. Also keep in mind a key point: Juji Gatame is versatile and adaptable. It can be applied from almost any position that takes place in most any kind of sport combat. Learn, practice and drill on as many situations and applications as possible in the dojo or gym so that you will instinctively react and be able to secure Juji Gatame from any position or situation (or the position or situation that you force your opponent into).

## APPLYING JUJI GATAME WITH ONE FOOT UNDER OPPONENT'S HEAT AND THE OTHER LEG OVER HIS TORSO

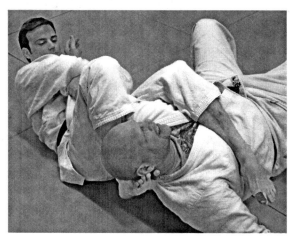

The attacker is using his right leg and foot to hook under the defender's head and using his left leg by placing it over the defender's torso to control his body. This proves that the most important thing is to stretch the defender's arm to get the tap out and if the attacker's legs and feet are useful in this position, then it's okay.

## APPLYING JUJI GATAME WITH OPPONENT "UPSIDE DOWN"

Here's a "belly down" application of Juji Gatame that shows how the armlock can be applied from any position. This situation often takes place when the defender is attempting to escape the attacker's Juji Gatame by kicking his legs and body over the attacker. There will be more on defense and escapes later in this book.

## APPLYING JUJI GATAME WITH OPPONENT ON ONE OR BOTH KNEES

Sometimes, the defender will attempt to get to one or both knees in an effort to escape. The attacker doesn't let go of his opponent's stretched arm and keeps up with the attack. Perseverance on the attacker's part is vital in getting the tap out.

## APPLYING JUJI GATAME WITH OPPONENT STANDING

Sometimes the defender will stand upright and as long as the attacker holds on tight to his opponent's stretched arm, he has a chance of getting the tap out. Here is another great example of how Juji Gatame can be applied from any position.

## TRAPPING YOUR OPPONENT'S ARM

Before you can stretch an opponent's arm you have to trap it first. Call it a trap, catch, snatch, scoop, hook, or anything you want but make sure to grab and hold the arm you intend to lock and get it as close to your torso (usually your chest) as possible. Trapping his arm to your chest or torso allows you to use the weight of your body to roll or arch back and straighten it. You are using the weight of your body and not simply your arm strength to pull, stretch or otherwise control your opponent's arm and elbow. Trap his arm as quickly as possible and make it part of your initial movement. Don't wait or hesitate to trap his arm, but instead make it part of your initial set-up to control your opponent.

When trapping your opponent's arm, make sure to trap it high enough on your torso (at your chest level) so that your opponent is unable to pull his arm back and get his elbow lower than your crotch. His elbow must not be lower than the pivot point of your fulcrum at your pubic bone, otherwise, he will be able to extract his arm free and all of your hard work at setting up the Juji Gatame will be for nothing.

Also keep in mind that you may need to lower your chest to his arm to help in trapping it tighter. Don't simply try to pull his arm to your chest, as you may have to meet it halfway by moving your chest to his arm and then letting the weight of your body straighten his arm.

## TRAPPING THE ARM: ATTACKER TRAPS IT TO HIS CHEST AND TORSO

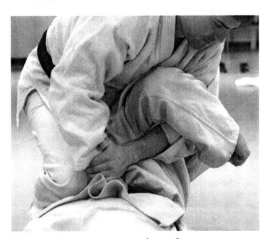

When trapping an arm, the idea is to get your opponent's arm (the one you intend to stretch) as close to your chest and torso as possible as quickly as possible and as firmly as possible. Remember, you're doing this quickly, often while moving and under pressure, so don't do anything fancy; get the job done and trap his arm so you have control of it and he doesn't. Presented in this chapter are some fundamental methods on how to trap your opponent's arm. These are some good, solid, practical ways to trap his arm that work with a high ratio of success but don't be limited by what you see

here. Later in this book, in the chapter on Levers, more information will be presented about how to trap an opponent's arm.

### ▮▮▮ TECHNICAL TIP ▮▮▮

**Trapping your opponent's arm is an integral part of levering and prying it free to be able to straighten his arm to secure the armlock. It's a strong controlling position. Before you can pry your opponent's arm out straight, you have to trap it first. Be sure to trap your opponent's arm as quickly as possible as you develop your roll, set-up or breakdown into Juji Gatame. Trapping your opponent's arm securely allows you more time to lever his arm and get the Juji Gatame. More on both trapping and levering an opponent's arm will be presented in the chapter on Levers later in this book.**

## TRAPPING THE ARM: TRAP IT QUICK

Trap your opponent's arm as quickly as possible. You will usually trap the arm you intend to stretch, but this may not always be the case. However, it usually is. The attacker latches onto the defender's arm and immediately traps it to his chest as shown in this photo. As you can see, the attacker is in the Shoulder Sit position, and trapping his opponent's arm is part of the entire controlling position.

**IMPORTANT:** You have to trap your opponent's arm before you can lock it. If you don't have control of your opponent's arm, he has a better chance of pulling it free and escaping.

# TRAPPING THE ARM: AN INTEGRAL PART OF THE ARMLOCK

This sequence of a Spinning Juji Gatame shows how the attacker has the defender's arm trapped as quickly as possible in the entire process of the attack.

The attacker (on bottom) immediately uses his left hand to trap his opponent's right arm to his chest and torso as he starts his spin into the armlock. The attacker doesn't make a "big deal" of trapping the arm. He quickly, and sometimes subtly, traps his opponent's arm as an integral part of the set-up.

As the attacker rolls his opponent over onto his back, look at how he continues us use his left arm to scoop and trap the defender's left arm to his chest. Important: The attacker makes sure that the trapped arm is as high on his chest as possible so the defender's elbow is not below the attacker's fulcrum point on his public bone.

The attacker uses both of his arms to literally hug his opponent's right arm to his chest. Making sure that the defender's right arm is firmly attached to his chest, the attacker will immediately roll back to secure the Juji Gatame, using the weight of his body to help straighten the defender's right arm.

**IMPORTANT:** As the attacker rolls, turns or applies the set-up to the armlock, he constantly traps or hugs his opponent's arm tighter and tighter to his chest and torso much in the same way a boa constrictor tightens its hold over its prey.

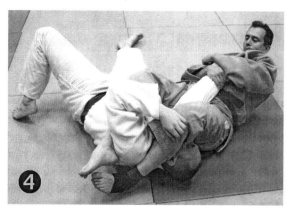

The attacker has rolled back with the defender's right arm completely straight and secured the armlock. Look at how the attacker keeps his arms hugging tightly to the defender's stretched arm. The attacker has trapped the defender's right arm to his chest and has used the weight of his body to stretch the defender's arm straight.

## TRAPPING THE ARM: THE ARM HUG-EFFECTIVE, QUICK AND USED OFTEN

This photo shows how the attacker crosses his arms and hugs his opponent's right arm to his chest as he is rolling him over. This is a common, and effective, way of trapping the arm. It is quick and leaves little room for the defender to extract his arm. Hugging an opponent's arm in this way may not be fancy, but it works and works with a high ratio of success at all levels of competition. **IMPORTANT:** There are many ways to trap an opponent's arm and a lot of them will be examined in the chapter on Levers later in this book.

### ▬▬ TECHNICAL TIP ▬▬

**When you trap your opponent's arm, you are not only controlling the arm you intend to stretch, you are controlling (or starting to control) his body as well. When you control your opponent's body, you control his position and how he moves. You are limiting his mobility and creating an opportunity for you to get your opponent into a leg press position or other controlling position to lever his arm loose and secure the Juji Gatame on him.**

## POSITION, THEN SUBMISSION: THE BASIC POSITIONS FOR APPLYING JUJI GATAME

While there are an almost infinite variety of positions that take place in any form of sport combat, there are some specific positions that take place directly relating to an effective application of Juji Gatame. As mentioned before, Juji Gatame can come from almost any position, but the two positions presented here (the Leg Press and the Shoulder Sit) are the dominant and primary positions used with regularity and with great success to control an opponent and finish him off with Juji Gatame.

### THE LEG PRESS

Your opponent knows he's in trouble when you have him on his back in what I have termed the "Leg Press" position. And on the other hand, you know that if you have your opponent on his back in a leg press, your chances of stretching his arm are pretty good.

Anytime your roll an opponent over or in any way get him onto his back, and you are seated at his side with one or both legs pressing him down to the mat, that is the leg press position. It is a common, and effective, position, yet for unknown reasons, I have never heard of a name for this position. There is no doubt that the leg press is a definite, controlling position where the attacker "rides" or controls his opponent. In some situations, the attacker may not ride his opponent in this position very long, and in other situations, the attacker may ride his opponent in the leg press for a fairly extended period of time. This is an ideal position for the attacker to trap his opponent's arm. The leg press allows the attacker control over his opponent's body, and as a result, additional time to lever, or pry, the defender's arm free and secure Juji Gatame. Sometimes, the attacker is unable to pry the defender's arms apart and straighten the arm to secure the Juji Gatame. In this case, the attacker can use the leg press position to switch to a pin or even control his opponent to such an extent that he can move into another armlock, choke or even use another application of Juji Gatame.

Study, practice and drill on the leg press on a regular basis. It's an effective position and one that is vital in your arsenal of skills.

## LEG PRESS: BASIC POSITION

This photo shows the basic application of the leg press. The attacker may keep his opponent on his back in the leg press for an extended period of time or for a short period of time, depending on the situation. The attacker is seated at the side of the defender with one leg over the defender's head, trapping it to the mat, and the other leg may be placed over the torso as shown here. In some cases, the leg may be jammed in the side of the defender's body as shown a bit later. The attacker uses this position to "ride," shifting his weight and moving as necessary to control the bottom grappler, giving the top grappler time to trap the defender's arm and secure further control over him to apply Juji Gatame. This leg press position also allows the top grappler the opportunity to switch to another position, such as a pin or other submission technique. Many variations of Juji Gatame in this book will use the leg press position.

### ▮▮▮ TECHNICAL TIP ▮▮▮

**When in the leg press position, the attacker will "ride" his opponent, shifting his weight and moving as necessary to control the defender and keep him on his back. The attacker will constantly try to assert more control and attempt to lever or pry his opponent's arms apart so he can stretch his opponent's arm and apply Juji Gatame.**

## LEG PRESS: ATTACKER MANIPULATES THE DEFENDER WITH HIS FEET AND LEGS

The attacker is wedging his left foot under the defender's left shoulder to keep the defender from placing his shoulder on the mat for stability. The attacker is using his right foot and leg to hook under the defender's left armpit to manipulate his arms and shoulders.

## LEG PRESS POSITION: HOOKING FEET TO CONTROL OPPONENT'S SHOULDERS

Sometimes, the top grappler will hook his feet or ankles together to better control and manipulate the bottom grappler's shoulders and arms.

## LEG PRESS WITH KNEE JAMMED IN OPPONENT'S SIDE AND THE OTHER LEG OVER OPPONENT'S HEAD

This photo shows how the top athlete, using the leg press for control, is jamming his left shin in the side of his opponent as he rides him for control.

## LEG PRESS TRAPPING OPPONENT'S LEG

Sometimes, the attacker will grab the defender's leg in order to lever the defender's arm loose and will use this to control the bottom athlete with the leg press.

## LEG PRESS: ATTACKER USES HANDS AND ARMS TO TAKE CONTROL OF THE ARM OR TO CONTROL HIS OPPONENT

The attacker constantly seeks to get more control of his opponent, and especially his opponent's arm so he can apply Juji Gatame. Each of the attacker's hands and arms has a specific function and the attacker must use each of them to constantly manipulate and control his opponent as the situation demands. This photo shows the attacker using his right arm to trap the defender's arm to his chest as he uses his left hand to control his opponent's hip.

## LEG PRESS: RIDE TO CONTROL

Sometimes it's a bumpy ride and the top grappler will have to do everything he can to keep his opponent on his back in the leg press. Look at how the top athlete is using his legs in an attempt to control the bottom grappler and how the top grappler is using his right hand to post on the mat for stability (the photo does not show that the attacker is using his left hand to trap the defender's right arm). The bottom grappler is doing his best to steal his right shoulder back (pull his shoulder down to the mat and away from the attacker) and shrimp into the top grappler to protect his right arm and shrimp into the top man to escape.

A resisting opponent on the bottom will bridge, arch, turn or do anything he can to escape from an attacker's leg press. This shows the defender on the bottom arching and doing a bridge in an attempt to get off of his back and initiate an escape.

# LEG PRESS: A SUCCESSFUL FINISH

By controlling your opponent in the leg press, you gain the time to pry his arm loose and secure your Juji Gatame. Your goal is to get the tap out or submission and the leg press position is probably the most often-used control position before applying Juji Gatame in any combat sport.

### ▰▰▰▰ TECHNICAL TIP ▰▰▰▰

**The leg press position has sometimes been called the "Juji Gatame Position." However, there are a lot of positions that Juji Gatame can be applied from and calling this position the "leg press" succinctly and accurately describes what the attacker is doing to his opponent.**

# RIDING AN OPPONENT WITH THE LEG PRESS

This series of photos shows how the attacker (on top in the leg press position) "rides" his opponent, shifting his weight and adjusting his leg position as needed to not only maintain control of the bottom grappler, but to gain more control of him.

The attacker has a good leg press and is controlling his opponent, but he wants to gain more control by placing his left leg over the defender's torso so he can use both of his legs and feet to manipulate and control the bottom grappler's shoulders and accordion (squeeze) them together to start the process of levering the bottom man's arm loose. The top grappler uses his right hand and arm to trap his opponent's left arm firmly to the attacker's body.

The top grappler uses his left hand to grab and control the bottom grappler's left hip as the top grappler shifts his weight to his right side (toward the direction of the bottom man's head). The top grappler continues to exert excellent control with his leg press over his opponent.

The top grappler continues to "ride" his opponent with his leg press as he starts to extract his left leg and foot from the side of the defender in preparation to quickly swing it over the defender's body.

The attacker quickly shifts his left leg over the bottom grappler's torso and uses his left hand to again grab the defender's left hip for control. Look at how the attacker's left toe is pointed so he can more easily drive his left foot over the defender's chest and torso and quickly slide it under the defender's right armpit and shoulder. Adjusting his leg position in this way has given the attacker a better chance of hooking both of his feet under the defender's far (right) shoulder to squeeze the shoulders together and making the entire shoulder area weaker and easier for the top grappler to lever the defender's left arm free to apply Juji Gatame.

The attacker has completely controlled his opponent with an effective leg press as he hooks his feet together to control and squeeze the bottom man's shoulders in order to lever his left arm free and stretch it to apply Juji Gatame. This series of photos shows how the leg press controls an opponent and gives the top grappler (applying the leg press) the time to control his opponent, which in turn gives him the opportunity to secure a successful Juji Gatame.

## THE SHOULDER SIT (OR SHOULDER SQUAT, SOMETIMES CALLED SITTING ON AN OPPONENT'S HEAD)

The "Shoulder Sit" position is another important position that directly sets your opponent up for Juji Gatame. It is a controlling position that is transitional and may not last very long. Think of this as when a vulture traps his prey. The attacker is hovering over his opponent just long enough to establish control and apply his Juji Gatame (or another technique). It is a transitional position that takes place most often from a throw (or takedown) or from a kneeling or squatting position or other dynamic, moving situation. This position gives the attacker time and opportunity to assert more control over his opponent. The attacker may be in this position for a split second, immediately following through after throwing or taking an opponent to the mat or ground, or transitioning from one ground attack to another; or the attacker may be in this position for several seconds in an effort to establish further control of the opponent. The attacker can quickly and effectively use this shoulder sit position to trap his opponent's arm to exert more control and secure Juji Gatame. While the attacker can often apply Juji Gatame from the shoulder sit, he can also quickly transition to any groundfighting skill that he may choose, or how the opportunity presents itself.

This position also enables the attacker to get lower and closer to his opponent and more effectively trap the defender's arm and roll into position to secure his Juji Gatame.

## SHOULDER SIT (OR SHOULDER SQUAT) POSITION: BASIC APPLICATION

Along with the leg press position, this is one of the most common positions used when applying Juji Gatame. Basically, the attacker squats directly over his opponent's shoulder and head as shown. This position is momentary and transient. The attacker may not be here very long; just long enough to trap his opponent's arm and secure more control before quickly applying Juji Gatame.

## FRONT VIEW OF THE SHOULDER SIT

The attacker has just thrown his opponent, turned him over or in some way broken him down and put him on the mat. The attacker immediately closes as much space as possible between his body and the defender's body by squatting over him as shown. As the attacker does this, he immediately uses his hands and arms to trap the defender's right arm (in this photo) to his torso.

The attacker exerts more control over his opponent and traps the defender's right arm to this chest as shown. Look at how the attacker has closed all space between him and his opponent. An important point is that the attacker is squatting at this point and not kneeling. By squatting, the attacker has more mobility and freedom of movement.

The attacker rolls back and pulls the defender's right arm out straight as he does. Look at how the attacker is effectively starting to apply Juji Gatame.

### ▬ TECHNICAL TIP ▬

**The shoulder sit allows the attacker to transition from one position to another with maximum control over his opponent. The shoulder sit is often done immediately after a throw or takedown and is done so quickly that most people don't view it as a controlling position.**

## BACK VIEW OF THE SHOULDER SIT

This back view shows how the attacker squats so low; he may actually sit on his opponent. The attacker is squatting over his opponent as shown, making sure to squat so he has more mobility. The attacker isn't merely squatting; he is also pressing his opponent down to the mat as he works to trap the defender's arms to the attacker's chest. The attacker's left shin is jammed into the side of the defender and the attacker's right leg is moving into position to swing over the defender's head.

The attacker has moved his right leg over the defender's head as he squats over him. The attacker is using his hands and arms to trap the defender's left arm to the attacker's chest.

The attacker closes all space between his body and the defender's body as he positions himself to roll back to apply Juji Gatame.

The attacker rolls back, stretching the defender's arm to secure Juji Gatame.

### TECHNICAL TIP

**Often, an attacker will follow-through from the Shoulder Sit position immediately stretching his opponent's arm or into the Leg Press position, relentlessly maintaining control of his opponent.**

## SHOULDER SIT FROM THROW

This shows how the shoulder sit is a transitional position that directly leads from a throw immediately into Juji Gatame.

The attacker has thrown his opponent to the mat and will follow through immediately into Juji Gatame. The attacker jams his right knee into his opponent's side.

The attacker immediately squats over his opponent as he starts to trap the defender's right arm to the attacker's chest. Look at how the attacker has used his left foot and leg to step over the defender's head. The attacker is now set to roll back and apply Juji Gatame in one smooth, quick transition from the throw to the armlock. There will be more on this transition in the chapter on Transitions later in this book.

The attacker rolls back from the shoulder sit to finish the Juji Gatame.

## SHOULDER SIT FROM KNEE OR A POSITION FROM THE GROUND

Sometimes, when the attacker has broken his opponent down or turned him onto his back, the attacker may be on one or both knees as shown here. The attacker immediately uses his hands and arms to trap the defender's arm. Look at how the attacker is positioned on his left knee and he is moving his right foot and leg over his opponent's head.

The attacker moves his left foot and leg over the defender's head and steps up off his left knee into a squatting position as shown. As he does this, the attacker squats or sits on the defender's left shoulder. From this position, the attacker will be able to roll back to apply Juji Gatame.

## SHOULDER SIT FROM A PINNING POSITION

Sometimes the attacker actually does "sit" on his opponent in the shoulder sit position as shown here.

The attacker has turned his opponent over onto his back and pinned him. The attacker has strong control over his opponent as is attempting to trap the defender's left arm or possibly secure a bent armlock. The attacker will sit on his opponent in this way as long as necessary to maintain control and methodically gain more control.

When the attacker has trapped the defender's left arm and he senses that he can successfully sit up and roll back to apply the Juji Gatame, he gets up on one knee and then the other in this squatting position. The attacker will now roll back to apply Juji Gatame.

## SHOULDER SIT WHEN OPPONENT IS FLAT

Here is another variation of the shoulder sit position where the attacker literally sits on his opponent. This is a rough, uncompromising position where the attacker can use the shoulder sit position to control his opponent and grind him into the mat. Being on the bottom is not pleasant and the attacker uses this dominant position to weaken his opponent and systematically secure Juji Gatame or another winning technique. The attacker has broken his opponent down or partially turned him onto his front side and sits on the bottom grappler's head, shoulder and upper back as the attacker uses his hands to secure more control or set up a technique. The defender on bottom is bearing the weight of the attacker's body as the attacker methodically controls the position. The attacker shifts his body weight and moves as necessary to keep his opponent flat on his front as long as necessary to further weaken the defender and methodically control him.

## SHOULDER SIT TO LEG PRESS POSITION

As often as not, the defender will immediately grasp his hands and arms together to keep them from being pulled apart. This can take place when the attacker has established a shoulder sit position and rolls the defender onto his back ending up in the leg press position. What takes place then is a fight for the arms of the defender. The attacker wants to pull them apart and stretch one for the Juji Gatame. The defender wants to keep his arms grasped together and bent at the elbows so they won't get pulled apart.

This is examined later in this book in the chapter on

Levers ("Trapping for Time"), but it's included in this chapter on Core Skills because transitioning from the shoulder sit to the leg press without losing control of the opponent is a fundamental and core skill.

The attacker has taken his opponent to the mat and immediately pounces on him stabilizing the situation with this shoulder sit position. From this shoulder sit, the attacker is using his left arm to hook his opponent's left arm to the attacker's chest; so far, so good for the attacker.

The defender offers some effective resistance and manages to pull his left arm free and attempts to use his right hand to grab it as he also attempts to curl up and roll onto his right side, away from the attacker. The attacker uses his right hand and arm as a post to stabilize his position as he shifts his body so that it continues to exert control over the bottom man. The attacker spent little time in the shoulder sit position before he transitioned to the leg press as it offered more control of his opponent.

The attacker has transitioned from the shoulder sit position to a secure leg press position with his right leg and foot over the defender's head for control of his upper body and is attempting to lever the defender's left arm free to apply Juji Gatame. The attacker will attempt to maintain the leg press position as long as possible, keeping his opponent on his back and vulnerable to having his arm levered free, scoring in a Juji Gatame win for the attacker.

### ▌TECHNICAL TIP ▌

Remember the phrase "Position, then Submission." This is the essence of what effective submission grappling is about. Grappling and fighting in any combat sport or self-defense situation is a series of position and many of them are linked together in some way. Maybe not every position or situation is connected together, but many are, especially in groundfighting. As the old saying goes, "one thing leads to another." Keeping this concept of "chain wrestling" or linking one movement to another allows you look at every situation as an opportunity to control your opponent and force him to give up to you. When groundfighting, there are many positions that a human body can be placed in, and this is the thing that keeps people like us up at night thinking. How well you control your opponent and his movement directly determines how well you control the situation and ultimately, the outcome of the fight or match. If you control the position, you are better able to secure the submission.

## THE ANGLE WHEN ROLLING TO FINISH

Sometimes, instead of rolling directly backwards, the attacker will have to roll at an angle in the direction of the defender's head or in the direction of the defender's hips and legs to apply Juji Gatame. The attacker the may, or may not, roll his body back so that he is directly sideways to the defender to apply the armlock.

## ROLL BACK TOWARD HEAD AND APPLY JUJI GATAME FROM AN UPWARD ANGLE

The attacker is controlling his opponent with a shoulder sit as he starts to trap and lever the defender's arms.

The attacker rolls back to an upward angle and as he does, he pulls and stretches his opponent's arm in the same direction as shown here. Look at how the attacker

is not sideways in relation to the defender and is situated as this extreme upward angle. This angle weakens the defender's (in this photo) left shoulder and makes it easier for the attacker to lever and stretch the defender's left arm.

The attacker rolls back and finishes the armlock at this upward angle.

### ▌ TECHNICAL TIP ▐

**If the defender's shoulders are not "square" or aligned with each other when he is lying on his back, they are weaker. Think of it this way: when you do the bench press in the weight room, are your shoulders square and aligned with each other, or is one shoulder situated higher than the other? Naturally, they are square and aligned with each other. To be able to effectively bench press, your shoulders must be aligned with each other to get the maximum use out of your entire upper body to perform the exercise. If one of the defender's shoulders is angled higher than his other, the defender's strength is compromised and the attacker is better able to trap and straighten the arm.**

## ROLL TOWARD HEAD, THEN ROLL TO LATERAL POSITION TO APPLY JUJI GATAME

World Judo Champion AnnMaria (Burns) DeMars demonstrates this application. The attacker first traps and then levers the defender's right arm free and as she does, she rolls to her left hips and side (toward the defender's head). The defender's shoulder is weaker in this compromised position, making it easier for the attacker to pry the arm loose. Look at how the attacker is leaning to her left to trap the defender's right arm closer to her body and is using the weight of her body rather than arm strength to control the defender's arm.

The attacker has her opponent's right arm firmly trapped to her chest and torso as she pulls the defender's hands apart and levers the right arm, starting to straighten it. The attacker now rolls from her left hip and side across her buttocks and is more sideways in relation to the position of the defender's body. Doing this further wrenches the defender's right arm free to straighten it.

The attacker has wrenched the defender's right arm free, straightening it and rolls back as she arches her hips to apply the Juji Gatame.

## ROLL BACK TOWARD OPPONENT'S FEET OR HIP AND APPLY JUJI GATAME: LOW ANGLE OF APPLICATION

While not often seen, stretching the defender's arm in a downward direction toward his hip or leg is an effective way of securing Juji Gatame. The attacker uses his left hand to trap the defender's right arm as shown and is using his left arm and hand to trap the defender's right leg as shown. This lever will be presented in the chapter on Levers later in this book.

The attacker traps the defender's arm and leg and rolls to his right side, prying the defender's arm loose.

The attacker applies Juji Gatame with the defender's right arm in a downward position and not extended out sideways as is usually done. This again shows the versatility of how Juji Gatame can be applied from almost any direction or position.

## FEET IN THE AIR: A SURE SIGN YOUR JUJI GATAME IS EFFECTIVE

Before we go on to the next chapter, let's take some time to admire our work. Sometimes, especially when the Juji Gatame is snapped on suddenly and with a lot of force, the defender's feet will leave the mat. This is a natural, defensive reaction to the pain and ballistic effect of the armlock as it is being applied. The defender may lift, swing, kick, bend or in some way move one or both legs. When he does this, he's finished. The armlock has definitely done its job. Shown here are a couple of instances where there is no doubt about the effectiveness of Juji Gatame.

The defender has drawn both of his feet up and together off the mat. This type of involuntary movement of the feet and legs is purely defensive and a sure sign of surrender. As you can see, the referee was on top of the action and already signaling to the attacker that the Juji Gatame was effective and the match was over.

When the defender swings his feet and legs straight up in the air, it's a sure sign he's had enough. The shock of the sudden, ballistic action of having the arm stretched and the elbow bent backward causes such an extreme reaction by the defender.

## THE ARCH: BOTH A NATURAL REACTION AND A DEFENSIVE MOVEMENT.

Another natural defensive movement is the arch. The defender may often arch or bridge up as the attacker applies pressure to his shoulder and arm. This arching action of the body is a natural one that eases the pain and pressure of the joint lock as it is being applied. In some cases, the defender may also be arching up in an effort to escape the armlock. While this isn't a sure sign that the defender is through, there's no doubt that he's definitely in trouble.

The next chapter examines the four basic ways to get an opponent into Juji Gatame. By systematically approaching the functional applications of Juji Gatame, you will have a better appreciation of how to apply this armlock in a variety of situations and positions.

# THE FOUR BASIC APPLICATIONS OF JUJI GATAME

## "THERE'S A METHOD TO MY MADNESS." SHAKESPEARE

## THE FOUR BASIC ENTRIES INTO JUJI GATAME

After studying this armlock for many years, it occurred to me that (as far as I could see), there was no "system" or "method" in the teaching of Juji Gatame. In other words, there was no structure in how athletes learned Juji Gatame other than learning the coach's favorite application or entry into the technique. If an athlete didn't have the opportunity to train on a regular basis with a coach who was steeped and well versed in both the fundamental, core skills as well as knowledgeable in the practical applications of the armlock, that athlete generally had a sketchy idea of how effective and versatile Juji Gatame really is.

I suppose the same could be said for any technique or skill of any subject, but what I sought to accomplish was to give some structure as to how Juji Gatame can be taught and learned most efficiently. These four basic methods of Juji Gatame were developed because of this.

By logically and systematically approaching this armlock from the very beginning to the most functional applications, anyone who wants to excel at Juji Gatame will be able to do so and have a solid understanding of how to perform it and be able to perform it under the stress of a real fight or match.

When it comes down to it, and no matter how the attack was initiated, there are four fundamental applications of Juji Gatame. Each of the four basic applications has been named based on their function and the direction in which the attacker moves to apply the armlock.

This chapter will examine these four basic approaches to the functional application of Juji Gatame. Each of the following chapters in this book will key in on the specifics and functional application of each of these four basic applications.

The four basic applications or entries to Juji Gatame are categorized in the following way:
1. Spinning Juji Gatame
2. Back Roll Juji Gatame
3. Head Roll Juji Gatame
4. Hip Roll Juji Gatame

In this chapter, each application will be presented and analyzed from three different views to show, at least from a fundamental perspective, how each entry is unique in its functional application of Juji Gatame. The first series of photos for each entry shows the basic application. The second series of photos show each entry from the back view to offer a different perspective of the movement of the basic application. The third series of photos for each entry shows one of its many functional applications for that particular entry. For a more thorough examination and analysis of each of these entries into Juji Gatame, please refer to the specific chapter dedicated to each later in this book.

Each entry's name describes the action of the move, and even if an athlete learns only the basic application of each of these four entries, he or she will have a thorough and systematic appreciation for how Juji Gatame really works and how it can be applied in a variety of situations.

## SPINNING JUJI GATAME: BASIC APPLICATION

This entry into Juji Gatame is unique in that the attacker applies the armlock while on his back and spinning under his opponent to gain control and momentum. The attacker's spinning movement rolls the defender over onto back to secure the armlock. As a result, this basic entry is named Spinning Juji Gatame.

While this is the most basic application of Juji Gatame, don't be fooled that it is only for novices. The Spinning Juji Gatame teaches more than just the armlock; it teaches important skills that every athlete will use for as long as he engages in groundfighting.

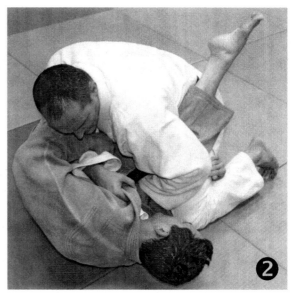

The attacker quickly rolls to his right side and hip (this is called "shrimping"). As he does this, the attacker uses his right hand to reach between the defender's legs and grab the defender's left leg immediately above the knee. The attacker uses his left hand to trap the defender's right arm to the defender's torso as shown. Look at how the attacker's body is curled, resembling a shrimp (that's why we call this movement shrimping). The attacker's right leg is placed on the defender's left side at about the ribcage.

The attacker is on his back with his opponent between his legs as shown.

The attacker swings his left leg over the defender's head and neck as shown. At this point, the attacker starts his spinning action to roll the defender over.

This photo shows how the attacker points his left toe, giving him more power in his left leg to control his opponent's head, neck and upper body. Look at how the attacker is perpendicular to the defender.

### TECHNICAL TIP

**The spinning action must be done with a lot of speed and force much in the same way one would throw an opponent to the mat. A fast, compact spinning action gets an opponent over quicker and with more control.**

The attacker rolls his opponent over as shown. Look at how the attacker is using his right hand and arm to scoop and control the defender's left leg as the attacker rolls him over. The attacker makes sure to use his left hand to continue to trap the defender's right arm as shown.

The attacker rolls the defender over onto his back and sits up to ensure that there is no space between the attacker's crotch, pubic area and hips and the defender's right shoulder and arm.

The attacker rolls onto his back and secures Juji Gatame.

## SPINNING JUJI GATAME: ANOTHER VIEW FROM THE BACK

This view from the backside of the attacker shows how the attacker "spins" under the defender. An important thing to mention is how close the attacker's hips and buttocks (seated on the left in this photo) are to the defender's knees. This close, compact space between the attacker and defender is necessary for the defender to quickly spin under his opponent. Some exponents of Juji Gatame prefer more space between the attacker and defender, but my preference is for the attacker to be as close as possible to this opponent when starting the spinning Juji Gatame.

### ▓▓▓▓ TECHNICAL TIP ▓▓▓▓

**When attacking with Juji Gatame, do not let go of your opponent's arm or give up on the attack. Keep a firm hold of his arm and continually try to gain more control of his body and the position. This situation where the defender attempts to stand or stands is a good example of how the attacker can secure the Juji Gatame and get the tap out if he keeps hold of his opponent's arm and stays round. Remember: stay round (doing this allows the attacker to keep rolling or turning an opponent) and never let go of his (or her) arm.**

This photo shows how closely the attacker spins under his opponent.

The attacker has spun under his opponent and is perpendicular to the defender's body at this point. Keep in mind that the spinning action of the attacker is fast and forceful. Do not attempt to slowly spin under an opponent.

The spinning action of the attacker starts to roll his opponent over as shown.

The attacker spins his opponent over onto his back as the attacker uses his right arm to trap the defender's left arm to the attacker's chest as shown.

The attacker sits upright on his buttocks to ensure that there is little or no room between his crotch, pubic bone and hip area and the defender's left shoulder and arm.

The attacker rolls back and secures Juji Gatame.

## SPINNING JUJI GATAME: A FUNCTIONAL APPLICATION

In this situation, the opponent attempts to stand to escape the Spinning Juji Gatame by the attacker.

This entry shows how Juji Gatame can be applied against an opponent who stands to escape, avoid or defend the attacker's Spinning Juji Gatame. The attacker continues to spin and turn under his opponent, preventing the defender from escaping and adding torque to the action of the armlock. The attacker should not give up on his attack if his opponent manages to get to a knee or stand. Some combat sports such as judo call a break to the action if one athlete pulls another up off the mat in this situation. I always tell my judo athletes to keep attacking until the referee orders them to stop.

Sometimes, the defender will stand in an attempt to escape the attack or pull the attacker off of the mat as a defensive move to avoid getting his arm stretched. In this photo, the defender has stood up as the attacker spins under him with a spinning Juji Gatame.

The attacker uses his left hand and arm to trap the defender's left leg as shown. As he does this, the attacker uses his legs to control the defender's upper body. Look at how the attacker hooks his left leg over his opponent's head preventing him from gaining an upright, standing position. As he does this, the attacker keeps spinning to his right and rolls the defender over.

The attacker has rolled his opponent over as shown.

The attacker secures Juji Gatame.

## BACK ROLL JUJI GATAME: BASIC APPLICATION

The Back Roll application takes place in a lot of circumstances when using Juji Gatame. This entry is often used as a follow-through from a throw or takedown and provides an excellent way to transition from a stable position such as a leg press position, shoulder sit position or from a mount position when pinning an opponent.

The name of this application describes what the attacker does; he rolls back as he applies Juji Gatame.

The attacker is at his opponent's left side in this photo and traps the bottom grappler's left arm as shown. The attacker places his left shin firmly onto his opponent's left side.

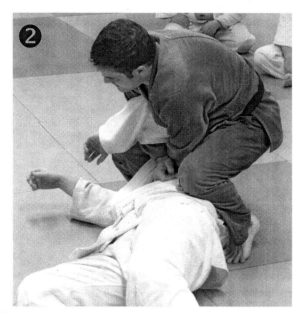

The attacker controls his opponent with a shoulder sit position, making sure to swing his right leg over his opponent's head as the attacker securely jams his left shin into the defender's left side at his ribcage area.

The attacker continues to trap his opponent's arm tightly to his chest as he squats low getting ready to roll onto his back.

The attacker rolls backward as he hugs his opponent's left arm to his chest, arches his hips and squeezes his legs together to secure the Juji Gatame.

## BACK ROLL JUJI GATAME: VIEW FROM THE BACK

This series of photos from the backside of the grapplers shows how the attacker literally rolls onto his back in order to apply the Juji Gatame.

Controlling an opponent from this position is called a "seated rodeo ride." The attacker is behind his opponent

and uses both hands to hook under the defender's arms to control his upper body. The attacker has his hooks in and is using his legs to control his opponent's hips and legs.

The attacker shifts his body weight to his left hip as he prepares to swing his right leg over his opponent's left shoulder and head.

The attacker swings his left foot and leg over his opponent's left shoulder and head as shown.

The attacker rolls the defender onto his back and applies the Juji Gatame.

## BACK ROLL JUJI GATAME: A FUNCTIONAL APPLICATON

In this situation, when the attacker has control over his opponent in a Mount or Vertical Pin. This is a common application often used in all forms of sport combat, but seen frequently in Mixed Martial Arts. The attacker has controlled his opponent by sitting on his chest or torso, establishing a dominant position that he can often hold for a good, long period of time. From this strong position, if the attacker's goal is to secure Juji Gatame, he will rotate over his opponent's body, swinging his hips and legs over, and roll onto his back to apply Juji Gatame. There are more variations of this application in the chapter on Back Roll Juji Gatame later in this book.

The attacker controls his opponent with a strong pinning position. Whether you call it a mount (in MMA or BJJ), Tate Shiho Gatame (in Judo or Jujitsu) or a schoolboy sit (in some forms of Catch Wrestling), this is a strong controlling position for the top grappler.

The attacker uses his right arm to trap his opponent's arms as the attacker uses his left hand to pull up on his opponent's head and wedge his right leg under it.

**IMPORTANT:** This series is a good example of how the attacker rolls back as he applies Juji Gatame. There are a variety of positions and situations where the roll back application is useful and effective presented later in the chapter on Back Roll Juji Gatame.

The attacker quickly switches the trapping hand to his left hand and secures the defender's arms to his chest as shown. As he does this, the attacker starts to spin or rotate his body so that he can swing his left leg over his opponent. The attacker uses his left hand to post onto the mat for stability.

The attacker rotates and as he does, he swings his left leg over his opponent as shown. The attacker continues to uses his left hand to trap his opponent's arms to his chest.

The attacker rolls back to apply Juji Gatame.

## HEAD ROLL JUJI GATAME: BASIC APPLICATION

The head roll application of Juji Gatame often comes from a fast tempo or flurry of action on the mat. This entry into Juji Gatame is really one of the most exciting to watch as the attacker literally rolls the defender over his head as he applies the armlock. The head roll Juji Gatame is an effective and often-used application and is used in every form of sport combat.

Anytime the defender is rolled over his head as the attacker applies Juji Gatame, it is the Head Roll Juji Gatame. There are different methods of how the attacker places his leg over his opponent's head as he rolls him, but the common theme of all head roll entries into Juji Gatame is the action of rolling the defender over his head to apply the armlock.

In this basic application, the attacker starts with a standing ride on his opponent who is on all fours.

The attacker drives his right leg over and under his opponent's body and places (anchors) his right foot

on the defender's left upper leg as shown. As he does this, the attacker positions his body over the defender as shown, placing the top of his head on the mat for stability. The attacker uses his left arm to hook and trap the defender's left arm to the attacker's body.

The attacker places his left foot and leg on the back of the defender's head as shown. The attacker is posting on the top of his head onto the mat for stability as he uses both of his arms to trap the defender's right arm to the attacker's body.

At this point, the attacker is in a stable position as shown in this photo. The attacker will often use his right hand and arm to grab or hook the defender's near (right) leg to help in rolling the defender over.

**⑤**

The attacker forcefully uses his left leg and foot to drive the defender's head down by swinging his left knee to the direction of the defender's lower body. Look at how the defender is starting to roll over his head.

**⑥**

The attacker uses his left leg and foot to drive the defender's head down by swinging his left knee toward the defender's lower body and rolling onto his left hip as shown. The defender's right leg and foot that has anchored the defender's left upper leg helps in the roll much in the way a pendulum swings.

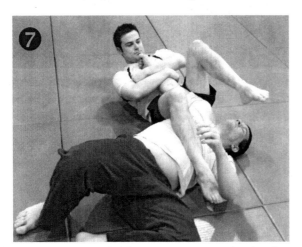

**⑦**

The attacker has rolled his opponent over his head onto his back as shown. The attacker immediately swings

his left leg over the defender's head. Look at how the attacker uses his right leg to trap the defender's body and how the attacker has used both of his hands to trap the defender's right arm to the attacker's chest.

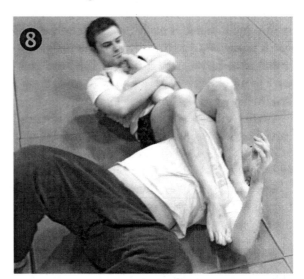

**⑧**

The attacker applies Juji Gatame.

**IMPORTANT:** While the head roll application of Juji Gatame may look difficult to execute, it is one of the most commonly used methods to turn an opponent onto his back to apply the armlock. Like the three other basic applications of Juji Gatame, the head roll entry is versatile and can be applied from a variety of positions and situations. Refer to the chapter on Head Roll Juji Gatame later in this book for many effective entries using this application.

# HEAD ROLL JUJI GATAME: ANOTHER VIEW FROM THE BACK

This application of the head roll Juji Gatame is seen often in grappling sports where the judogi or jujitsugi are used. This sequence of photos shows how the attacker uses the defender's pant leg to assist in the action of rolling the defender over his head to apply the armlock.

The attacker places his right shin over the back of the defender' neck as shown in this photo. As he does this, the attacker continues to uses his right arm to trap the defender's left arm to the attacker's chest. The attacker starts to roll onto his right side as he starts the head roll action.

The attacker drives his left foot and leg under the defender's body as shown. Look at how the attacker uses his left hand and arm to post onto the mat for stability.

The attacker drives his right knee and leg downward and toward the defender's lower body as the attacker rolls onto his right hip as shown. This forces the defender's head and shoulders down and starts the action of rolling the defender over his head. The attacker uses his left hand to grab the defender's left pant leg.

The attacker places the top of his head onto the mat for stability as he uses his right arm to hook and trap the defender's left arm. The attacker moves his right leg over the defender's body as shown in preparation for using the right foot and leg to jam onto the back of the defender's neck and head.

The attacker uses his left hand to pull the defender's left leg and drag it over and across the attacker as shown to assist in the head roll action.

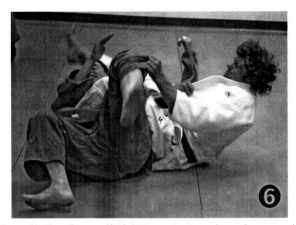

The attacker has rolled his opponent directly over the opponent's head and onto his back.

The attacker secures the Juji Gatame.

## HEAD ROLL JUJI GATAME: A FUNCTIONAL APPLICATION

In this situation, head roll Juji Gatame is applied from the guard position or when the attacker is fighting off of his back, buttocks or hips.

This series of photos shows how the head roll application is named for the direction that the attacker rolls his opponent over and can be applied from any starting position. Some might say that this is simply a variation of the Spinning Juji Gatame, but in reality, the attacker is placing his left leg and foot over his opponent's head and rolling him directly over his head.

The attacker (in the bottom) uses his left arm to trap

his opponent's right arm. As he does this, the attacker rolls to his right hip and wedges his right foot onto the defender's left hip. Doing this creates an anchor, giving the attacker more control of his opponent and a pivot point to attack from.

The attacker rolls onto his right side as he swings his left leg over his opponent's body as shown. As he does this, the attacker uses both arms to trap the defender's right arm to the attacker's chest. Look at how the attacker is using his right foot to anchor onto the defender's left hip and upper leg.

The attacker rolls over onto his right side as he continues to swing his left leg over his opponent. Look at how the defender is already starting to lose his balance toward his head.

The attacker places his left leg and foot on the back of the defender's neck as the attacker rolls over onto his front.

The attacker sits through with his left leg and knee and rolls onto his left hip as shown. As he does this, the attacker continues to use his left hand to trap the defender's right arm and uses his right hand to grab the defender's right leg. The attacker rolls the defender over the defender's head.

The attacker has rolled his opponent over onto his back and swings his left leg over the defender's head to control it in this leg press position.

The attacker applies Juji Gatame.

## HIP ROLL JUJI GATAME: BASIC APPLICATION

This application is similar to the head roll Juji Gatame, but instead of rolling the defender over his head, the attacker rolls in the direction of the defender's hip to secure the Juji Gatame making it a unique entry into the armlock. As in all of the basic entries into the armlock, the rolling action initiated by the attacker builds momentum and adds to the control that the attacker has in securing Juji Gatame.

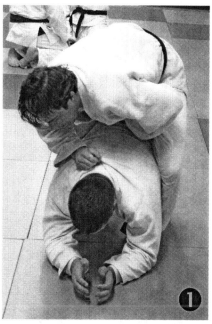

The attacker has taken his opponent to the mat and the defender is on all fours.

The attacker hooks his right leg under the defender's body as the attacker reaches over the defender. The attacker posts on the top of his head for stability and is sideways to the defender's body.

The attacker uses his left leg and foot to hook under the defender's head as shown, all the while posting on the top of his head for stability. The attacker uses both of his arms to grab the defender's right arm to trap it to the defender's body.

The attacker rolls over his right shoulder, in the direction of the defender's right hip. Look at how the attacker uses his left leg to hook under the defender's head to initiate the rolling action of the defender.

The attacker continues to roll over his right shoulder

and rolls the defender over as shown. Look at how the attacker continues to trap the defender's right arm tightly to his chest as he rolls the defender over.

The attacker rolls the defender over onto his back.

The attacker rolls his opponent over onto his back and the attacker comes into an upright, sitting position as shown.

The attacker rolls back to secure the Juji Gatame.

# HIP ROLL JUJI GATAME: ANOTHER VIEW FROM THE BACK

In this situation, the hip roll Juji Gatame is applied when an opponent is lying flat on his front in a defensive position. Not many athletes expect to be rolled into a Juji Gatame from this defensive position. This sequence clearly shows that the attacker rolls in the direction of the defender's hips when applying this entry.

This series of photos shows how even when an opponent if lying flat on his front, the last thing he may think the attacker will do is roll him over onto his back to secure Juji Gatame. This hip roll Juji Gatame application shows how this armlock can be applied from a wide variety of situations.

The defender is lying flat on his front. Amazingly, many athletes lay in this position, thinking they are safe or waiting for the referee to call a break in the action to save them from the opponent. In this situation, the top grappler has a decided advantage. The top grappler uses his left hand to grab his opponent's collar (if there is no collar to grab, the top grappler would use his left hand and arm to hook under the defender's right shoulder). Look at how the attacker sits sideways on the bottom man's back as the attacker uses his right hand to grab his opponent's belt.

The top grappler uses his left arm to hook under his opponent's right shoulder and arm as shown. The attacker traps the defender's right arm to his chest. As he does this, the attacker uses his left foot and leg to step over the defender's head and jam the left foot under the

head and neck of the defender as shown. The attacker's right foot is wedged in the defender's midsection.

The attacker rolls over his right shoulder as shown, in the direction of the defender's right hip.

This photo shows how the attacker rolls over his right shoulder.

The attacker continues to roll over his right shoulder and rolls the defender over as shown in this photo. Look at how the attacker's left leg and foot is controlling the defender's head and forcing the defender to roll.

The attacker completes his roll and turns his opponent onto his back. The attacker immediately applies Juji Gatame.

# HIP ROLL JUJI GATAME: A FUNCTIONAL APPLICATION

In this variation of the hip roll Juji Gatame, the attacker is controlling his opponent in a mount position or from a vertical pinning situation in judo or sambo.

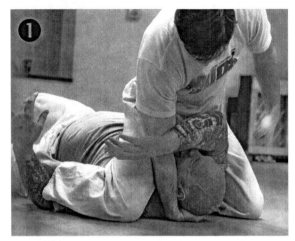

The attacker is on top of his opponent and controlling him as shown. The attacker uses his right knee to pin the defender's left arm to the mat.

The attacker starts his attack by using his left arm to scoop the defender's right arm and trap it to the attacker's chest. The attacker stabilizes his position as he comes off the mat with his left foot.

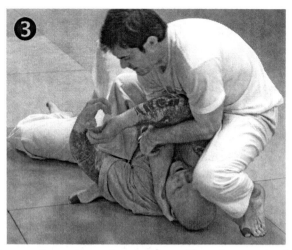

The attacker spins to his right quickly as he uses his left hand and arm to continue to trap the defender's right arm. The attacker uses his right hand to hook under the defender's head to keep the defender from attempting to bridge or arch to escape. Grabbing the defender's head also gives the attacker a stable base to better spin. Look at how the attacker moves his left leg as he squats.

The attacker uses his left leg to hook over the defender's head as shown as the attacker rolls over his right shoulder (rolling toward the defender's right hip).

The attacker rolls over his right shoulder, all the while scooping the defender's right arm tighter to the attacker's chest as he rolls.

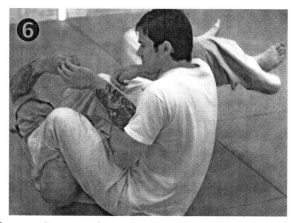

The attacker completes the shoulder roll and comes up to a seated position as shown. Doing this places the attacker very close to the defender.

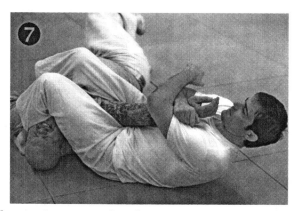

The attacker secures Juji Gatame.

## THE FOUR BASIC APPLICATIONS ARE INSTRUMENTAL IN UNDERSTANDING JUJI GATAME AND ITS MANY VARIATIONS

The four primary applications of Juji Gatame: 1) Spinning Juji Gatame, 2) Back Roll Juji Gatame, 3) Head Roll Juji Gatame, and 4) Hip Roll Juji Gatame are in some way used in every functional application of this versatile armlock.

The following chapters will examine and analyze a variety of functional entries, turns, rolls, breakdowns and set-ups, classified (sometimes loosely) into the four primary applications. Many of the applications tend to blend together, but in an effort to systematically present, and thoroughly examine and analyze, the many forms of Juji Gatame, the four primary entries will be used as a guide.

The next chapter examines Spinning Juji Gatame and its many functional applications.

**▬▬ TECHNICAL TIP ▬▬**

**The four basic applications provide a framework for the study and understanding of Juji Gatame. From these four primary applications, there are an infinite number of ways to stretch an opponent's arm with Juji Gatame.**

# SPINNING JUJI GATAME

## "A CLEVER FIGHTER IS ONE WHO NOT ONLY WINS, BUT EXCELS IN WINNING." SUN TZU

What has come to be called Spinning Juji Gatame is the first of the four basic applications of the Juji Gatame presented in this book. From a coaching perspective, I recommend teaching this application before the other three for a number of reasons. First, this is a dynamic and active application of Juji Gatame. It works and it works on a consistent basis with a high ratio of success. Second, all the fundamental movements necessary to trapping the opponent's arm, establishing a good fulcrum, using the legs and all the elements that make up an effective armlock are found in this application. Third, this basic application of Juji Gatame teaches, and reinforces, good groundfighting skills such as staying round, working off the buttocks or hip, mobility, using the hands, arms, legs and feet to manipulate and control the opponent, the ability to shift body weight and other key factors that make up a successful and effective armlock. These skills are used in all phases of groundfighting, not only in this specific application of Juji Gatame, so this is an ideal initial skill to teach to novices (and reinforce on a regular basis in drill training with more advanced and elite athletes). Fourth, learning this application initially sets the stage for the learning of the other three basic applications more easily. Through the years, I have experimented with teaching each of the four basic applications initially and have found that the skills necessary for success in this application are more easily transferred to the other basic applications and for groundfighting in general.

This spinning application can be used against opponents who are on both knees, on one knee, standing on both feet or pretty much in any position seen in any form of submission grappling, judo, sambo, jujitsu or sport combat. Spinning Juji Gatame is a versatile and adaptable set-up and used in all levels of competition and fighting. For this reason, it's recommended that you drill on this form of Juji Gatame every practice; make no excuses to avoid it. It is a fundamental position weapon in your arsenal, and like any weapon, if you don't train with it on a regular basis, you won't have the instinctive skill necessary under stressful, real-world conditions. Drilling on the Spinning Juji Gatame every workout will definitely enhance the skill level of every athlete who makes it a daily part of his or her practice.

Some of these spinning Juji Gatame applications may look alike at first glance, but take the time to study each of them and their individual, unique differences (as well as their particular uses) will become apparent. As with all the variations of Juji Gatame in this book, there will be subtle, yet significant, differences in each of the applications presented.

The word "shrimp" or "shrimping" will be used often when describing what goes on when doing a spinning Juji Gatame. "Shrimping" is the action of the attacker rolling to one side, mostly on his hip, and curling up to make his body as round as possible. This shrimping movement allows the attacker maximum mobility and is a vital (and often-used) movement when doing spinning Juji Gatame.

## SPINNING JUJI GATAME (THE BASIC APPLICATION WITH OPPONENT ON BOTH KNEES)

Presented here is the basic application of spinning Juji Gatame. Use this as your starting point in your study of this armlock. As many aspects of this basic spinning Juji Gatame will be shown here as possible, so it may seem a bit like "overkill" but to have a comprehensive understanding of Juji Gatame, it is important to cover as many details as possible. By the way, even though this is the "basic" way of applying spinning Juji Gatame, it works at all levels of competition. The best advice is to drill on this every workout, without fail (refer to the chapter on Exercises and Drills).

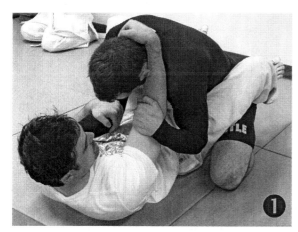

The attacker is reclining and sitting on his buttocks very close to his opponent with his buttocks touching (or very close) to the defender's knee as shown. The attacker uses his left arm to trap the defender's right arm at the elbow and upper forearm and the attacker uses his right arm and hand (if necessary) to control his opponent's head as shown.

What is presented here is the basic application of spinning Juji Gatame and it is done with the defender on both knees. On the following pages, spinning Juji Gatame (when the defender is on one knee or standing) will be presented as well. When teaching, learning and practicing spinning Juji Gatame, work on this basic version of having the defender on both knees, then progress to the application with the defender kneeling on one knee and then progress on to the variation with the defender standing or even squatting. It's recommended that you drill on all three variations on a regular basis to develop an aggressive mindset and approach to doing Juji Gatame from this position.

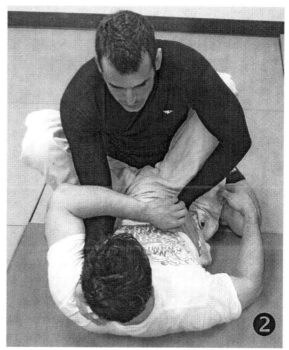

There is minimal space between the attacker (on bottom) and the defender when initiating this entry. Some people may like a bit more room at the hips when starting the spin into this application than I recommend. However, it's been my experience that the attacker's hips have to be very close to the defender for the highest ratio of success when doing spinning Juji Gatame. This allows no (or little) room for the defender to escape and still affords the attacker the ability to spin to his hip or side and shrimp under his opponent to create the rolling action. When setting this up, the attacker should try to sit as close to the defender's knee (or knees) as possible.

The attacker rolls to his right side (in this photo) and mostly onto his right hip. As he does this, the attacker rolls or curls into his opponent so that the attacker's body is now sideways in relation to the defender's body as shown. The attacker drives off of his left foot. Doing this gives the attacker more power into his shrimping action and allows him to spin with more mobility under his opponent. The attacker's left foot and leg are also in good position to quickly swing over the defender's head.

This side view of the attacker's shrimping action shows a number of important things. 1) Notice how close the attacker's head is in relation to the defender's left knee. This is important for the attacker to be curled up in this way so he can quickly roll his opponent over. 2) Look at how the attacker is using his left arm to trap his opponent's right arm to the attacker's chest. 3) The attacker uses his right hand to reach between his opponent's legs and grabs his opponent's left leg near the knee as shown here. Grabbing the defender's leg in this way gives the attacker a handle to grab as he rolls the defender over and onto his back. Grabbing the leg in this way also gives the attacker a good anchor or pivot point so he can pull himself in closer to his opponent's knee. 4) The attacker's right leg is placed against the defender's left side at about the ribcage. The attacker

will use this leg to help drive and roll his opponent over. 5) This is an important point; the attacker is shrimped or curled up and is on his right hip (and not flat on his back). This shrimping action is vital to staying round and allowing the attacker to have greater freedom of movement when doing the spinning Juji Gatame.

The attacker swings his left leg and foot over his opponent's head as shown. Look at how the attacker continues to use his left arm to trap his opponent's right arm to the attacker's chest.

The attacker swings his left foot and leg over his opponent's head and uses his left leg to hook the defender's neck and head tightly as shown. The defender's neck is being tightly controlled with the bent left leg of the attacker. Look at how the attacker points his left foot to gain more power into this hooking action. As he does this, the attacker uses his right leg to drive and push against the defender's left side at about the ribcage. As he is doing this, the attacker continues to shrimp and spin into his opponent. This spinning action builds momentum to help roll the defender over onto his back, and it also gets the attacker closer to the defender's body to exert more control in the entire movement. The attacker uses his right hand and arm to hook under his opponent's left leg at about the knee and the attacker uses his right arm to help left the defender over as he rolls him.

The attacker continues to roll his opponent over as shown. Look at how round the whole action is, giving the attacker more mobility and added momentum in the rolling action.

This photo shows the rolling action from a different view. Look at how the attacker's left leg is used to drive the defender's head over. The attacker's right leg continues to drive hard against the defender's side and the attacker uses both of his legs to "steer" the defender's body as the attacker rolls him over. Look at how the attacker uses his right hand and arm to help lift and roll the defender's left leg over. The bodies of the attacker and defender are locked together with the attacker in complete control.

The attacker completes his spin and rolls his opponent onto his back. At this point, it is important that the attacker sit up on his buttocks as shown here, establishing his position and making sure that his body is as close to his opponent as possible. This way, the attacker's hips, crotch and pubic bone are jammed up against the defender's left shoulder and arm, with the attacker's crotch serving as the fulcrum for the armlock. The attacker is now controlling his opponent to the mat in the leg press position.

The attacker completes his spin and rolls his opponent onto his back. At this point, it is important that the attacker sit up on his buttocks as shown here, establishing his position and making sure that his body is as close to his opponent as possible. This way, the attacker's hips, crotch and pubic bone are jammed up against the defender's left shoulder and arm, with the attacker's crotch serving as the fulcrum for the armlock. The attacker is now controlling his opponent to the mat in the leg press position. Look at how the attacker continues to trap his opponent's right arm to his chest.

This photo catches the action of the attacker using his arms to trap the defender's right arm tightly to the attacker's chest. The attacker will roll backward and the trapping action of the defender's right arm and the body weight of the attacker rolling back will extend and stretch the defender's right arm.

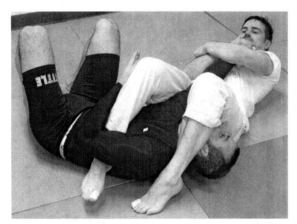

The attacker rolls back, and as he does, arches his hips so that there is more power at the fulcrum, locking the extended right arm of the opponent and secures the Juji Gatame.

Okay, the previous sequence of photos showed the basic application of spinning Juji Gatame. It can't be stressed enough that this entry is the basis of every Juji Gatame application that is presented in this book. Learn the spinning Juji Gatame and practice it often; it will serve you well. What follows are some specific points that make for a successful spinning Juji Gatame on a consistent basis and with a high ratio of success.

## SHRIMPING: THE FUNDAMENTAL SKILL IN MOBILITY FOR SPINNING JUJI GATAME

Shrimping, or the ability to curl the body making it round, is an essential skill when doing Juji Gatame, especially the spinning application. An important rule in doing spinning Juji Gatame is: do not lay flat of your back. You must be round, so be sure to shrimp or curl into your opponent, curling over onto the hip closest to the defender. In the following photos, it is the attacker's right hip. If you stay flat on your back, you limit your mobility severely and will not be able to move your body into position to apply the spinning Juji Gatame.

A key feature of spinning Juji Gatame is the shrimping action of the attacker. This photo shows how the attacker curls his body as he rolls over onto the hip and side (in this photo, the attacker's right side) of his opponent. An important element of Juji Gatame is to stay round, as it allows the attacker greater mobility and explosive speed.

This view shows how the attacker shrimps to his right side. It also shows how the attacker uses his right hand to grab and hook himself onto his opponent's left leg. Grabbing the opponent's leg in this way helps the attacker shrimp in deeper, which give him more mobility when rolling his opponent. Look at how close the attacker's head is to the defender's left knee. The attacker is as round as possible, allowing for a smooth, effective roll into Juji Gatame.

## TRAPPING THE DEFENDER'S ARM

The following photos show how the attacker traps the defender's arm in spinning Juji Gatame. Remember, the idea is to control the defender's arm and stretch it to secure Juji Gatame. Trapping his arm is essential in the success of this armlock.

As discussed in the chapter on Core Skills and later in the chapter on Levers, trapping the opponent's arm is essential in a successful Juji Gatame. The attacker uses his left arm (in this photo) to trap the defender's right arm. It is important to quickly trap the defender's arm and not make a big production about doing it. Don't get so wrapped up in trapping the opponent's arm perfectly that it takes too long (and the opponent pulls his arm free). Quickly trap the opponent's arm as part of the shrimping and spinning movement.

As the attacker spins under his opponent, he uses his left arm to tightly trap the defender's right arm to his chest and torso.

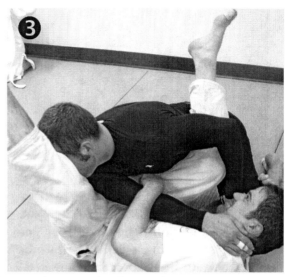

The attacker never lets loose of the trapped right arm as he continues the entry by swinging his left leg over the defender's head.

The rolling action of both bodies helps trap the defender's right arm even tighter to the defender's chest as shown in this photo. At this point, the armlock is almost complete and the action of the attacker rolling up onto his buttocks secures the defender's right arm even tighter to the defender's chest and torso. The attacker's left arm traps the defender's right arm at the elbow area.

The attacker now uses his right arm to hook onto the defender's right forearm near the wrist. The attacker's left arm trapping at the elbow and the attacker's right arm trapping at the forearm and wrist area of the defender's right arm completely control the defender's arm. The attacker "hugs" the defender's arm to his chest.

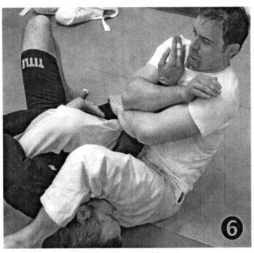

The attacker has complete control of the defender's right arm at this point and the attacker rolls backward as shown. The weight of the attacker's body (and not the strength of his arms) as it rolls backward stretches and extends the defender's right arm.

The attacker secures the Juji Gatame, making sure to arch his hips as he stretches the defender's right arm.

## GRABBING, HOOKING, BLOCKING AND CONTROLLING THE DEFENDER'S LEG WHEN ROLLING HIM

How the attacker uses his hand and arm to hook, grab and control the defender's leg and knee is a matter of preference and opportunity. As a rule of thumb, it's a good idea to grab and control the defender's leg as you roll him over onto his back. This allows the attacker more control in the rolling action as well as an ideal position to be in when the defender is rolled over onto his back in the leg press position. Presented here are a few ways to control the defender's leg, and in one instance, how to use the opponent's jacket instead of grabbing his leg to roll him over. Learn and become skillful at the basic method of grabbing the defender's leg when applying spinning Juji Gatame. After becoming skillful at the basic approach, work on a variety of ways of controlling your opponent's leg as you roll him over.

## BASIC LEG GRAB

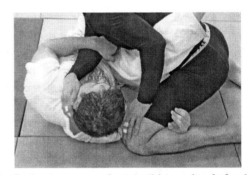

This is the basic approach to grabbing the defender's leg when shrimping and spinning under him. The attacker uses his hand to hook and grab directly under the defender's knee as shown.

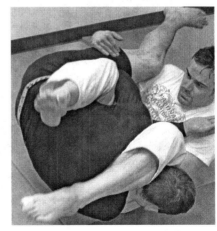

This view shows how the attacker uses his right hand to control the defender's leg (and lower body) in the roll. Everything is a handle, so make every effort to control every handle possible every chance you get.

# ARM HOOK

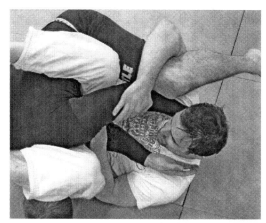

Sometimes, the attacker will use his entire arm to hook the defender's leg at the knee. This gives the attacker a lot of control and a very secure, compact rolling action.

This photo shows the attacker using his arm to hook lower on the defender's leg at about the ankle area.

# ARM HOOK AND GRAB OPPONENT'S JACKET, SLEEVE OR ANYWHERE ON HIS UNIFORM

Sometimes, when hooking with the entire arm, the attacker may be able to grab onto his opponent's jacket, sleeve or pants. The attacker may also grab onto his own lapel, sleeve or any part of his own jacket or pants.

# GRAB PANT LEG

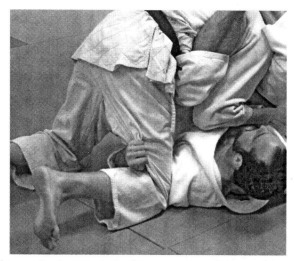

This is the basic method to grab the defender's leg at the pants when in a judo or jujitsu uniform. The pants provide a good handle to control an opponent. The ideal situation is for the attacker (in this photo) to reach between the defender's legs and grab the defender's pants immediately above the knee as shown. Look at how the attacker has used his left hand to grab and pull himself in closer to his opponent's right knee, enabling him to become rounder and better able to roll his opponent over.

The attacker was not able to uses his left hand to reach between his opponent's legs to grab, but has been able to use his left hand to grab on the outside of the defender's right pant leg as shown. As this photo shows, this can often be the case when the defender stands or squats.

## HAND BLOCK

Some athletes prefer to use the (in this photo) right hand to block the defender's left leg as shown. Instead of grabbing or hooking with the arm, the attacker uses his arm and hand to block the defender. Using the arm in this way provides a useful anchor for the attacker to spin deeply under his opponent.

## GRAB DEFENDER'S ANKLE

The attacker may use his hand to grab the defender's ankle or lower leg as shown here. This usually takes place when the defender has been able to come to a standing position, but can also be done if the defender is kneeling on one or both legs.

## NO LEG HOOK

Sometimes, the attacker may not grab the defender's leg at all. Instead, he may use his right hand (in this photo) to push the defender's jacket or upper body over and into the roll. There will be more on this entry later in this chapter.

Let's now turn our attention to various spinning Juji Gatame situations. Not every spinning Juji Gatame application is shown, but a lot of them are. Take what is presented and alter these moves so that they fit your needs specifically within the context of your sport or activity. Necessity is the mother of invention, so make it a point to change anything in this chapter or in this book and make it work for you.

## SPINNING HEAD ROLL JUJI GATAME

There are times when the attacker (on the bottom) spins under his opponent and rolls him almost directly over the defender's head. What the attacker does in this situation is to adapt to the movement of the defender, and as a result, often spins more deeply under his opponent to set up the rolling action. There are some fairly common reasons that this may take place. Sometimes, the defender may simply be stronger than the attacker and offer a great deal of resistance, or the defender may be able to move away sufficiently that the attacker may have to spin in more deeply under him to initiate the rolling action. Another reason the attacker may choose to use this deeper spin and roll his opponent directly over his head is that the attacker may simply like this variation of spinning Juji Gatame. In these situations, the attacker shrimps and spins so deeply under his opponent that he forces the defender to roll over his head and onto his back. You will see this application later in this chapter when spinning Juji Gatame is done against an opponent kneeling on one knee or against a standing opponent. This deeper spin resulting in rolling the defender directly over his head may seem like a subtle change from the basic spinning Juji Gatame application, but it is something that actually takes place, and as a result merits some attention here.

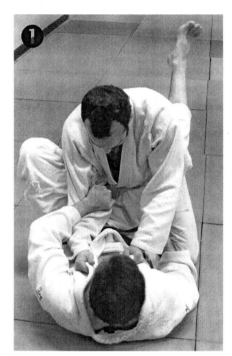

The first photo shows the initial position with the attacker on his back with his opponent between his legs.

The attacker shrimps and spins to his right as shown.

The attacker swings his left leg up in preparation to hook over his opponent's head. As he does this, the attacker continues to spin to his right deeply under his opponent.

The attacker continues to spin deeply as he uses his left leg to hook over his opponent's head. Look at how the defender is rolling forward and over his head.

The attacker continues to spin deeply, using his legs to drive and roll his opponent directly over his head.

This photo shows how the defender rolls forward and over his head.

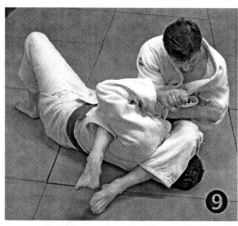

The attacker completes the spin and roll and has his opponent controlled in the leg press position.

The spinning action of the attacker continues and rolls the defender over.

The attacker secures Juji Gatame.

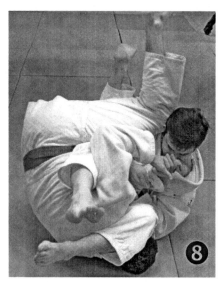

Look at how the defender is rolling mostly over his head and partially over his shoulder.

# SPINNING AND ARCHING JUJI GATAME

Sometimes, the attacker may not be able to roll his opponent over onto his back from a spinning Juji Gatame. If the opponent offers a strong resistance or moves away enough to prevent the attacker from rolling him, the attacker may be able to arch his hips from the bottom position and secure Juji Gatame. This sequence of photos shows the attacker (on bottom) spinning under his opponent at the AAU Judo Grand Nationals.

The attacker has managed to pull and extend the defender's left arm enough that the defender's left elbow is positioned at the attacker's pubic bone giving the attacker a stable fulcrum to apply the armlock. As the attacker uses both hands and arms to trap and then pull the defender's left arm, the attacker arches his back and hip and drives his pubic bone (the fulcrum) into the extended arm and elbow of the defender. Look at how the attacker hooks his right leg over the defender's head, pulling the defender's head down and preventing him from getting to an upright posture. The attacker doing this also adds a counter-pressure to the action of his arching hips and pelvis area, creating more pressure on the defender's left elbow.

The attacker spins under his opponent to apply Juji Gatame.

### TECHNICAL TIP

**More armlocks from this position where the defender remains on his knees or is taken to the mat on his front side will be presented later in the chapter on Belly Down, On the Knees and Various Other Finishing Positions.**

The attacker spins deeply under his opponent and has his left leg placed across the defender's right side and is in the process of using his right leg to hook the defender's head for maximum control. The attacker traps the defender's left arm to the attacker's chest tightly.

## SPINNING AND ARCHING JUJI GATAME (A CLOSER LOOK)

The attacker (on bottom) uses his left hand and arm to trap his opponent's right arm as shown.

The attacker shrimps to his right as he uses his right hand to reach between the defender's legs and grab the defender's left leg. As he does this, the attacker starts to swing his left leg up and over the defender's head.

The attacker hooks his left leg over his opponent's head as shown. At this point the attacker's body is round and his head is placed close to his opponent's left knee. Look at how the attacker has the defender's right arm trapped to his chest. It is important for the attacker to make sure that the defender's right arm is trapped tightly to the attacker's chest and the defender's elbow is placed at, or near, the attacker's crotch and pubic bone (the fulcrum).

Instead of rolling the defender, the attacker quickly and forcefully arches his hips and uses both hands to pull hard on the defender's extended arm. This creates a strong Juji Gatame to get the tap out.

## SPINNING JUJI GATAME
## COUNTER TO GUARD PASS

If the top grappler gets past the legs of the bottom grappler and is in the process of passing his guard, the bottom grappler can still pull off a Juji Gatame. The top grappler moves to his right and to the left of the attacker (on bottom). The attacker immediately rolls onto his left hip, making sure to not be flat on his back.

The attacker continues to roll to his left side and hip as he uses his left hand and arm to trap the top man's left arm. The attacker also starts to swing his right leg up and over his opponent's left shoulder and head.

IMPORTANT: In many instances, the attacker may be able to arch his hips, stretch his opponent's arm and apply the arching type of Juji Gatame from the next position (as presented previously) to get an immediate tap out, but if that is not possible, the attacker will continue.

The attacker hooks his right leg over his opponent's neck as shown. The attacker also now uses both of his hands and arms to trap the defender's left arm to the attacker's chest. The attacker has rolled over to his left and is on his left side and shoulder.

The attacker rolls forcefully onto his left side and hip as he uses his right leg to hook and roll his opponent over.

The attacker has rolled his opponent over onto his back and is ready to secure the Juji Gatame.

## SPINNING JUJI GATAME COUNTER TO CAN OPENER

This is a tough predicament for the bottom grappler who is trapped in a can opener. The can opener is an effective neck crank, so the bottom grappler must react quickly to escape this situation. The top grappler (applying the can opener) is between the bottom grappler's legs. The bottom grappler is actually the attacker in this sequence of photos. The attacker is using his left hand to trap the top grappler's right arm.

The attacker (on bottom) shrimps and spins deeply to his right as he continues to use his left hand and arm to trap the defender's right arm. The attacker uses his right hand to reach through the defender's legs and grab the defender's left leg as shown. The attacker's head is close to the defender's left knee, showing how deeply the attacker spins under his opponent. At this point, the attacker starts to swing his left leg up and over his opponent's head.

The attacker swings his left leg over the defender's head and hooks it forcefully. All the while, the attacker continues to spin under his opponent creating momentum to roll the defender over onto his back.

The attacker rolls his opponent over onto his back. The attacker uses both hands and arms to trap the defender's right arm to the attacker's chest.

The attacker secures the Juji Gatame.

# SPINNING JUJI GATAME IF OPPONENT MOVES BACKWARD AND AWAY TO AVOID THE ARMLOCK

Sometimes, an opponent will move directly back and away as the attacker attempts a spinning Juji Gatame. This sequence of photos examines what to do in this situation.

The attacker (on bottom) is preparing to do the spinning Juji Gatame, but the top grappler anticipates this and starts to move directly back and away from the attacker.

In a lot of situations, the defender may even come up on one knee as shown here. He does this in an effort to stabilize his position and possibly get past the bottom grappler's legs. The attacker shrimps and spins deeply under the top grappler, and most likely will have to spin very deeply to his right and to the opponent's left side. The attacker does this to close the space between his body and the defender's body as the defender moves away.

**IMPORTANT:** It is essential for the attacker to perform the spinning action as fast as possible to prevent the top grappler from moving away and out of range of the effectiveness of the spinning Juji Gatame.

The attacker continues to shrimp and spin deeply under his opponent and starts to swing his left leg over his opponent's head as shown.

The attacker (on bottom) has closed the gap between his body and his opponent's body and most likely will have to use his left leg that is hooking over his opponent's head to pull the two bodies closer together. The attacker may even use his right leg that is hooked over the defender's left side to pull the two bodies closer so he can roll the defender over and onto his back.

The attacker rolls his opponent over and onto his back. He will quickly trap the defender's right arm and roll back to secure Juji Gatame.

## SPINNING JUJI GATAME USING LAPEL CONTROL INSTEAD OF GRABBING OPPONENT'S LEG

Sometimes, it is not possible for the attacker to reach in and hook the defender's leg to assist in rolling the defender over onto his back. In this situation, the attacker may choose to control the defender's body with the lapel of his jacket. Obviously, this is not a move for "no gi" grappling but is useful for any combat sport that uses a jacket.

The attacker (on bottom) uses his left hand to grab this opponent's right sleeve and uses his right hand to grab his opponent's left lapel as shown in this photo. As he does this, the attacker starts to shrimp to his right side as he places his right leg against the defender's left side at about the ribcage.

The attacker performs a standard spinning Juji Gatame with the exception of using his right hand to grab and push his opponent's left lapel (instead of using his right hand to reach between his opponent's leg and grab the defender's left knee). The attacker shrimps and spins to his right.

The attacker swings his left leg over his opponent's head as he continues to spin to his right under his opponent.

Without his opponent's leg to grab, the attacker uses his right hand by forcefully pushing on his opponent's left lapel and controlling the opponent's chest. The spinning action of the attacker, coupled with the pushing action of the attacker's right hand on the defender's chest, rolls the defender over.

This photo shows how the attacker uses his right hand to push the defender as the attacker uses his left hand and arm to trap the defender's right arm to the attacker's chest and torso.

The attacker rolls his opponent over and onto his back as shown.

The attacker rolls back and secures Juji Gatame.

## LEG KICK OVER SPINNING JUJI GATAME

Not everyone can shrimp and spin under an opponent or the situation may not warrant a spinning movement under the defender. This variation of spinning Juji Gatame is for this type of person or for this situation. Basically, the attacker (on bottom) rolls to his right side and hip and does not spin under his opponent to apply this variation of Juji Gatame.

The attacker has his opponent between his legs as shown.

The attacker quickly rolls to his right side and hip as he starts to swing his left leg over his opponent's head. The attacker uses his left hand to trap the defender's right arm.

The attacker rolls completely onto his right side as he uses his left leg to hook over his opponent's head. As he does this, the attacker uses both hands and arms to trap his opponent's right arm firmly to the attacker's chest.

The attacker forcefully rolls across his buttocks and lower back to his left as he uses his left leg to hook over the defender's head.

The attacker rolls his opponent over and onto his back. Look at how the attacker also uses his right leg that is placed against the defender's left side at the ribcage to force the defender over.

The attacker rolls his opponent over and onto his back as shown and has the defender controlled in the leg press.

The attacker rolls back to secure the Juji Gatame.

# KNEE JAM (ALSO CALLED BELT LINE) SPINNING JUJI GATAME

Sometimes, the attacker (on bottom) may not have both of his legs on the outside of his opponent's body and have one of his legs wedged across the belt line of his opponent as shown in this photo. Look at how the attacker has his right knee positioned with his right leg wedged against the midsection at about the belt line of his opponent.

Here is another view of the starting position for this spinning Juji Gatame variation. Look at how the attacker (on bottom) wedges his right leg across his opponent's midsection at about the belt line.

The attacker shrimps to his right and spins under his opponent as shown. The attacker's right lower leg and shin is wedged across his opponent's midsection at the belt line.

The attacker swings his left leg over his opponent's head as he rolls the defender over and onto his back.

The attacker rolls his opponent over. Look at how the attacker keeps his right knee bent with his right shin jammed against the right ribcage of the defender.
**IMPORTANT:** The attacker should not move or swing his right leg (wedged in the right side of his opponent) over the defender's body. Doing this will give the bottom grappler an opportunity to escape, so it is important for the attacker to control his opponent with his right knee (in this case) wedged as shown. The attacker has the defender's right arm trapped with his left arm.

The attacker rolls back to secure Juji Gatame.

## BELTLINE SPINNING JUJI GATAME WITH UNDERHOOK

Sometimes, instead of grabbing the defender's leg to control him, the attacker can uses his hand and arm to hook under the defender's arm and shoulder. The attacker starts his spinning Juji Gatame from the beltline (or knee jam) guard position.

The attacker shrimps and spins under his opponent and as he does, the attacker uses his right hand to grab under his opponent's left arm and armpit.

This photo shows how the attacker uses his right hand to hook under his opponent's left arm to control it.

The attacker continues to spin under the defender as he uses his right hand to control the defender's left armpit. The attacker uses his left leg to hook over his opponent's head and the attacker has his right shin and lower leg wedged along the belt line of the defender. The attacker starts to roll the defender over as shown.

Look at how the attacker uses his right hand to hook under the defender's left armpit along with the attacker's right leg to force his opponent to roll over.

The attacker rolls his opponent over and onto his back and controls him with the leg press position.

The attacker rolls back and secures his Juji Gatame.

# ELEVATOR SPINNING JUJI GATAME

The attacker (on bottom) uses his right leg and foot to wedge against the defender's left hip as shown.

The attacker starts to move his right foot and leg in and between his opponent's legs, with the attacker's right foot at his opponent's left inner thigh.

The attacker wedges his right shin firmly in the defender's left inner thigh as shown.

The attacker shrimps to his right and spins under his opponent as he swings his left leg up and over the defender's head. As he does this, the attacker uses his

right hand to reach between his opponent's legs and grab the defender's left leg immediately above the knee.

The attacker spins deeply to his right and rolls his opponent over and onto his back as shown. Look at how the attacker's right knee is bent and his right shin is jammed into his opponent's torso.

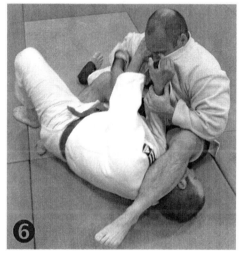

The attacker rolls his opponent over and onto his back. The attacker's right leg remains placed between his opponent's legs as shown.

The attacker's right lower leg traps the defender's right upper leg in this application as the attacker rolls back to secure the Juji Gatame.

## FOOT HOOK SPINNING JUJI GATAME (SINGLE ARM)

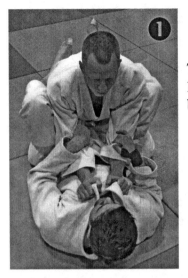

The attacker (bottom) has his opponent between his legs.

The attacker swings his right leg and foot up and across the defender's head. The attacker places his right foot on the right side of his opponent's neck as shown.

The attacker shrimps to his right side as he quickly swings his left leg and foot up and across his opponent's head as shown. Look at how the attacker places his left leg over the top of his right leg (that is still hooked onto the defender's neck). As he shrimps to his right, the attacker uses his left hand to trap the defender's right arm as shown. The attacker uses his right hand and arm to reach through and between the defender's legs and uses his right hand to grab the defender's left leg at about the knee area. The attacker has rolled onto his right hip and side.

The attacker continues to shrimp and spin to his right as he rolls his opponent over as shown.

The attacker rolls his opponent over and onto his back as shown in this photo.

The attacker rolls his opponent onto his back and controls him in the leg press.

The attacker secures the Juji Gatame.

## FOOT HOOK SPINNING JUJI GATAME (BOTH ARMS)

This is a variation of the previous application of spinning Juji Gatame where the attacker traps and locks both of the defender's arms.

The attacker swings his left leg and foot up and across the defender's head and neck. As he does this, the attacker arches his hips and rolls slightly to his right hip and side. As he does this, the attacker uses both of his hands and arms to trap the defender's arms to the attacker's torso. Look at how the attacker's crossed legs and both of his hands isolate and extend both of the defender's arms.

The attacker places his right leg over his opponent's head with the attacker's right foot wedged at the right side of the defender's neck. The attacker uses both of his arms to trap both of his opponent's arms as shown.

The attacker continues to roll to his right hip and side. Doing this causes more torque and places a great deal of stress on both of the defender's extended arms.

The attacker rolls the defender over and onto his back as shown, all the while applying pressure on both of his opponent's arms with his crossed legs and hands.

The attacker rolls his opponent over and onto his back with both of the defender's arms extended, stretched and trapped.

The attacker rolls back, applying pressure on both of his opponent's arms in this both arm variation of Juji Gatame.

## NO ROLL SPINNING JUJI GATAME

This application proves that you don't always have to spin under your opponent and roll him onto his back when doing Juji Gatame from the bottom. Sometimes, as shown here, you can trap your opponent and secure the armlock. If an opponent is strong and the attacker is unable to roll him over, the attacker can uses this variation of Juji Gatame. The attacker (on bottom) has his opponent between his legs in his guard.

The attacker uses both of his hands and arms to trap the defender's right arm as shown.

The attacker starts to shrimp and roll to his right side. The attacker may need to use his left hand to push against the defender's left shoulder to create more room to move to his right side.

The attacker spins under his opponent as he swings his left leg up and over the defender's head.

**5**

The attacker uses both of his legs to trap the defender's head and body from escaping. The attacker uses his legs to pull the defender's body down and arches his hips forcefully to apply pressure on his opponent's extended right arm at the elbow joint.

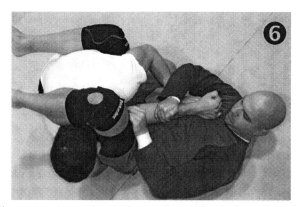

**6**

This top view shows how the defender's right arm is extended and the elbow joint is directly over the attacker's pubic point, serving as the fulcrum. The forceful upward arching action of the attacker's hips along with his legs trapping his opponent's head and body creates the pressure to get the tap out. Also, look at how the attacker is positioned sideways in relation to the defender to create more pressure on the elbow.

## AIR SPIN JUJI GATAME

**1**

This variation may work on some opponents, as it is so audacious. The attacker (on bottom) has both of his feet wedged in his opponent's hips as shown. The attacker uses both hands to grab and hold both of the defender's arms at the forearms or sleeves. **IMPORTANT**: It is essential for the attacker to have his hips deeply under his opponent as shown in this photo.

**2**

The attacker uses both legs to lift his opponent and as he does this, the attacker uses both of his hands to pull his opponent to him.

As the attacker lifts his opponent into the air, the attacker uses his feet to manipulate the defender's hips by pushing hard with his right foot on the defender's left hip and pushing with less force with his left foot on his opponent's right hip. This foot and leg action by the attacker causes the defender to spin to his right while in the air.

This shows how the attacker uses his feet to spin his opponent over and onto his back.

As the defender lands on his back, the attacker quickly applies Juji Gatame. While this variation isn't done often, it is possible and worth learning.

## SPINNING JUJI GATAME WHEN AN OPPONENT IS ON ONE KNEE

Sometimes, an opponent will bring his knee up and support himself on one knee. There are two general reasons for doing this. 1) Your opponent is attempting to stabilize his position so he can "posture up" or make his body upright to give himself more room to work or he may come up on one knee so he can attempt to pass your guard. A skilled opponent may also come up on one knee in an attempt to stand up in an effort to pick you up off the mat to nullify your Juji Gatame attempt. Your opponent may also attempt to "stack" you or pull your hips out toward him and roll you high up onto your shoulders or head. Doing this negates the stability that the bottom grappler has from his position on his hips or buttocks and prevents the bottom man from freely moving. 2) Your opponent may be merely trying to get to one knee for a more comfortable and stable position for himself. Novices or athletes who are not highly skilled in groundfighting often do this. But, whatever the reason, train for this situation so that when it happens you are prepared and can instinctively react to secure the armlock.

This shows the top grappler kneeling on one knee and posturing up to gain space and possibly attempt to stand and lift the bottom grappler off the mat to nullify his armlock or choke from this position. Look at how the top grappler is also using his hands to push down on the bottom grappler's hips to pin them to the mat limiting his mobility. If the bottom grappler is skilled at doing Spinning Juji Gatame and has the wherewithal after drilling on this situation many times in the dojo or practice room, he can grab the defender's left leg with his right hand and use the Spinning Juji Gatame from this awkward position.

This photo shows the defender on one knee making an effort to pass his opponent's guard. The attacker (on the bottom) is tying the top grappler up with a Sankaku (Triangle) position to set him up for a choke or a spin into Juji Gatame. The top grappler is using his close proximity with his right leg and hips to "crowd" the bottom grappler. The top grappler will use his right leg to move the bottom man's left leg in an attempt to pass by it.

The obvious weakness of coming up on one knee for the defender (on top) is that it gives his opponent on the bottom a good "handle" to grab onto and to gain more control and use to roll him over. If you are the bottom grappler attempting a Juji Gatame from this position, make sure to methodically, step by step, gain as much control over your opponent as possible. The first step is to grab and control his leg so that you can use it to prevent him from getting away and also use it to pull yourself in closer so you can spin under him and roll him over for the Juji Gatame. If your Juji Gatame isn't a

viable attack at this point, switch to a Sankaku (Triangle Choke) or other move. Remember to continually take control away form the defender so he can't escape.

![TECHNICAL TIP]

Use one or both of your legs to hook over your opponent's head, shoulders or body and use the strength of your legs to pull him back down to you (as seen in some of the previous photos). By using your legs and feet in this way, you keep him from gaining an upright and stable position and you have a better chance of securing your Juji Gatame (or any other technique from this position such as a Triangle Choke).

## SPINNING JUJI GATAME WITH OPPONENT ON ONE KNEE (BASIC APPLICATION)

The defender (on top) steps up with his left foot so that his right knee is on the mat and his left foot is positioned as shown. The attacker uses his left hand to trap the defender's right arm and immediately starts to shrimp to his right (in the direction of the defender's upright knee).

The attacker shrimps to his right as he uses his right hand to reach under the defender's left leg and uses his right hand to grab the defender's lower leg. Look at how the attacker continues to use his left hand to trap the defender's right arm.

The attacker spins to his right and under his opponent as he uses his right hand to hook the defender's left lower leg. The attacker starts to swing his left leg up and over the defender's head.

### ■ TECHNICAL TIP ■

**Don't wait to see that your opponent has come up on one knee. By constant drill training, you can "feel" when he makes the move with his leg to come up on it. This kinesthetic reaction will enable you to immediately catch your opponent's leg and use your hand to hook under it. If you wait until your opponent posts up on one leg in this way, he may already be passing your guard or making a move to escape your attack.**

The attacker spins to his right and under this opponent as he places his left leg over the defender's head. Look at how the attacker is sideways in relation to the defender's body as he starts to roll the defender over.

The attacker uses both of his legs to drive his opponent over as he uses his right hand and arm to trap the defender's left leg as shown.

The attacker rolls his opponent over and onto his back. During this entire shrimping, spinning and rolling action, the attacker uses his left hand to firmly trap the defender's right arm to the attacker's chest and torso. Look at how the attacker continues to use his right hand and arm to control the defender's left leg, ensuring that the defender rolls over onto his back.

The attacker does not let go with his right hand on his opponent's left leg until the very end of the rolling action. By doing this, the attacker ensures that the defender has been rolled completely over and onto his

back. The attacker has the defender in the leg press at this point.

The attacker rolls back to secure the Juji Gatame.

## RUSSIAN DRAG SPINNING JUJI GATAME

If the attacker (on bottom) is unable to spin under his opponent to roll him over, he may grab and pull (or drag) the defender's foot toward the attacker's head to disrupt the defender's balance and pull him off of his base. There are other Russian Drag variations in other chapters of this book as well.

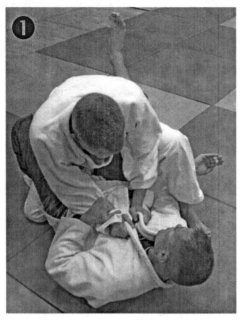

As the defender steps up with his left leg, the attacker uses his right hand and arm to reach under it and hook the lower leg. The attacker uses his left hand to trap his opponent's right arm to the attacker's chest.

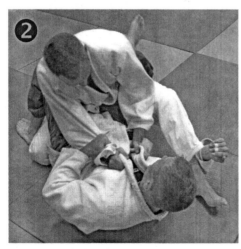

The attacker uses his right arm to hook his opponent's left leg at about the ankle and the attacker pulls (or drags) the opponent's left leg toward the attacker's head. This action literally pulls the defender's left foot out from under him.

As he drags the defender's left leg to him with his right hand, the attacker swings his left leg up and over his opponent's head and rolls to his left his and side. The attacker uses his left leg to drive down on his opponent's head, forcing the defender to roll over toward his right side and shoulder.

The attacker continues to roll to his left side as shown. As this rolling action takes place, the attacker uses his right hand to continue to hook his opponent's left lower leg. The attacker uses his right hand to grab his opponent's left sleeve as shown. The attacker continues to use his left hand to trap his opponent's right arm. This action wraps up the defender with the attacker completely in control of the rolling action.

The attacker rolls over onto his left side as shown, never letting go of the defender's left leg with his right arm. As he does this, the attacker uses both hands to pull hard on the defender's right lower arm (or sleeve in this photo) to extend and stretch it. The attacker arches his hips as he stretches the defender's right arm across his crotch (the fulcrum) to get the tap out with this Juji Gatame.

## ELEVATOR LEG CONTROL SPINNING JUJI GATAME

When the defender (on top) raises up on one knee as shown, the attacker may choose to use this spinning Juji Gatame variation.

The attacker places his right knee under his opponent's left thigh as the attacker uses his left hand to trap the defender's right arm to his chest.

This view from the back shows how the attacker uses his right leg and foot to hook under the defender's left

knee and thigh as the attacker starts to shrimp and spin under his opponent.

The attacker shrimps to his right as he swings his left leg over the defender's head as shown. Look at how the attacker is on his right side and hip as he shrimps and spins to his right under his opponent (in the direction of his opponent's upright leg). Look at how the attacker's right hand is holding onto the defender's left lapel.

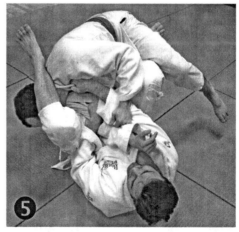

The attacker uses his right hand that is holding the defender's left lapel to push and steer the defender over. As he does this, the attacker uses his left leg and foot to drive his opponent over, working in unison with his right leg that is hooked under the defender's left thigh and knee.

This photo shows how the attacker rolls his opponent over.

IMPORTANT: The attacker uses his left leg to push down on the defender's head and neck as he uses his right leg and foot to lift the defender's left inner thigh and knee. This action whips and rolls the defender over.

The attacker rolls his opponent over and onto his back and controls him with the leg press.

The attacker rolls back and secures his Juji Gatame.

## BELTLINE (KNEE JAM) SPINNING JUJI GATAME WHEN DEFENDER IS ON ONE KNEE

The attacker (on bottom) has a belt line or leg jam guard position with his right leg bent with his right knee to his right (as shown) and his right lower leg and shin wedged across the defender's midsection at the belt line.

This photo from the opposite side shows the attacker's right foot anchored against the defender's right hip.

The top grappler may take this opportunity to step up on his left knee for stability or in an effort to pass the bottom grappler's legs and guard.

As the top grappler steps up with his left leg, the attacker (on bottom) shrimps to his right and uses his right hand to reach under the defender's left leg as shown. The attacker uses his left hand to trap his opponent's right arm.

The attacker continues to spin to his right and under his opponent as he swings his left leg up and over his opponent's head.

The attacker spins deeply under his opponent as he uses his left leg to hook and drive downward on his opponent's head and uses his bent right leg to drive and push upward on his opponent's torso. This action creates a turning and whipping effect and rolls the opponent over. All the while, the attacker continues to use his right hand and arm to hook and lift his opponent's left leg as the attacker continues to use his left hand to trap the defender's right arm to his chest.

The attacker rolls his opponent over onto his back and controls him with a leg press.

The attacker secures his Juji Gatame.

## SPINNING JUJI GATAME COUNTER TO KNEE ON CHEST

Here is a position where an opponent is definitely on one knee; that knee is planted on the bottom grappler's chest and he is controlling him.

The bottom grappler is in a tough situation and must actively take the offensive to escape. The top grappler has his right knee wedged on the bottom grappler's torso.

The bottom grappler (the attacker) shrimps to his right (into the direction of the top grappler) and as he does, he uses his right hand and arm to reach under the top grappler's extended left leg. Ideally, the bottom grappler grabs his opponent under the opponent's knee, but the bottom grappler must grab any part of the leg or foot to start this move.

The bottom grappler shrimps to his right and under the top grappler as he uses his right hand (holding onto the opponent's left knee and leg) to pull himself toward the opponent's foot. As he does this, and as he gets close enough with his body, the bottom grappler swings his left leg over his opponent's head as shown.

The attacker (on bottom) spins under his opponent and he uses his right hand and arm to lift upward on his opponent's left leg and knee. The attacker jams his right bent knee into the top grappler's torso as he uses his left leg to drive downward on the top grappler's head. This action causes the top grappler to roll over his right shoulder and head as shown. Look at how the bottom grappler uses his left hand to trap the top grappler's right arm.

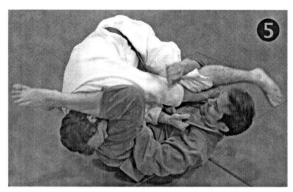

To assert more control, the attacker uses his right hand and arm to hook deeply under the top grappler's left leg and knee as shown. The attacker's body is round and he rolls his opponent over.

The attacker continues to roll his opponent over as shown.

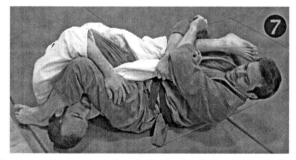

The attacker traps the defender's right arm and leg together as the attacker arches his hips to secure the Juji Gatame.

## SPINNING JUJI GATAME WHEN AN OPPONENT IS STANDING

This photo shows why Juji Gatame is so versatile and can be applied from any position, even when the attacker is on the top of his shoulders or on his head. Sometimes your opponent will stand, or attempt to stand upright, when you are under him in the guard position. Standing upright and attempting to pull the bottom attacker off the mat is a common way for a defender to escape the armlock. The bottom grappler's main goal is to secure the armlock, but to get this done, he must prevent the defender from standing upright as much as possible and to spin under him to prevent the defender from picking him up off the mat. As the attacker (the bottom man) does this, he must also use his legs to control the defender and prevent him from getting to an upright position. This Juji Gatame was successful from this position, reinforcing the fact that this armlock can be applied from almost any position or situation.

While these different applications may look alike, they are all distinctive and effective in securing Juji Gatame when the defender attempts to stand up or attempts to pull the attacker up off the mat to stop the attack.

## SPINNING TO PREVENT DEFENDER FROM STANDING

This photo shows how the attacker has spun under his opponent and used his left leg to hook over the defender's head. Doing this prevented the defender from standing upright and the attacker is now in the process of applying Juji Gatame. In this situation during a freestyle judo match, the defender managed to get to one knee and then attempted to stand but the attacker on the bottom stayed round and spun under the defender, rolling the top grappler over and into Juji Gatame. The attacker applied some basic principles of Juji Gatame very well. For starters, he did not let go of his opponent's arm. The attacker firmly trapped the defender's arm (that the attacker wanted to stretch) to the attacker's torso. The attacker also shrimped in with his body making himself rounder. Doing this helped prevent the defender from pulling the attacker off of the mat to stop the armlock. The attacker also used his left leg well in hooking it over the defender's head and neck, preventing the defender from standing all the way up and gaining a stronger, upright posture with which he could use to initiate an escape.

## ATTACKER GRABS DEFENDER'S LEG FOR CONTROL

This photo shows how the top grappler managed to stand up, but the bottom grappler has used his left hand and arm to grab his opponent's right leg in an attempt to take him back down to the mat. The bottom grappler's goal is to take the top man back to the mat, or at least prevent him from standing upright and pulling free form the armlock or pulling the bottom man off of the mat. Also, notice how the attacker was not able to hook either leg over the defender's head, but used his left leg to hook the defender's body in an attempt to keep the defender from standing upright and escape. It worked; the bottom grappler took his opponent back to the mat and applied Juji Gatame.

## SPINNING JUJI GATAME WHEN OPPONENT STANDS (LEG GRAB)

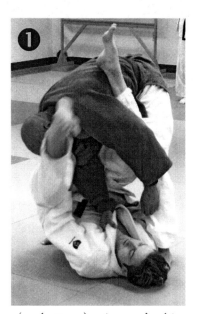

The attacker (on bottom) spins under his opponent to apply Juji Gatame, but the top grappler manages to stand in an effort to stop the attack.

The attacker uses his right hand to reach through the defender's legs and will use his right hand and arm to hook the defender's left leg.

The attacker uses his right hand and arm to hook the defender's left leg, grabbing between the ankle and knee. Look at how close the attacker's head is to the defender's left leg and foot.

The attacker uses both of his legs to hook and force the defender to roll as the attacker uses his right hand and

arm to hook deeply around the defender's left lower leg. This action starts the defender rolling over his right shoulder.

The attacker rolls his opponent over as shown.

The attacker rolls his opponent over and onto his back in the leg press position.

The attacker secures Juji Gatame. The attacker has the option to let go of the defender's left leg as he secures the armlock. Often, trapping both the leg and arm of the defender weakens him because it places the defender on his side and takes away one of the appendages that he could use for stability.

## ATTACKER SPINS UNDER OPPONENT TO PREVENT HIM FROM ESCAPING

The attacker (on bottom) spins under his opponent in an effort to prevent the defender from standing upright and pulling his arm free. By spinning under his opponent, the defender "corkscrews" with his body and this action often prevents the defender from standing completely upright and pulling his arm free from the armlock. This corkscrew action by the attacker also helps in rolling the defender over and back down to the mat.

## ATTACKER HOOKS DEFENDER'S HEAD WITH HIS LEG FOR CONTROL

This photo shows how the top grappler managed to stand up, but the bottom grappler has used his left hand and arm to grab his opponent's right leg in an attempt to take him back down to the mat. The bottom grappler's goal is to take the top man back to the mat, or at least prevent him from standing upright and pulling free from the armlock or pulling the bottom man off of the mat. Also, notice how the attacker was not able to hook either leg over the defender's head, but used his left leg to hook the defender's body in an attempt to keep the defender from standing upright and escape. It worked; the bottom grappler took his opponent back to the mat and applied Juji Gatame.

## SPINNING JUJI GATAME WHEN OPPONENT STANDS

The attacker (on bottom) is applying Juji Gatame from this position and the defender is attempting to pull the attacker up and off the mat.

To prevent the defender from pulling him up and off the mat, the attacker spins to his right across the back of his shoulders forcefully. The attacker's goal is to spin so much that his head is actually between the defender's legs. Look at how the attacker uses his left leg to hook over the defender's head to control it and prevent the defender from standing upright.

This forceful spinning action by the attacker "corkscrews" both of the grapplers and forces the defender to roll over his right shoulder.

In some cases, the attacker may use his right hand to grab the defender's lower leg, or ankle or pant leg to assist in rolling the defender over and onto his back.

The attacker rolls the defender over and onto his back and will pursue his Juji Gatame from this point.

## SPINNING JUJI GATAME WHEN OPPONENT STANDS (EMPHASIS ON SHOWING HOW THE HAND ASSISTS IN THE TECHNIQUE)

This sequence of photos shows how the attacker (on bottom) spins deeply under the defender and how the attacker uses his hand to manipulate and control the defender's leg to assist in rolling him over.

The attacker (on bottom) has his opponent in his guard and the defender stands in an effort to stop the attack.

The attacker spins to his right. As he does, the attacker uses his right hand to grab his opponent's left lower leg. Look at how the attacker's head is close to the defender' left leg and sideways in relation to the defender's body position.

The attacker swings his left leg up over his opponent's head and the attacker uses his left hand and arm to hook the defender's left leg. The attacker uses his right hand, hooking the defender's left leg to pull himself in closer to his opponent's right leg for more control in the spin.

The attacker now uses his right hand to reach further and grab his opponent's right lower leg. If the defender is wearing pants, the attacker should grab them for a stable handle. Look at how the "corkscrew" action along with the hooking and controlling action of the attacker's legs is causing the defender to bend forward off balance.

The attacker continues to spin hard to his right, under his opponent causing the defender to start to roll forward.

The attacker uses his right hand to grab the pant leg of the defender. In a "no gi" situation, the attacker can simply grab his opponent's ankle instead of grabbing the pant leg.

The attacker spins under the defender and forces him to roll over as shown. The attacker uses his right hand (in this case) to grab the defender's lower pant leg to assist in rolling him over.

The attacker rolls his opponent over and onto his back where the attacker will control the defender with a leg press and secure his Juji Gatame.

## DEFENDER SQUATS (OR CATCHES DEFENDER BEFORE HE CAN STAND)

Sometimes, as the attacker (on bottom) attempts a spinning Juji Gatame, the defender will squat in an initial effort to stand. This photo (taken at the AAU Freestyle Judo Nationals) shows such a situation. The bottom grappler lost control of his opponent's right arm (the arm the attacker was trying to lock), but the attacker wants to keep the top grappler from getting away, so he has grabbed the defender's left arm as the attacker uses his right hand and arm to hook under the defender's left leg at the knee.

The defender uses his right hand to pull downward on the attacker's left knee to prevent the top grappler from standing. While the defender was able to escape, this shows how the bottom grappler can attempt to do spinning Juji Gatame on an opponent in a squatting position.

## SPINNING JUJI GATAME AS THE DEFENDER SQUATS IN AN EFFORT TO STAND OR ESCAPE

The attacker (on bottom) has his opponent in his guard. The top grappler is squatting.

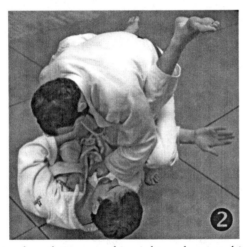

The attacker shrimps to his right as he uses his right hand and arm to reach under his opponent's left leg at about the knee area. Look at how the attacker spins hard to his right and is sideways in relation to the defender's body. The attacker uses his left arm to trap the defender's right arm to the attacker's body.

The attacker performs spinning Juji Gatame as shown.

The attacker uses his right hand to hook deeply under the left knee of the defender as he rolls the defender over.

This view shows how the attacker uses his right hand and arm to hook under the defender's leg at the knee area.

The attacker rolls the defender over. Look at how the attacker uses his right hand to grab the defender's sleeve (or any part of his jacket or body) to bundle him up and control the defender more in the rolling movement.

The attacker rolls his opponent over and onto his back and controls him with the leg press.

The attacker secures his Juji Gatame.

## STAY WITH IT AND KEEP TRYING TO STRETCH HIS ARM

The attacker has spun under his opponent but the defender has managed to get to both feet. The attacker uses both of his hands and arms to trap the defender's left arm and uses his right leg to hook over the defender's head in an effort to pull the defender back down to the mat. The defender has managed to use his right hand to grab his left hand and will pull the defender off of the mat to escape the armlock.

The defender has managed to pull his left arm in enough to get his left elbow below the pubic bone of the attacker, thus enabling him to bend his left arm and escape the armlock. On the other hand, the attacker is not letting go of his opponent's left arm and is now arching his hips in an effort to re-straighten the defender's left arm. This dogged, determined attitude is what it takes to make opponents tap out. In this instance, however, the defender managed to keep his left arm bent and pull the defender up and off the mat to escape. You can't get them every time, but if you are known as an arm stretcher, you have a psychological advantage over your opponents.

### ▰▰ TECHNICAL TIP ▰▰

Some grapplers may squat when positioned between the legs of an opponent in his guard. This is often a good tactic and allows the top grappler (who is squatting) more mobility in an effort to get past his opponent's legs.

## ALMOST A SUCCESSFUL JUJI GATAME

Not every Juji Gatame attack is successful but this photo shows how determined the attacker was. The defender successfully picked the attacker up off the mat even though his arm was fully stretched and he was almost ready to tap out. In judo as well as some other combat sports, when the defender lifts the attacker off of the mat in this way, the referee calls a halt to the action for the safety of the athletes. Preventing this from taking place is why we work so hard on spinning Juji Gatame in an effort to secure the armlock before the defender escapes in this way. There will be more on this later in the chapter on Defenses and Escapes.

## DEFENDER PULLED HIS ARM FREE TO ESCAPE JUJI GATAME

Here's what the bottom grappler doesn't want to happen. The defender has managed to stand upright and gain his stability enough to be able to pull his arm free and escape the Juji Gatame. As he extracted his arm, the defender managed to pull it completely loose from the attacker's grasp, causing the attacker to fall to the mat. There will be more on how to escape Juji Gatame in the chapter on defense and escapes later in the book.

### ■■■ TECHNICAL TIP ■■■

More often than not, the grappler who is defending against an opponent's Juji Gatame, Sankaku (Triangle) or any number of attacks from the bottom will attempt to stand and pull the attacker (who is on the bottom) off of the mat. The bottom grappler should make every effort to prevent his opponent from standing and by all means, keep hold of his opponent's arm and keep trying to apply the submission technique until the referee orders him to stop.

## SPINNING JUJI GATAME WHEN THE DEFENDER IS ALREADY STANDING OR STANDING OVER THE ATTACKER

Sometimes, the attacker is positioned on the mat and the defender is standing. The attacker may be kneeling on one or both knees, on his backside in the guard position, seated on his buttocks or in any number of positions. In other words, the attacker may not always be in the dominant position so make it a point to practice what to do when this happens. The next photo sequences offer some ideas for this type of situation.

The bottom grappler steps up onto his left foot as shown but must take caution to not stay in this position more than a split second. The top grappler can apply an Uchi Mata (Inner Thigh Throw) easily from this position if the bottom grappler stays on his knee too long. The various photos that follow pick up the action from this point.

Here is a situation where the bottom grappler is on his knees having been knocked down or, for any number of reasons, is facing his opponent who is standing over him. Several situations will be shown on the following pages and while they are all similar, they are distinct in application. The grappler on both knees must get from the weaker position and in the process will attempt a Juji Gatame.

## TECHNICAL TIP

**If you are on both knees or on one knee and your opponent is standing over you dominating you, it's obvious that you are in trouble. Attacking your opponent is your best option and knowing how to attack him effectively means the difference between winning and losing.**

## SPINNING JUJI GATAME FROM KNEELING AGAINST A STANDING OPPONENT

The attacker is on his knees with his opponent standing over him as shown.

The attacker rises to one knee with his left knee (the knee close to his opponent) up. It is important for the attacker to not stay in this position very long at all as the attacker may use an Uchi Mata (Inner Thigh Throw) or other throw or takedown to take him to the mat. The top grappler may also simply snap the bottom grappler back down to the mat. With this in mind, the grappler on one knee should immediately start his attack. The bottom grappler positions his body to the extreme right side of his opponent who is standing.

The attacker immediately pushes off of his left foot and swings his right foot and leg to his opponent's left hip (the hip farthest from the attacker).

The attacker swings his body to the right, spinning under his opponent. The attacker uses his left hand to hold the defender's right arm tightly to trap it for the eventual armlock. It is important that the attacker stay round when spinning under his opponent so he can get as much momentum as possible to roll his opponent.

The attacker spins under his opponent swinging and securing his left leg over the defender's head as shown.

The attacker spins deeply under his opponent and rolls him over and onto his back.

The attacker rolls his opponent over onto his back and will secure the Juji Gatame.

## PULL GUARD FROM A KNEELING POSITION AND ATTACK WITH SPINNING JUJI GATAME

Sometimes, the best thing to do is to swing under your opponent and pull him into your guard. This can possibly neutralize the situation and buy you some time to set your opponent up for a spinning Juji Gatame (or other technique) as shown here.

The attacker (on bottom) is on one knee and positioned as shown in relation to his opponent.

The attacker pushes off of his left foot and swings his right leg on the outside of his opponent.

The attacker swings under his opponent and pulls the top grappler down and into his guard as shown.

When the attacker senses that he can attack, he starts his spinning Juji Gatame as shown.

The attacker spins deeply under his opponent and uses his left leg to hook over his opponent's head.

The attacker shrimps and spins deeply under the defender and rolls the defender over and onto his back.

The attacker rolls his opponent over and controls him with the leg press.

The attacker secures the Juji Gatame.

## SPINNING JUJI GATAME FROM GUARD WITH FOOT IN OPPONENT'S HIP

Sometimes, the bottom grappler will be fighting from the guard position or somehow end up on side or back as shown. In some instances, the standing grappler may be attempting to get past the bottom man's leg and pass his guard. In any event, the bottom grappler can apply spinning Juji Gatame from this position. The attacker (on bottom) jams his right foot in his opponent's left hip as he uses his hands to grab and hold his opponent's right arm. Look at how the attacker is positioned on his right hip and not flat on his back. The bottom grappler has better mobility from this position.

The attacker is using his right foot that is wedged in his opponent's left hip as an anchor enabling him to spin to his right so that the attacker's head is closer to his opponent's left foot. The attacker (on bottom) attempts to spin as much as possible under his opponent, but eventually, he won't be able to get any closer. As the attacker spins to his right and under his opponent's body as shown, the attacker starts to swing his left leg upward.

**IMPORTANT:** The attacker's right foot is anchored on his opponent's left hip. The attacker uses this anchor foot as a stable base to spin under his opponent more effectively.

The attacker swings his left leg up and over his opponent's head as shown. Notice that the attacker has been using his arms to trap his opponent's right arm tighter to the attacker's chest all the while he has been under him.

The attacker hooks his left leg over his opponent's head as he uses both hands to further trap the defender's right arm to his chest as shown. Look at how the attacker's right leg is placed across the defender's left side. All this time, the defender is spinning to his right to get as deep as possible under his opponent.

The attacker continues to spin under his opponent and uses his left leg to hook forcefully over his opponent's head as shown. The attacker is rolling his opponent over and onto his back at this point.

The attacker rolls his opponent over onto his back and immediately sits up on his buttocks to ensure that his hips and crotch as are close as possible to the defender's right arm and shoulder for maximum control and to provide a strong fulcrum to apply the armlock.

The attacker secures the Juji Gatame and gets the tap out.

## SPINNING JUJI GATAME WHEN THE ATTACKER IS STANDING AND THE DEFENDER IS KNEELING

It may not happen often, but there are times when the attacker chooses to do a spinning Juji Gatame from the standing position when his opponent is kneeling. Some people may consider it risky, but this move has proven to be successful for athletes who are willing to practice it often and attempt it when unexpected.

## JUMP-IN SPINNING JUJI GATAME WHEN OPPONENT IS ON KNEES

The attacker is standing and leading with his left leg and foot as his opponent kneels on both knees.

The attacker swings his right leg to, and past, his opponent's left hip (the hip farthest from the attacker).

The attacker swings down and under his opponent and onto the attacker's right hip and side.

The attacker spins under his opponent and is positioned sideways in relation to the defender's body as shown.

The attacker swings his left leg up and over the defender's head as the attacker spins under the defender.

### ▣ TECHNICAL TIP ▣

**This technique is also a good way to initially learn and safely practice jumping or "flying" Juji Gatame (refer to the chapter on Transitions later in this book). These jumping techniques are so audacious that they sometimes work, even against experienced opponents.**

The attacker sins and rolls his opponent over as shown.

The attacker rolls his opponent onto his back and controls him with the leg press.

The attacker stretches his opponent's arm to secure the Juji Gatame.

## JUMP-IN WITH KNEE JUJI GATAME WHEN OPPONENT IS ON KNEES

The attacker stands while the defender kneels as shown. Look at how the attacker leads with his left foot and leg.

The attacker curls his body up as shown as he spins under his opponent. Look at how the attacker bends his right leg and places his right shin against the defender's right hip or side.

The attacker continues to curl up as he spins under his opponent as shown.

The attacker's right shin is wedged against the defender's right side and torso as the attacker spins under his opponent. The attacker starts to swing his left leg up and over his opponent's head.

The attacker continues to spin under the defender. Look at how the attacker uses his left leg to hook, pull down and control his opponent's head.

The attacker rolls his opponent over and onto his back.

The attacker rolls his opponent onto his back and into the leg press position where he will secure Juji Gatame.

Spinning Juji Gatame is effective and develops a great many athletic, technical and tactical skills in groundfighting. As has been said several times already in this chapter: learn spinning Juji Gatame well and practice it often. It won't let you down.

Let's now turn our attention in the next chapter to another of the four basic entries: the back roll Juji Gatame.

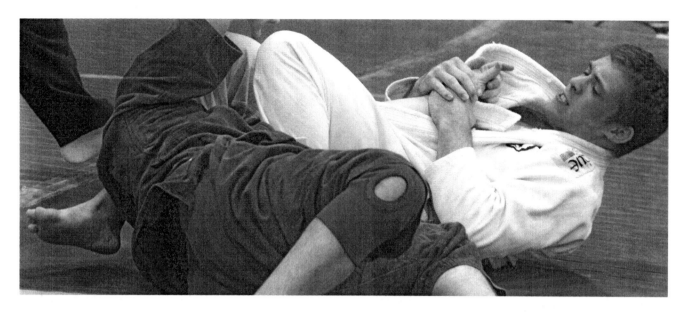

# BACK ROLL JUJI GATAME

"THESE THINGS AREN'T TRICKS. THEY'RE SKILLS. SKILLS ARE RELIABLE AND DEPEND ON SOLID FUNDAMENTALS AND PROPER EXECUTION. TRICKS ARE UNRELIABLE AND DEPEND ON LUCK AND A WEAK OPPONENT."
BOB CORWIN

The primary action of the back roll Juji Gatame is the attacker rolling onto his back or backside in some way to apply the armlock. In almost all variations of Juji Gatame, the attacker rolls onto his back, but in this specific entry, the primary action that makes the armlock work is the movement of the attacker rolling backward. The attacker does not roll over his shoulder in the direction of his opponent's hip. He does not roll over his side in the direction of the opponent's head and he doesn't spin under his opponent as part of the entry. The attacker simply rolls backward. Granted, this is pretty basic, but then again, the basics work and work at all levels of sport combat, from local to international and from novice to professional.

Actually, almost all variations of Juji Gatame entries end up with the attacker trapping his opponent's arm, hugging it tightly to his body and rolling backward to stretch the arm and apply pressure to secure the tap out. So, in essence, the back roll Juji Gatame is the workhorse of all the entries and it makes sense to become as proficient as possible in this basic, yet vital, approach to performing Juji Gatame.

This chapter examines a variety of entries, set-ups, breakdowns and turns where the back roll Juji Gatame is done. But, before that is done, the basic skills of the back roll Juji Gatame will be analyzed.

## BACK ROLL JUJI GATAME (BASIC APPLICATION-VIEW FROM THE FRONT)

The attacker controls his opponent with the shoulder sit position as shown in this photo. Look at how the attacker is already starting to trap the defender's right arm to the attacker's chest.

The attacker starts to lever the defender's arm free. Look at how the attacker's right shin is jammed in the right side and back of the defender. The attacker's left leg is already placed over his opponent's head. The attacker is squatting low as he brings his chest to his opponent's right elbow and his body is round.

The attacker rolls back, trapping the opponent's right arm to his chest and using the weight of his body to stretch his opponent's right arm out straight.

The attacker rolls onto his back and arches his hips, making sure that the defender's right arm is extended with the defender's elbow located at the attacker's pubic bone (the fulcrum).

## BACK ROLL JUJI GATAME (BASIC APPLICATION-VIEW FROM THE BACK)

From this view, you can see how the attacker's body is round as he controls his opponent in the shoulder sit position. The attacker's right shin is wedged in the right side and back of his opponent.

The attacker rolls back, keeping his right shin jammed firmly in his opponent's back and side.

The attacker continues to roll onto his back, levering his opponent's right arm free.

The attacker secures Juji Gatame.

### ▮▮▮▮ TECHNICAL TIP ▮▮▮▮

**The back roll Juji Gatame is the simplest of the four basic applications of the armlock, but an essential one in performing every variation of Juji Gatame used.**

## ATTACKER MUST GET ROUND QUICKLY

The attacker should squat and get round and compact as quickly as possible. By staying round, the attacker will roll back with control. Do not fall backward, instead roll back with control.

The starting position varies depending on the situation. In this case, the attacker was kneeling, so he is positioned on one knee as shown. Remember, if you are kneeling as you start, do not stay kneeling. Get off of your knee or knees and squat quickly. Otherwise, your knees resting on the mat will block your opponent from rolling back.

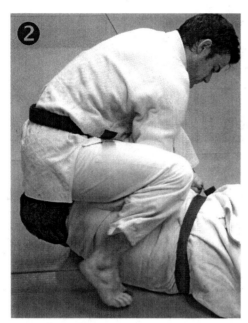

The attacker immediately squats and as he traps his opponent's arm, the attacker lowers his body, rounding it in the process.

The attacker's rounded body enables him to roll back quickly and with control of the situation and position. If he were to reach back with his hand to catch himself as he lowers his body, the attacker would lose control of his opponent. Also, by trapping the defender's arm to his body and rolling backward, the attacker uses the weight of his body to stretch and extend his opponent's arm.

## ATTACKER USES HIS FOOT AND LEG TO TRAP AND CONTROL OPPONENT'S HEAD

The attacker's right foot and leg trap his opponent's head much in the same way a nutcracker squeezes and cracks a nut. The attacker's right heel is jammed tightly against the defender's head as shown here. Look at how the attacker sits low and his upper leg and buttocks are actually sitting on the defender's head. This is an uncomfortable position for the bottom grappler and assures that the attacker controls his opponent's head.

As the attacker sits and rolls onto his buttocks to apply the armlock, he draws or pulls his right foot in tightly so that his right heel is jammed hard onto the side of the defender's head. The defender's head is trapped, making it easier for the attacker to control the bottom grappler as he applies Juji Gatame.

## BACK ROLL JUJI GATAME (AS EXECUTED IN COMPETITION)

This sequence of photos shows how the back roll Juji Gatame is done when it counts. These photos were taken at the AAU Freestyle Judo Nationals, proving that good, solid basics work at all levels of competition.

The back roll Juji Gatame takes place anytime the attacker rolls onto his back to apply Juji Gatame. In this photo, the attacker has his opponent in the leg press and is working to lever the defender's arm free.

## ATTACKER JAMS HIS SHIN IN OPPONENT'S BACK AND SIDE

Often, when executing the back roll Juji Gatame (especially in its basic application), the attacker will wedge the leg that does not go over his opponent's head (in this photo, the right leg; the leg that is at the opponent's torso) firmly in the back and side of his opponent. The attacker should not be in a hurry to swing his leg over his opponent's body in the notion that he must always place his leg over the opponent's chest. If the situation calls for it, the attacker may adjust his leg position so that his leg is placed over his opponent's body, but initially, the attacker should secure and control the position, and then get to the business of levering or prying his opponent's arm so that the attacker can extend it and get the armlock.

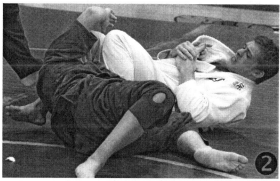

The attacker has trapped his opponent's left arm firmly to the attacker's chest as he rolls back stretching the arm.

This photo shows how attacker arches his hips to apply the most pressure possible on his opponent's left arm and elbow.

## BACK ROLL JUJI GATAME FROM THE MOUNT OR STRADDLE PIN

Sitting on an opponent in the mount or straddle pin is probably the most basic (and often used) set up for the back roll Juji Gatame in combat sports, proving again that good, solid fundamentals work and work with a high ratio of success. There are a variety of applications and a few of them will be presented on the following pages.

## BACK ROLL JUJI GATAME FROM A HIGH MOUNT

The attacker has a "high mount" controlling his opponent. In this version of the mount, the attacker is sitting high on the defender's chest and using his knees and legs to crowd and wedge the bottom grappler's arms and shoulders together. The attacker uses his hands and arms to start to trap his opponent's arms.

The attacker uses his right arm to trap the defender's left arm as he swings his right leg under the defender's left shoulder. The attacker uses his left hand to pull up on the defender's head to make room for his right foot and lower leg under the defender's head. The attacker's left knee is still on the mat and used to stabilize the attacker.

The attacker now switches hands, placing his right hand on the mat for stability as he uses his left hand to trap the defender's arms to the attacker's chest. Look at how the attacker starts to shift his weight and body position to swing to his back right. Look at how the attacker's left foot is driving off the mat as he lifts his left knee.

The attacker swings his body over his opponent as shown in this photo. Look at how the attacker's left leg has swung over the defender's head and the attacker's left foot is wedged firmly onto the left side of the defender's head. The attacker is using his left hand to trap the defender's right arm firmly to the attacker's chest.

The defender has now swung around and over his opponent and rolls back to secure Juji Gatame.

## BACK ROLL JUJI GATAME FROM THE "WATSON JITSU" MOUNT

The attacker controls his opponent by using his right leg and knee to trap his opponent's left arm and shoulder to the mat as shown here. The attacker is in a "high mount" with the attacker sitting on the defender's chest. The attacker's left knee is placed on the mat. The attacker uses his right hand to grab and hook behind his opponent's head.

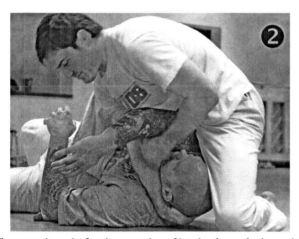

The attacker shifts the weight of his body and places his right foot on the mat under the defender's left armpit. The attacker moves his left knee close to the defender's head as he shifts his position. Look at how the attacker uses his right hand to trap the defender's right arm as he continues to control the defender's head.

The attacker uses his right hand and arm to trap the defender's right arm as the attacker pushes off of his right foot (on the mat) as he swings his left leg over the defender's head.

The attacker swings his left leg over the defender's head and controls the bottom grappler with the leg press position.

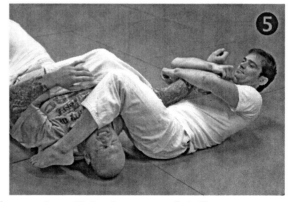

The attacker rolls back to secure Juji Gatame.

## BACK ROLL JUJI GATAME FROM THE MOUNT

This variation of Juji Gatame from the mount or vertical pin position is pretty standard and definitely should be included in this chapter. The attacker (on top) controls his opponent in the mount position. The attacker uses his right hand to scoop and start to trap the defender's left arm to the attacker's chest and torso. As he does this, the attacker uses his left hand to push on the defender's chest. This stabilizes the attacker as he starts to apply the Juji Gatame. Notice that the attacker is seated on the defender and on his knees with the attacker's body positioned low on the attacker's chest at about the stomach area.

The attacker pushes off the defender's chest with his left hand as the attacker springs up off of his knees and into a squatting position.

The attacker spins his body to his right as he swings his right leg over the defender's head as shown. As he does this, the attacker bends forward slightly to control his balance, but also to lower his body so that he can continue to trap the defender's left arm tightly to the attacker's chest as he spins over the defender. The attacker continues to squat and stay low over his opponent.

The attacker rolls back and secures Juji Gatame.

## HALF NELSON BACK ROLL JUJI GATAME FROM A MOUNT

This variation of the back roll Juji Gatame from the mount emphasizes a lot of upper body control where the attacker sets his opponent up with a half nelson to control the defender's shoulders. The attacker starts out of a high mount as he shifts his body weight to his right (to the defender's left side). The attacker uses his right hand to roll his opponent over onto the defender's right said. The attacker sinks in his left hand and arm under his opponent's left arm. This sets up the half nelson.

The attacker controls his opponent's left shoulder and upper body with a half nelson. The attacker applies pressure with the half nelson and turns the defender over onto the defender's right side as shown.

The attacker quickly shifts his right knee near the defender's head. The attacker continues to control his

opponent with his left hand that is applying the half nelson on the opponent's left shoulder. The attacker's body is directly over the defender's left shoulder.

The attacker continues to roll his opponent over onto the opponent's right side as the attacker starts to swing his right leg over the defender's head. The attacker continues to use his left hand to trap his opponent's left arm. The attacker uses his right hand to push on his opponent's head for stability. (The attacker can also uses his right hand to grab the defender's lapel.)

The attacker swings his right leg over the defender's head and controls him with a leg press as the attacker continues to trap the defender's left ram more tightly to the attacker's chest.

The attacker rolls back and secures Juji Gatame.

## SIDE POSITION KEYLOCK TO BACK ROLL JUJI GATAME

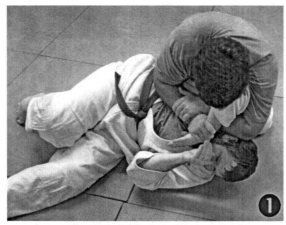

This is a basic, and very good, set up for Juji Gatame from the side position or any pin applied from the side. The attacker starts by controlling his opponent with a keylock on the defender's right arm as shown.

This shows a closer view of the attacker's keylock on the defender's right arm.

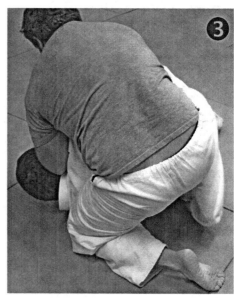

The attacker steps up with his right foot and leg and jams his right shin in the defender's back and side, as he does this the attacker makes sure to wedge his left knee under the defender's right shoulder as shown. As he does this, the attacker starts to trap the defender's right arm to the attacker's chest.

The attacker quickly springs up off of his left knee and swings it over the defender's head. The attacker's right shin is still jammed firmly in the defender's right side and back. The attacker firmly traps the defender's right arm to the attacker's chest as the attacker controls his opponent with the leg press as shown.

The attacker rolls back and secures the Juji Gatame.

## KNEE ON TORSO TO BACK ROLL JUJI GATAME

Often, when following through from passing his opponent's guard or from a takedown or throw, the attacker will jam his knee (in this photo, the attacker's right knee) in the right side of the defender's body. This knee serves as is a controlling and stabilizing point for the attacker.

The attacker moves toward his opponent's head with his right knee still pressing down on the defender's torso. The attacker starts to use both hands to scoop and trap the defender's right arm.

The attacker moves up toward his opponent's head and places his left leg over the defender's head as shown. As he does this, the attacker starts to trap the defender's right arm. The attacker's right shin is jammed in the right side of the defender's body.

The attacker squats, making sure that his hips and buttocks are close to the defender's right shoulder. The attacker starts to apply the roll back Juji Gatame on his opponent.

The attacker rolls back and secures Juji Gatame.

## SPIN AND STRETCH TO JUJI GATAME

The attacker spins the defender over as shown.

The attacker (standing) controls his opponent with a started neck and arm grip. The defender is kneeling as shown.

The attacker spins his opponent over and immediately jams his right shin in the right side of the defender's body. The attacker starts to uses his right hand to scoop and trap the defender's right arm as shown.

The attacker moves his right foot and leg across and to the side (important: not directly in front) of the defender's body. The attacker's right heel is placed at the side of the defender's right knee. As the attacker does this, he starts to spin the defender over to the defender's right side.

The attacker immediately follows through to the mat and controls his opponent with a shoulder sit position as shown.

The spin and stretch Juji Gatame is a great drill to develop the skills necessary to immediately transition from a throw (or takedown) to Juji Gatame. It is recommended that athletes perform 3 or 4 sets of 5 repetitions each at every practice. The spin and stretch is also a good move to use if the attacker is standing and the defender is kneeling.

## JUDO STACK WHEN OPPONENT IS ON ALL FOURS TO JUJI GATAME

If the defender is on all fours (as shown in this photo), the attacker moves to the defender's side (in this case, the defender's left side) as shown. The attacker uses his left hand to grab the defender's jacket at about the shoulder are or upper right sleeve. The attacker uses his right hand to grab the defender's right upper leg as shown. The attacker is squatting and not on his knees.

The attacker quickly uses both hands to trap his opponent's right arm.

The attacker springs backward out of his squatting position as he uses both hands to pull and drag his opponent over onto the defender's left side as shown.

The attacker rolls back as shown.

The attacker secures his Juji Gatame to get the tap out.

The attacker immediately controls his opponent with the shoulder sit position.

The attacker quickly traps the defender's right arm as shown.

The attacker rolls back after making sure to control the defender and trap his right arm to the attacker's chest.

The attacker rolls back and applies Juji Gatame.

## JUDO STACK WHEN OPPONENT IS FLAT ON FRONT TO JUJI GATAME

The attacker squats to the left side of the defender (in this photo) and uses his left hand to grab at the defender's far (right) shoulder and triceps area on the jacket as shown. The attacker uses his right hand to grab the defender's right pant leg immediately above the defender's knee.

The attacker springs up backward out of his squat and uses both hands to pull and drag the defender over onto the defender's left side.

The attacker immediately steps over the defender's head with his left leg.

The attacker squats, making sure to jam his right shin in the defender's right side and back. The attacker uses both hands to trap the defender's right arm.

The attacker rolls back as shown.

The attacker secures Juji Gatame.

## KNEE ON TORSO (UKI GATAME-STRADDLE HOLD) TO BACK ROLL JUJI GATAME

This is a standard application of Juji Gatame when the attacker controls his opponent with his knee in the knee on chest or torso position (also called Uki Gatame in judo). The attacker uses his left knee placed on his opponent's torso to control him.

The attacker starts to trap the defender's left arm with both of his arms as he moves to his left. The defender is in a squatting position as shown. Look at how the attacker's left shin is jammed in the defender's left side.

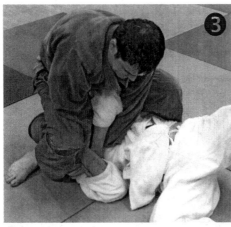

The attacker quickly moves his right foot and leg over the defender's head. Look at the angle of the attacker relative to his opponent. He has swung his body around so that he is now facing the defender's hips and leg. The attacker does this to better lever and pry the defender's left shoulder and arm free to apply the armlock.

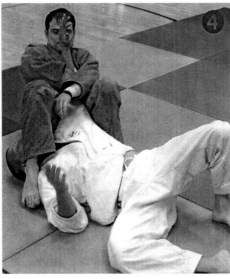

The attacker rolls back at a high angle in relation to the defender's body as he starts to secure the Juji Gatame. The defender's left shoulder and arm are weaker from this angle than if the attacker were directly sideways to his opponent.

The attacker rolls back to secure Juji Gatame.

## KNEE ON TORSO SPIN TO JUJI GATAME

The attacker controls his opponent with an Uki Gatame o knee on chest position. In this case, the attacker jams his righ knee on his opponent's torso.

This photo shows another view of the knee on torso position

The attacker uses his right hand and arm to scoop under the defender's left arm as shown.

The attacker jams his right knee deep onto his opponent's chest as the attacker moves his body toward the defender's head. The attacker moves his left foot and leg over the top of the defender's head as shown.

The attacker swings around the defender's head as shown. Look at how the attacker uses his right arm to trap the defender's left arm.

The attacker swings around completely so that he is now facing the direction he started. As he does this, the attacker, squats low and jams his left shin in the left side of the defender's body. The attacker now uses both hands and arms to trap the defender's left arm to the attacker's chest.

The attacker rolls back and applies Juji Gatame.

## JUJI GATAME COUNTER AGAINST NEAR LEG BENT LEGLOCK

This is a counter-move if you are on the bottom and the attacker sinks his leg in for a near leg ride or attempts a bent knee lock from this position.

The top grappler is attempting to secure a bent knee lock on the bottom grappler's right leg after sinking in his near leg ride with his right leg.

As the attacker sits back to secure the leglock, the attacker (on bottom) rolls over the shoulder nearest to his opponent (in this photo, the right shoulder). Doing this takes the pressure off of the bent knee lock.

The attacker completes his shoulder roll and quickly swings his left foot and leg over his opponent's head.

The attacker must work quickly as his opponent will continue to attempt the leglock. The attacker quickly uses both hands and arm to trap his opponent's right arm (to the attacker's chest) as shown.

The attacker quickly arches his hips, applying pressure for the Juji Gatame to work.

This photo shows a different view of the action with the attacker securing the Juji Gatame.

## RUSSIAN DRAG TO BACK ROLL JUJI GATAME

The defender (on top) comes up on one knee in an attempt to stabilize himself or pass his opponent's guard. The attacker (on bottom) uses his right hand and arm to reach under the top grappler's left foot and leg as shown.

**IMPORTANT:** This set up is also a good "plan B" is the bottom grappler's attempt at a spinning Juji Gatame does not work.

The attacker uses his right arm to hook and pull his opponent's left leg to the attacker's right shoulder and straight as shown.

This view shows how the attacker uses his right arm to hook the defender's left lower leg and pull (or drag) it straight. This action upsets the top grappler's balance to his back side as shown.

The attacker drives forward and toward his opponent, placing his right leg across the defender's torso as shown.

This photo shows the back side and we will switch to this view to complete the sequence. Look at how the attacker drives off of his left foot and leg to drive his opponent onto his back.

The attacker drives his opponent onto his back and the attacker sits on his opponent as shown.

The attacker now pins his opponent as shown. The attacker uses his left arm to trap his opponent's right arm to the attacker's chest.

The attacker swings his left leg over the defender.

The defender has swung his left leg over his opponent's head and is using his left arm to trap the defender's right arm firmly to the attacker's chest.

Switching back to the front view, the attacker is squatting as shown, having just swung his left leg over his opponent's head. The attacker continues to use his left arm to trap his opponent's right arm and is now using his right arm to assist in trapping the defender's right arm. Look how round the attacker's body is.

The attacker rolls back and applies Juji Gatame.

## NEAR SHOULDER SIT TO BACK ROLL JUJI GATAME

This is a good move that Neil Adams showed me. The attacker is positioned at the head of the defender, who is on all fours.

The attacker moves to his right (to the defender's left side) as shown. The attacker swings his right leg over his opponent's low back and hips.

The attacker wedges his right foot and leg in the defender's right hip and upper leg as shown. Look at how the attacker uses his left had to post onto the mat for stability. It is recommended that the attacker also uses his right hand to grab the defender's right wrist and pull the defender's right wrist into the defender's right stomach area.

The attacker moves his left knee toward the defender's head as the attacker shifts his body position to the defender's head as shown.

This back view shows how the attacker jams his left knee in the back of his opponent's head and left shoulder. The action of the attacker's left knee jamming in the defender's left shoulder and head is the pivot point to roll the defender onto his back. As he does this, the attacker uses his right leg, which is jammed in the defender's right hip and upper leg, to manipulate the defender's lower body over as well.

The attacker rolls the defender over onto the defender's back.

This view shows how the attacker rolls the defender onto the defender's back. This photo also shows how the attacker uses his right leg and foot to lift and manipulate the defender's lower body. Look at how the attacker rolls onto his left hips and buttock.

The attacker sits back onto his buttocks and rolls the defender onto his back.

The attacker swings his left leg over the defender's head as the attacker uses both hands to trap the defender's right arm to the attacker's body.

The attacker rolls back and secures Juji Gatame.

## SIT BACK JUJI GATAME

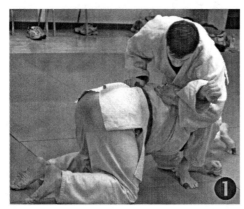

The attacker starts his attack from the head of the defender, who is on all fours as shown. The attacker places his left foot and leg on the right side of the defender's head by his right shoulder. The attacker uses his left hand to hook under the defender's right shoulder and arm.

The attacker uses his right leg to step over the defender's upper body and right shoulder. The attacker wedges his right foot in the right hip area of the defender. The attacker uses his right hand to grab the defender's belt and continues to uses his left hand to scoop up under the defender's right upper arm as shown.

The attacker uses his left arm to firmly trap the defender's right arm to the attacker's chest. As he does this, the attacker starts to sit on his opponent's right shoulder and roll backward. The attacker uses his right hand to pull on the defender's belt.

This view shows how the attacker rolls backward, pulling the defender onto his back. Look at how the attacker uses his right foot to help lift and control his opponent as he rolls him backward.

This view from the back shows how the attacker rolls backward. You can see how the attacker uses his left hand to trap the defender's right arm to the attacker's chest and how the attacker uses his right hand to pull on the defender's belt.

The attacker rolls his opponent onto his back, and as he does this, the attacker quickly uses both hands to grab and trap the defender's right arm to the attacker's chest.

The attacker rolls onto his back, rolling his opponent with him as the attacker secures the Juji Gatame.

## JUJI GATAME AGAINST LEG SCISSORS OR HALF GUARD

A common defensive position for the bottom grappler is to use his legs to scissor the top grappler's leg in the half guard position. In this photo, the attacker's right leg has been scissored by the bottom grappler.

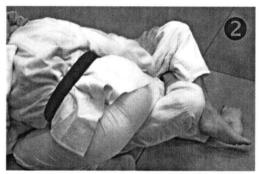

The attacker starts the move by using his right hand to push down on his opponent's left knee. As he does this, the attacker starts to pull his right leg out as much as possible. If possible, the attacker will pull his leg out completely to free it, giving him the advantage in the position.

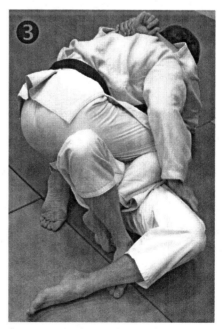

The attacker extracts his right leg as much as possible from his opponent's leg scissors. The attacker bends his right knee and jams it down on the defender's left upper leg and hip area. The attacker's left knee is on the mat near the defender's left shoulder and head area.

As the attacker extracts his right leg as much as possible, he uses both hands to hook and trap his opponent's right arm. Look at how the attacker leans his body into the defender so the attacker's chest is close and he is better able to trap the defender's right arm. The attacker springs up off of his left knee into a squatting position.

The attacker swings his left foot and leg over the defender's head. As he does this, the attacker uses both hands to trap the defender's right arm tightly to the attacker's chest. Look at how the attacker is squatting over the defender at this point.

The attacker rolls backward and secures the Juji Gatame. Look at how the attacker's right foot and leg is still being scissored by the defender. There is no need for the attacker to pull his right foot and leg free.

## SIT AND DRAG TO JUJI GATAME

This is similar to the sit back Juji Gatame except that in this variation, the attacker does not roll his opponent onto the opponent's back. This is a painful variation of Juji Gatame as the attacker really cranks the defender's arm and shoulder at an extreme angle. The attacker starts the move from the top as shown. The attacker uses his left hand to hook under his opponent's right arm and shoulder as the attacker uses his right foot to step over the defender's lefts shoulder and side.

The attacker steps forward with his left foot and leg as he sits onto his buttocks. As he does this, the attacker uses his right hand to scoop under the defender's right elbow (and will use his right hand to quickly grab his left upper leg) and the attacker uses his left arm to hook and trap the defender's right arm firmly to the attacker's chest. The attacker jams his right foot and lower leg under the defender's left his and upper leg.

The attacker uses his right hand to grab his left upper leg (this serves as a strong anchor to lever the defender's arm loose). As he does this, the attacker leans to his left hip and side and uses his left hand to post on the mat for stability. At the same time, the attacker rolls to his left his and levers the defender's right arm loose. Look at how the attacker is sitting on his opponent's head.

The attacker leans to his left backside and uses his left hand to hook under the defender's compromised right arm (look at how the attacker's left hand scoops near the defender's right upper arm and wrist area). This action creates pain in the defender's extended right shoulder and arm and levers the defender's arm loose so the attacker can secure his Juji Gatame.

## GLAHN SPECIAL TO BACK ROLL JUJI GATAME

The Olympic medal winner Klaus Glahn used this set up as an effective strangle. We've adapted it so that it can be used as both a strangle as well as an effective Juji Gatame, making this technique "double trouble" for the opponent.

The attacker (on top) is positioned relative to his opponent as shown. The attacker uses his left hand to reach under the defender's right arm and the attacker uses his left hand to grab the defender's left lapel. The attacker uses his right hand to grab the defender's jacket. Look at how the attacker's right elbow is pointed downward.

This photo shows the side view and you can see how the attacker's left arm is hooked tightly under the defender's right armpit area. The attacker is on his knees and at the defender's right side near the defender's shoulder.

The attacker places his left foot on the defender's right knee as shown.

The attacker uses his hands and arms to roll the defender over to the attacker's left (and defender's right). Look at how the attacker uses his left foot to prop or block the defender's right knee.

The attacker rolls the defender over onto his back.

The attacker continues to roll over and on top of the defender. Look at how the attacker's body is in the shape of a tripod with the attacker's head posted on the mat with each of the attacker's feet and legs spread wide. This is a stable position for the attacker to further launch this attacker from.

The attacker pops his head up and off the mat and leans back a bit as shown.

The attacker uses his right arm to firmly trap the defender's right upper arm to the attacker's chest as the attacker moves his left foot forward near the defender's head area.

The attacker swings his left foot and leg around toward the defender's head as the attacker continues to trap the defender's right arm to the attacker's chest. The attacker starts to roll backward and onto his buttocks.

The attacker rolls backward, securing the Juji Gatame as shown.

## POWER HALF TO JUJI GATAME

The attacker (on top) sinks a power half nelson on his opponent's left shoulder as shown.

The attacker jams his left foot in the defender's left hip as he moves to his right and over his opponent's back. The attacker continues to apply a lot of pressure with his power half on the defender's left shoulder and head.

The attacker moves his body to his right and behind his opponent. The attacker places his right knee on the mat near and behind the defender's head as shown. As he does this, the attacker uses his arms to trap and pry the defender's left arm up and to the attacker's chest.

The attacker quickly swings his right leg over his opponent's head as he rolls back to apply Juji Gatame.

## NEAR WRIST RIDE TO JUJI GATAME

Controlling the defender's wrist is a good way to control his entire body as this application demonstrates. The attacker (on top) uses his right hand to grab his opponent's right wrist (this is the wrist ride).

The attacker moves to his right, keeping his chest and head low and near the defender's upper back and head. The attacker is on both feet with good mobility.

The attacker continues to move to his right and around the defender's right side. Look at how the attacker has used his right hand to grab and control the defender's right wrist and forearm. Look at how the attacker uses his right elbow to drive down toward the mat, cranking the defender's right arm and bending the defender's right wrist down and inward.

The attacker moves around toward the top of his opponent and uses his right wrist ride to control the defender's right arm. The attacker uses his left hand to grab under the defender's right elbow.

The attacker scoops the defender's right forearm up with both hands. The attacker uses his right elbow and forearm to exert pressure on the defender's back; doing this cranks and pulls the defender's right arm upward.

The attacker pulls and hooks the defender's right bent arm to the attacker's chest. Look at how the attacker has bent forward so that his chest meets the defender's right elbow. This pulls the defender up off the mat a bit.

The attacker's action has pulled the defender onto his left side. The attacker continues to trap the defender's right elbow and arm firmly to the attacker's chest. The

attacker is kneeling on his right knee (placed directly behind the defender's upper back). The attacker stabilizes his position by posting with his left foot as shown.

The attacker quickly moves his left foot over the defender's head.

The attacker jams his right shin in the back and right side of the defender's body as the attacker uses both hands to hook and trap the defender's right arm to the attacker's chest. The attacker's left foot and leg hooks the defender's head tightly as the attacker rolls back.

The attacker rolls his opponent onto his back into the leg press.

The attacker applies Juji Gatame.

## HECK LEG HOOK TO JUJI GATAME

World Open Sambo Champion Chris Heckadon has used this breakdown to Juji Gatame for much of his career with success. He demonstrates it in this sequence of photos.

The attacker applies this entry from the top and head area of the defender. The attacker uses his left hand to hook under the defender's right arm. The attacker uses his right hand to grab the defender's belt.

The attacker uses both hands to grab the defender's belt as the attacker sits onto his buttocks, actually sitting on the defender's head and upper shoulders. As he does this, the attacker jams his right foot and lower leg under the left hip and upper leg of the defender.

This photo shows how the attacker sits on his buttocks, grabbing the defender's belt with both hands as shown.

The attacker's right lower leg and foot is wedged in the defender's left upper leg and hip area.

The attacker rolls to his right hip and side, and as he does, he uses his right foot to hook firmly in the left hip area of his opponent and whips him over as shown. Look at how the attacker's left leg and foot is placed over the defender's head controlling it. The attacker continues to hold onto the defender's belt with both of his hands, pulling the defender over.

The attacker pulls his opponent over and onto his back.

The attacker immediately applies Juji Gatame. Look at how the defender's right arm is pulled high and at an awkward, weak angle (for him). This adds more pressure to the shoulder and arm.

# THE "CBW" (CRUDE BUT WORKS)

This is a crude, simple and ugly way to get an opponent into Juji Gatame, but it works as often as not and should be included in this chapter.

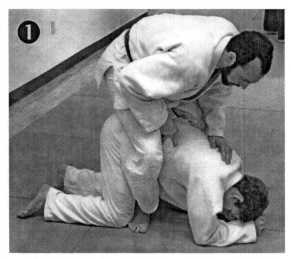

The attacker (on top) rides his opponent who is on all fours.

The attacker uses his right hand and arm to hook under the defender's right shoulder and arm.

The attacker bends forward and pivots off of his right foot to swing his left leg over the defender's head. As he does this, the attacker traps the defender's right upper arm to the attacker's chest.

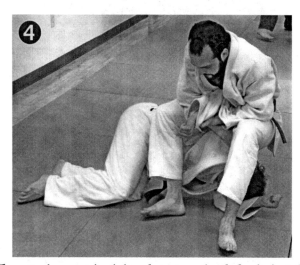

The attacker uses both hands to trap the defender's right arm at about the elbow area. As he does this, the attacker sits on his opponent's upper back and rolls backward.

The attacker tucks his head and stays round, pulling the opponent back and extending and stretching the defender's arm as shown. Hey, it's crude, but it works.

## GIBSON JUJI GATAME

Named for Greg Gibson, the first American to win a World Sambo Championship, who used this armlock with devastating effect. It may not be pretty, but it worked for Greg.

The defender is on all fours and the attacker sets him up from a standing ride as shown.

The attacker sinks his feet and legs in the defender's hips (gets his hooks in) and as he does, the attacker uses his right hand and arm to hook under the defender's right shoulder and upper arm.

The attacker pivots on his right foot and swings his left leg over the defender's head. As he does this, the attacker uses both hands to scoop and pull the attacker's right arm up toward the attacker's chest to trap it.

The attacker drops onto his right knee then immediately drops onto his left knee as well. This traps the defender's upper body, arm and head.

The attacker kneels on both knees and sits on his opponent's right shoulder. As he does this, the attacker uses both hands to grab the defender's forearm. The attacker pulls up on the defender's arm as shown.

A lot of pressure is placed on the defender's right shoulder and arm (including elbow) when the attacker sits backward directly on the defender's right shoulder. This is a painful hold, so be careful when practicing it.

## CLIMB UP GUARD PASS TO JUJI GATAME

The attacker grabs and hugs both of the defender's legs to start this method of passing his opponent's guard.

The attacker works his way up the defender's body and works to the side of the defender as shown.

The attacker has successfully worked his way up and past the defender's legs and is positioned at the defender's left side.

The attacker uses both of his hands and arms to hook and trap the defender's left arm to the attacker's chest.

The attacker comes up on one knee as shown. The attacker's right knee is placed at the side of the defender's head. The attacker's left shin is jammed in the left side of the defender at about the ribcage.

The attacker springs up as shown and starts to move his right foot and leg over the defender's head.

The attacker moves into the shoulder sit position and continues to use both of his arms to trap the defender's left arm to the attacker's chest.

The attacker starts to roll backward to apply his armlock.

The attacker rolls back and secures Juji Gatame.

## BELT AND NELSON BREAKDOWN WHEN OPPONENT IS FLAT ON FRONT TO BACK ROLL JUJI GATAME

This is a personal favorite of mine and athletes from my club have been using it with success for many years. It's an ideal way to break an opponent down to either a pin or an armlock (as shown here).

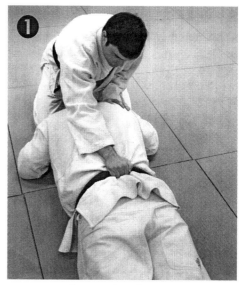

The opponent is flat on his front side in a defensive position. The attacker uses his right hand to grab the defender's belt as shown. Look at how the attacker's hand is palm down as he grabs the belt.

---

### TECHNICAL TIP

**Almost any breakdown, turnover, guard pass or transition from a throw or takedown can be turned into an opportunity to get an opponent into Juji Gatame. Experiment with a variety of breakdowns, turnovers, guard passes and transitions from standing to groundwork positions to come up with your own variations of Juji Gatame from any of these situations.**

---

The attacker moves to his left a bit and is positioned above the defender's right shoulder. The attacker uses his left hand to hook and scoop the defender's right upper arm upward toward the attacker's chest. The attacker continues to use his right hand to hold the defender's belt.

The attacker uses his left hand to grab his right wrist as shown. This creates a strong hold on the defender's right shoulder.

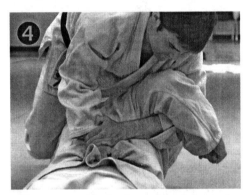

The attacker moves his body to his right and over the defender's head, making sure to keep a firm hold as shown.

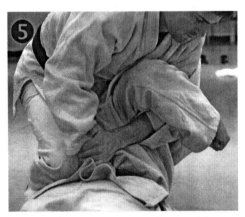

The attacker moves to his right and behind his opponent, trapping the defender's right arm and shoulder to the attacker's chest as shown.

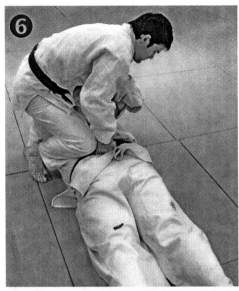

This shows how the attacker has moved into position behind his opponent and uses his right shin to jam in the back of the defender. The attacker continues to use his left hand and arm to trap the defender's right shoulder and arm.

The attacker moves his left foot and leg over the defender's head as he continues to jam his right shin in the defender's right ribcage. Look at how the attacker now uses both hands and arms to hook and trap the defender's right arm to the attacker's chest.

The attacker rolls back, extending the defender's trapped arm as he does.

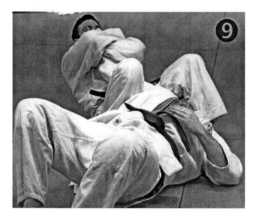

The attacker secures Juji Gatame.

## BELT AND NELSON DRAG TO JUJI GATAME

If the defender is on a stable base on all fours and offering a lot of resistance, the attacker can use this breakdown to Juji Gatame with effective results.

The attacker uses the belt and nelson grip to control and pull the bottom grappler forward, pulling him off of his

stable base on all fours and flat onto his front.

The attacker moves his right foot and leg over the defender's body and sits on the defender's left shoulder and head area. The attacker continues to pull his opponent into him with the belt and nelson grip, trapping the defender's right shoulder and arm tightly to the attacker's chest. The attacker's left foot and leg are hooked over the defender's head.

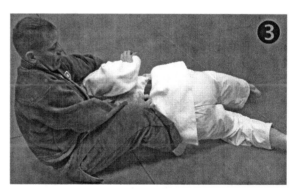

The attacker sits back onto his buttocks as he drags the defender's left shoulder and upper arm into his chest. Look at how the attacker wedges his right foot under his opponent's left hip.

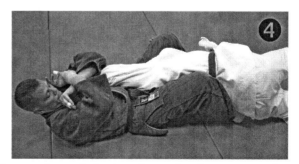

The attacker rolls back and stretches his opponent's arm to apply Juji Gatame.

## KEYLOCK TO BACK ROLL JUJI GATAME

The attacker has followed through to the ground or mat from a throw or takedown or may have turned his opponent over onto his side as shown. The attacker uses his right hand and arm to trap the defender's right upper arm to the attacker's chest. The attacker traps the defender's head with both of his legs, pinching his knees together to trap the defender's head.

The attacker continues to uses his knees and legs to trap the defender's head as he applies a keylock on the defender's right arm.

■■■■    TECHNICAL TIP    ■■■■

Keylocks provide the attacker a strong controlling position, allowing him time to trap his opponent's arm more effectively when setting him up for Juji Gatame. There are two types of keylocks used in gi and no gi grappling sports. The first, presented here, is the standard keylock. This keylock does not use the opponent's uniform in any way and can be used in any grappling situation whether a jacket and belt are used or not. The second keylock is the "judo keylock" that uses the opponent's jacket and belt to literally tie him up and control him. The judo keylock will be presented after this standard keylock is shown here.

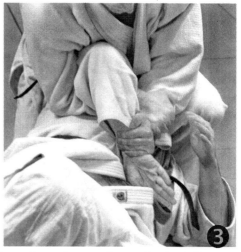

This photo shows how to form a keylock. It is important for the attacker to use the keylock and pull the defender's elbow to the attacker's chest, trapping the arm firmly.

The attacker moves to his right and around to the back side of his opponent's upper back and head. As he does this, the attacker uses his left foot and leg to trap the defender's head as shown. The defender's right knee is placed on the mat.

The attacker springs up into a squat, jamming his right shin in the defender's right side. Look at how the attacker hooks and traps the defender's right arm to the attacker's chest.

As the attacker rolls back, he levers the defender's right arm free, using the momentum of the attacker's body weight rolling backward.

The attacker rolls back and levers the defender's right arm loose, extending it.

The attacker rolls back, stretches his opponent's right arm and secures Juji Gatame.

### TECHNICAL TIP

A keylock is a good method of controlling an opponent's arm for both "gi" and "no gi" situations. Keylocks are used to control an opponent for a variety of submission and pinning techniques.

## JUDO KEYLOCK TO BACK ROLL JUJI GATAME

This application of the keylock uses the opponent's jacket and sleeve to help control him. The attacker uses both hands and arms to scoop the defender's right elbow up and off the mat.

The attacker uses his right hand and arm to slide through the defender's right upper arm. As he does this, the attacker continues to use his left hand to pull up on the defender's right elbow to accommodate his right hand and arm sliding through.

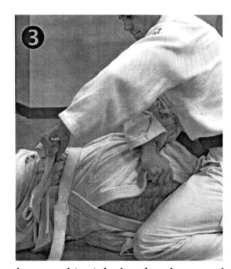

The attacker uses his right hand and arm to hook and trap the defender's right arm. Doing this pulls the defender onto his left side as shown. As he does this, the attacker uses his left hand to grab the defender's jacket apron (the portion of the jacket below the belt).

The attacker uses his left hand to grab and pull his opponent's jacket apron up and over forearm of the defender's bent right arm as shown. This traps the defender's right arm to his body.

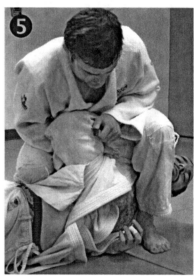

The attacker moves to his right side, squatting. As he does this, the attacker jams his right shin in the back and right side of his opponent. The attacker moves his left leg over his opponent's head, trapping it.

The attacker maintains his judo keylock control with his

right hand as he controls his opponent in the shoulder sit.

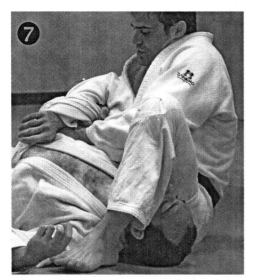

The attacker rolls back onto his buttocks with the trapped right arm of the defender.

The attacker uses his right hand to scoop under the defender's right arm as shown. Look at how the attacker has his right hand palm up. Doing this give him more power to lever the defender's arm loose.

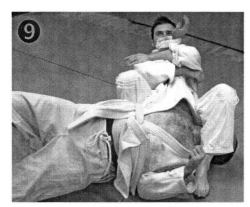

The attacker traps his opponent's right arm to his chest as he rolls back and applies Juji Gatame.

## BURNS BREAKDOWN TO BACK ROLL JUJI GATAME

This breakdown is named for AnnMaria (Burns) DeMars, the first American to win a World Judo Championship, who used it during her career.

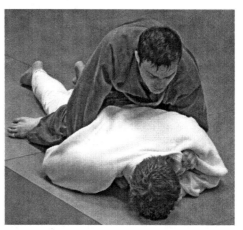

The defender is flat on his front in a defensive position. The attacker uses his left hand to scoop and hook under the defender's left shoulder and grab the left lapel of the defender. The attacker uses his right hand to scoop and hook under his opponent's right arm and grabs the defender's right forearm. Look at how the attacker is straddling his opponent.

The attacker shifts his body to his left and to the right of his opponent. As he does this, the attacker firmly holds onto his opponent's left lapel and right forearm.

The attacker quickly jumps to his right, over his opponent's body with a lot of force, continuing to hold onto his opponent with both hands.

As the attacker jumps to his right, he pulls his opponent over. The attacker makes sure not to fall onto his side or buttocks, but rather lands on both of his knees.

This photo shows the back view. The attacker is positioned on both of his knees. It is important for the attacker to not be seated on his buttocks, hip or side. He must be on his knees.

This photo shows how the attacker controls his opponent with his hands and arms as he pulls the defender over.

The attacker springs up and jams his left shin in the side and back of his opponent. As he does this, the attacker uses both hands to hook and trap the defender's left arm to the attacker's chest.

It's a good idea for the attacker to keep his chin tucked on his opponent's left shoulder. At this point, the attacker is positioned on both of his knees, kneeling. Look at how the attacker uses his hands and arms to control the defender.

This photo shows how the attacker is positioned as he traps the defender's left arm to the attacker's chest.

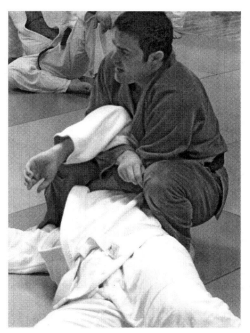

The attacker moves his right foot and leg over his opponent's head.

The attacker rolls back to apply Juji Gatame.

The attacker rolls back, stretches his opponent's arm and gets the tap out.

## SEATED RODEO RIDE TO BACK ROLL JUJI GATAME

This position takes place more often than people realize. Anytime the attacker is seated behind his opponent in this position, it is called a seated rodeo ride. Often, the attacker has rolled his opponent over into this position from a stable position where the defender was initially on all fours. Actually, there are any number of situations where the attacker can roll his opponent over into this position and apply Juji Gatame.

The attacker controls his opponent from the back with a rodeo ride.

The attacker moves to his right, shifting his weight to his right and to the left side of his opponent. As he does this, the attacker places his right lower leg across the front of the defender and wedges his right foot at the defender's left hip as an anchor. Look at how the attacker's body is now sideways and behind his opponent with the attacker's left foot and leg posted on the mat for stability. The attacker continues to use both hands to grab his opponent's lapels.

The attacker continues to use his right leg and foot to anchor the defender's left hip. As he does this, the attacker uses his right arm to hook and trap the defender's right arm to the attacker's chest. The attacker is now ready to swing his left foot and leg over the defender's head. The attacker's body is sideways to the defender's body as shown. The action of the attacker also helps in pulling the defender's upper body downward to the mat.

The attacker now uses both hands to trap the defender's right arm as the attacker swings his left foot and leg over his opponent's head.

The attacker swings his left foot and leg over his opponent's head to control the defender's upper body.

The defender swings his left foot and leg over the defender's head and applies Juji Gatame.

### TECHNICAL TIP

Move from one controlling position to another, all the while doing everything possible to hook, grab and control your opponent's arm so that you can trap him with your Juji Gatame. It is important to be methodical and not to hurry or force a move. Remember the phrase, " get the position, and then get the submission."

## BURNS BREAKDOWN TO SEATED RODEO RIDE TO BACK ROLL JUJI GATAME

The attacker uses both hands to reach and hook under the defender's arms from a top ride position.

The attacker uses both hands to hook and control the defender's wrists. As he does this, the attacker rolls to his left, rolling his opponent with him.

This photo shows how the attacker uses both hands to grab his opponent's forearms and wrists.

The attacker rolls the defender over and as he does, the attacker moves his feet and legs around the defender's body to secure a rodeo ride.

The attacker controls his opponent from behind with a seated rodeo ride.

The attacker shifts his body position to his left and as he does, he uses his right hand to help hook and trap the defender's left arm. The attacker shifts his body position to his left and to the left side of his opponent.

The attacker swings his right foot and leg over his opponent's head as he uses both hands to trap the defender's left arm to his chest.

The attacker applies his Juji Gatame.

## HIP SHIFT BREAKDOWN FROM STUCK ON BOTTOM TO JUJI GATAME

Sometimes, the attacker may be stuck in this position where he is on his back with his opponent lying on top of him. A possible situation might be where the attacker tired to roll his opponent, but for some reason, the opponent managed to stop the roll and stabilize himself in this way. Sometimes, the defender (on top) may be in the attacker's guard and has turned this way in an effort to roll out. In other circumstances, the defender may have been in the attacker's seated rodeo ride and pushed off of his feet in an effort to arch or bridge out of it. In any event, this is an odd position, but it does happen, and because of that, the smart grappler will plan for it and train for when this situation takes place.

The bottom grappler (the attacker) has his hooks in and controls his opponent with a rodeo ride from the bottom position. The attacker is attempting to bridge and turn into the attacker to get out of the ride.

The attacker moves his left foot and leg behind the defender's left knee as shown.

The attacker uses his left foot and leg to kick his opponent's left leg out straight. This flops the defender back down and onto his buttocks as shown.

The attacker now has his opponent in the seated rodeo ride. The attacker shifts his position, moving to his right and to the right side of the defender. The attacker moves his right foot and leg in front of his opponent for control.

The attacker swings his left foot and leg over his opponent's head. As he does this, the attacker uses his right hand and arm, which is controlling the defender's right shoulder to pull the defender down to the mat.

The attacker is sideways to his opponent. The attacker uses his right hand to secure a quarter nelson on the right shoulder and head of the defender. This helps control the defender's upper body and traps his right arm to the attacker's chest.

The attacker now has the defender in the leg press and is controlling him. The attacker uses both hands and arms to trap the defender's right arm to the defender's chest.

The attacker scoots back as necessary, making room to swing his left leg over the defender's head as shown.

The attacker rolls back to apply Juji Gatame.

## SIDE SHIFT WHEN STUCK ON BOTTOM TO JUJI GATAME

Here is another situation where the attacker is on bottom and has a rodeo ride to control his opponent.

The attacker uses his right hand to grab his opponent's right hip. If it is a "no gi" situation, the attacker can use his right hand to push on the defender's right hip rather than grabbing it.

The attacker shifts his upper body and head to his right as he swings his right leg across the defender's body as shown.

The attacker moves his upper body to his right and sideways to his opponent as shown. As he does this, the attacker uses his left hand and arm to secure a lapel choke on his opponent (this isn't required, but is helpful as it puts the defender in "double trouble").

The attacker is sideways to his opponent with his right leg across the defender as shown. The attacker's left foot is placed on the mat. Look at how the attacker continues to have control of his opponent's hip with his right hand.

The attacker swings his left foot and leg over his opponent's head as shown.

The attacker now uses his right hand to help hook and trap the defender's right arm to the attacker's chest as he continues to move his left leg over his opponent's head.

The attacker rolls back and secures his Juji Gatame.

The back roll Juji Gatame is one of those skills that, while simple in concept, has many functional applications. And because of its simplicity, the many entries, rolls, breakdowns and turns where it is applied all have a high ratio of success in competitive situations. As with every move in this book, take what you see and modify it so that it works for you.

The next chapter focuses on the head roll Juji Gatame; a skill that has been used at all levels of competition in judo, sambo, submission grappling, sport jujitsu, BJJ, catch wrestling and MMA and is a favorite of some of the best armlock technicians in the world.

# HEAD ROLL JUJI GATAME

"SOMETIMES YOU
HAVE TO PLAY
FOR A LONG TIME
TO PLAY LIKE
YOURSELF."
MILES DAVIS, JR.

## THE HEAD ROLL JUJI GATAME: AN INTRODUCTION

The head roll juji Gatame is probably the most popular of the four primary applications of Juji Gatame in the real world of sport combat. It is also the most technical and requires the most study and practice. While it takes some time to learn (like anything of value), this entry has proven to have a high ratio of success for athletes of all weight classes, male and female, in every form of sport combat. The head roll Juji Gatame is distinct from the other basic applications in that the attacker rolls or turns his opponent over the defender's head in something that resembles a somersault. Because of this, I named this application the "head roll" because it accurately describes what takes place.

The head roll Juji Gatame is (depending on someone's point of view, I suppose) the most technically challenging of the four basic applications of Juji Gatame. It takes more time to learn and instinctively perform this armlock than the other three, but then again, this entry is used more often than any other application of Juji Gatame by a wide spectrum of athletes.

As G. K. Chesterton said, "to appreciate anything, we must isolate it." This is certainly true with this application of Juji Gatame. To better appreciate and understand how and why this application works, this chapter will isolate, analyze and "disassemble" the various parts of the head roll Juji Gatame, and then "reassemble" them into the functional and successful technique that it is. There are a number of technical skills that must be mastered to be able to pull this off in competition, and to master them; we first must understand them and why and how they work. That takes some analysis of the many parts that make the whole of this armlock application. Let's get to it.

## MAT TEMPO

Think of the head roll Juji Gatame in the same way you would a throw or takedown. Often, to control the opponent's balance, position and movement, a throwing technique comes out of a fast tempo. Tempo is the phrase I use to describe how fast or how slow the athletes move about on the mat. An effective head roll Juji Gatame often results from a flurry of activity on the mat. The skill of rolling the defender over his or her head and into Juji Gatame is, in many ways, the exact same as a throwing technique. In a throwing technique, the goal of the attacker is to get his opponent's back on the mat with total control. This describes what you are doing in a head roll Juji Gatame (but then again, it accurately describes what you are doing in any of the four basic applications of Juji Gatame).

The action of rolling a resisting opponent over his head in a somersault does not come out of a slow, ponderous motion. Instead, it comes out of a fast, explosive (and controlled) series of movements. In many cases, a successful head roll Juji Gatame takes place when one athlete gains control over the other in a scramble, or flurry of activity where neither grappler has the initial advantage. When training on the head roll Juji Gatame, design your drills so that the way you are performing the set up and armlock is how you would like it to look like in a real match. Train realistically for the best results.

## THE PRIMARY WAYS OF DOING HEAD ROLL JUJI GATAME

There are three principle variations on how the attacker uses his leg to control his opponent's head when rolling the defender over his head and into Juji Gatame. It doesn't matter what combat sport it is, these three methods are used in some variation by every successful Juji Gatame technician who specializes in the head roll application: 1) Bent Knee Head Control Application, 2) Extended Leg Head Control Application and 3) "No Head" Control Application.

## BENT KNEE HEAD CONTROL APPLICATION

This variation places emphasis on the attacker's bent leg, which drives the defender's head downward, somersaulting the defender over onto his back.

The attacker places his left shin and the top of his left foot on the back of his opponent's head and neck. The attacker posts on the top of his head as he traps the defender's right arm.

The attacker anchors his right foot at the defender's left hip and upper leg as shown. As he does this, the attacker uses his left foot and shin to drive downward on the defender's head. The attacker drives his left knee to the right, toward the defender's lower body.

The attacker continues to sit through and onto his left hip as he uses his left bent leg to drive down on the defender's head. As he does this, the attacker uses his right leg to lift the defender's body and roll him over his head.

## EXTENDED LEG HEAD CONTROL APPLICATION

This variation of the head roll Juji Gatame features the attacker's extended (or slightly bent) leg, which drives the defender's head downward, somersaulting him over onto his back.

The attacker sinks his right leg and foot in and anchors his right foot on his opponent's left hip or upper leg as shown. The attacker posts on his head to the side of the defender and starts to lever the defender's right arm loose. As he does this, the attacker places his extended left leg across the back of the defender's head and neck. (The attacker's leg may be slightly bent or fully extended.)

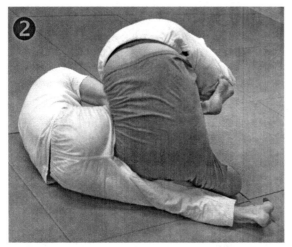

The attacker turns or rolls onto his left hip and drives his left leg forcefully downward on the back of his opponent's head and neck. The attacker uses his right leg and foot to lift the defender's body as shown.

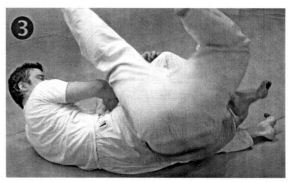

The fast and forceful action of the attacker turning or rolling onto his left hip and side, coupled with the whipping action of his legs, forces the defender to somersault over and onto his back.

### TECHNICAL TIP

**How the attacker somersaults the defender, rolling him over his head and onto his back is a matter of preference as well as opportunity. All of these variations work.**

## "NO HEAD" CONTROL APPLICATION

This variation of the head roll Juji Gatame takes place when the attacker does not place a leg over the top of the defender's head. Instead, the attacker hooks his leg under the defender's head using the turning movement of his body to somersault the defender over onto his back.

The attacker drives both of his feet and legs under his opponent. The attacker's right leg is wedged under the defender's head and the attacker's left leg is wedged across the defender's torso. As he does this, the attacker, uses his hands and arms to hook and trap the defender's left arm as shown. The attacker is posted on the top of his head for stability (and to see what is going on).

The attacker quickly and forcefully turns or rolls to his right side. As he does this, the attacker starts to lever his opponent's arms apart.

The fast turn of the attacker's body to his right side, along with the attacker pulling on the defender's left arm, forces the defender to somersault over his head.

## KEY POINTS FOR A SUCCESSFUL HEAD ROLL JUJI GATAME

Presented here are some of the key (and necessary) components of the head roll Juji Gatame.

## ATTACKER AND DEFENDER ARE IN THE SHAPE OF THE LETTER "L"

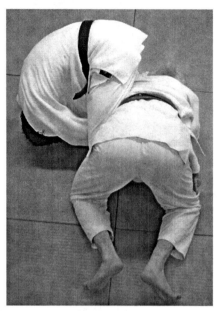

Often, the attacker is positioned sideways relative to his opponent's body as shown here. The attacker is posted on the top of his head and positioned at the (in this photo) left shoulder and upper body of the defender. The defender may be on his knees or flat on his front, or in any variation of these positions.

## ATTACKER POSTS ON THE TOP OF HIS HEAD FOR STABILITY

The attacker should post on the top of his head to stabilize his body (as well as the body of his opponent). By posting on the top of his head, the attacker has the option to roll to his left or to his right, depending on the opportunity and situation. By posting on the top of his head like this, the attacker also has a good view of what it going on.

This photo shows how the attacker posts on the top of his head as he applies the head roll Juji Gatame at the AAU Freestyle Judo Nationals. The attacker has a clear view of what is taking place by posting on the top of his head.

## ATTACKER'S LEG FOOT ON THE BACK OF DEFENDER'S HEAD AND NECK

The attacker places his bent leg on the back of his opponent's head and neck. Look at how the attacker's left lower shin and top of the left foot are placed on the defender's head. The attacker has good control of the defender's head and can force him to somersault over and onto his back with this leg and foot placement.

## THE ANCHOR FOOT IN DEFENDER'S HIP AND LEG

The attacker drives his (in this photo) left foot and leg and "anchors" or places his left foot on the defender's right hip and upper leg. This give the attacker strong control of the position, as well as provides the attacker a stable pivot point to initiate his action of turning the defender over in a somersault.

This shows how the attacker has anchored his right foot low on the defender's leg showing that as long as the attacker has a stable anchor to work with, it doesn't matter if the anchor foot is at the defender's hip or upper leg.

## THE ATTACKER SITS THROUGH ONTO HIS HIP

The attacker forces his opponent to somersault over by the quick, driving sit through action of the leg that is closest to the defender's head. In this photo, the attacker's right foot and leg are placed at the back of the defender's head and neck.

The attacker quickly and forcefully drives his right knee toward the feet (or lower body) of the defender as shown. The attacker (in this photo) turns onto his right side and hip.

The attacker sits through with his right knee as shown so that the attacker is now on his right side. Look at how this action forces the defender's head down so that it is easier to roll him over his head and onto his back.

## THE ATTACKER'S LEG ACTION: THE LEG WHIP

As a tie-in to the skill of sitting through with the leg on his opponent's head, the attacker uses his legs to manipulate and "whip" the defender over as shown in this sequence of photos.

The attacker has anchored his left foot on the defender's right hip and upper leg. The attacker starts to place his right leg on the back of the defender's head.

The attacker has both of his feet and legs in place for the head roll Juji Gatame. The attacker now turns so that he rolls or turns onto his right side.

The attacker turns onto his right hip and side as he uses his left foot and leg to drive the defender's head down. As he does this, the attacker uses his left leg to lift the defender's body (at the belt line of the defender) upward. This forceful, whipping action of the attacker's legs resulting from his quick turn (sit through) onto his right hip and side forces the defender to roll over his head as shown.

This photo shows how the attacker continues to sit through and onto his right side, causing the whipping action of his legs to roll the defender over his head.

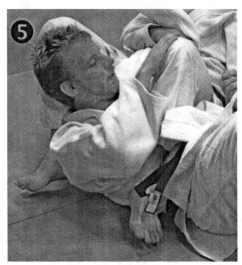

The attacker rolls the defender over and onto his back as shown in this photo taken immediately after the attacker has somersaulted over his head. Look at how the attacker's right foot and leg are still at the back of the defender's head. The attacker's left leg and foot are still across the defender's torso.

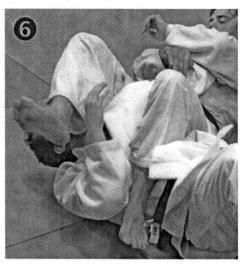

The attacker immediately swings his right leg over the defender's head in order to trap it to the mat.

## LEG GRABS AND HOOKS

Often, the attacker will use the arm that is not trapping his opponent's arm to assist in pulling, lifting, swinging or hooking the defender's leg or legs over to roll the defender over and onto his back. There are two primary methods of doing this: 1) Leg Grabs and 2) Leg Hooks.

## GRABBING THE DEFENDER LOW ON HIS PANT LEG

The attacker uses his left hand to grab low on the defender's pant leg to lift and drag the defender over and across the attacker's body as the attacker executes the head roll Juji Gatame.

## GRABBING THE DEFENDER HIGH ON HIS PANT LEG

The attacker uses his right hand to grab at the knee area or higher up on the pant leg at the hip area to help roll the defender over onto his back.

## GRABBING THE PANT LEG IN COMPETITION

This photo shows how the attacker (with his back to the camera) uses his right hand to grab his opponent's right pant leg at the hip area in an effort to pull and drag him over during a head roll Juji Gatame.

## HOOKING THE DEFENDER'S LEG

This is useful in both "no gi" and "gi" grappling sports. This method of controlling the defender's leg has been popular in sambo for many years due to the fact that sambo wrestlers wear shorts and not long pants as in judo or jujitsu. The attacker uses his left hand and arm to hook and trap the defender's left arm as he uses his right hand and arm to hook the defender's right leg to assist the head roll action.

## ATTACKER HOOKING DEFENDER'S LEG AND GRABBING LOCKING HIS HANDS TOGETHER

Sometimes, the attacker can grab his hands together locking his grip during the rolling action as shown here.

## ATTACKER HOOKING DEFENDER'S LEG AND GRABBING HIS OWN PANT LEG

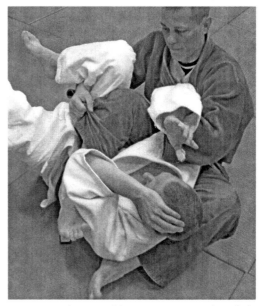

In some cases the attacker can use one hand (in this photo, his right hand) to hook around the defender's right leg. The attacker grabs his right pant leg as shown.

## HEAD ROLL JUJI GATAME: THE BASIC APPLICATION

The attacker approaches on the defender's left side as shown. In this basic entry, the defender is on his elbows and knees.

The attacker drives his right leg under the defender's right side so that the attacker's right foot is anchored at the defender's left upper leg or hip. The attacker extends himself over the defender so that the attacker's head is posted on the mat to the right of the defender's shoulder. The attacker uses his left arm to hook the defender's right arm and start to trap it.

The attacker moves his left leg over onto the back of the defender's head and neck as shown.

The attacker places his left leg and foot on the defender's head and neck. The attacker is posted on the top of his head for stability as he continues to use his left arm to hook and trap the defender's right arm.

The attacker starts to drive his left knee downward to the mat and will quickly drive the left knee to the attacker's right and toward the defender's lower body.

The attacker drives his left knee downward and in the direction of the defender's lower body. Look at how the attacker is starting to swing his left knee to his right and toward the defender's lower body and legs. At this point, the attacker is starting to sit through so that he will be on his left side and hip.

This view shows how the attacker drives his left knee toward the attacker's right so that he will be on his left side. As he does this, the attacker's right foot is still anchored on the defender's left hip.

The attacker forcefully sits in (on his **left** side) and as he does, he uses his left foot and leg to **drive** the defender's head downward. The attacker uses his right leg and foot to swing forcefully upward and into the torso of the defender. This action forces the defender to roll directly over his head.

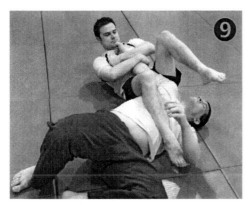

The attacker rolls across his buttocks so that he rolls over as shown. As he does this, his rolling action forces the defender to somersault over his head and onto his back. The attacker immediately swings his left leg over the defender's head as shown.

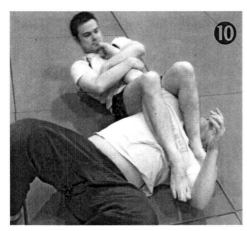

The attacker has rolled the defender over the defender's head and applies Juji Gatame.

## HEAD ROLL JUJI GATAME WITH LEG DRAG

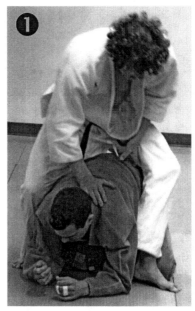

The attacker starts his attack from a standing ride.

The attacker digs his left foot and leg in under the torso of the defender. Look at how the attacker is using his left hand to post onto the mat for stability.

The attacker posts his head on the mat for more stability and he uses his right arm to hook and trap the defender's left arm.

The attacker quickly jams his right knee and shin down onto the back of the defender's head and neck. As he does this, the attacker starts to turn to his right and in the direction of the defender's lower body.

While he is doing this, the attacker uses his left hand to grab the defender's near (in this case, the defender's left) pant leg.

The attacker sits through with his right knee and onto his right side as shown.

As the attacker sits through, he uses his left hand to pull the defender's left leg up and over the attacker's body and head.

This view from the other side shows how the attacker uses his left hand to drag and lift the defender's left leg over. Look at how the attacker rolls the defender over the defender's head.

The attacker completes the head roll with the leg drag and rolls the defender over and onto his back.

The attacker immediately applies Juji Gatame.

## HEAD ROLL JUJI GATAME WITH LEG HOOK

The attacker starts his attack and uses his left arm to hook the defender's right arm.

This view shows how the attacker posts on the top of his head and positions his body over the defender.

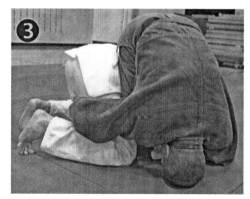

The attacker uses his right arm to hook the defender's right upper leg as shown.

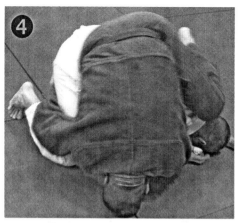

At this point, the attacker moves his left leg up and over the back of the defender's head. The attacker uses his left leg to drive down on the back of the defender's head and neck.

The attacker uses both hands and arms to hook and trap the defender's right arm and right leg. Often, the attacker can grab his hands together. At this point, the attacker starts to roll onto his left side as shown.

The attacker rolls his opponent over the defender's head as shown in this photo.

The attacker rolls the defender over his head and onto his back. Look at how the attacker has grabbed his hands together, completely trapping the defender's right arm and right leg.

This photo shows an alternative way for the attacker to use his right hand to grab his own pant leg if he has chosen not to grab his hands together (or has been unable to grab his hands together for some reason).

The attacker can now apply Juji Gatame.

## HEAD ROLL JUJI GATAME WITH EXTENDED LEG

The attacker controls his opponent with a rodeo ride. As he does this, the attacker uses his right hand to grab the defender's right forearm and wrist as shown.

The attacker sinks his right leg and foot in and anchors his right foot on his opponent's left hip or upper leg as shown. The attacker posts on his head to the side of the defender and starts to lever the defender's right arm loose. As he does this, the attacker places his extended left leg across the back of the defender's head and neck. (The attacker's leg may be slightly bent or fully extended.)

The attacker places his extended left leg across the back of the defender's head and neck. The attacker's leg may be straight or slightly bent.
**IMPORTANT:** The attacker's left upper leg or knee is driving downward on the back of the defender's head and neck.

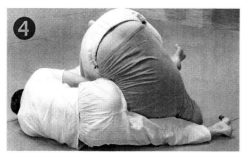

The attacker turns or rolls onto his left hip and drives his left leg forcefully downward on the back of his opponent's head and neck as shown. The attacker uses his right leg and foot to lift the defender's body.

The fast and forceful action of the attacker turning or rolling onto his left hip and side, coupled with the whipping action of his legs, forces the defender to somersault over and onto his back.

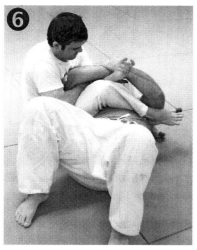

The attacker rolls his opponent over the opponent's head and onto his back.

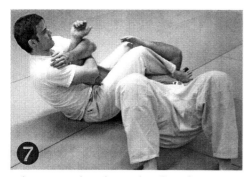

The attacker immediately applies Juji Gatame.

## "NO HEAD" ROLL INTO JUJI GATAME

The attacker applies a "belly-down" Juji Gatame as shown here. Look at how the attacker does not have his right leg placed on the back of the defender's head. Instead, the attacker's right leg is hooked under the defender's head and neck. Look at how the attacker uses both of his hands and arms to trap the defender's left arm. The attacker is posted on the top of his head.

The attacker forcefully and quickly rolls or turns onto his right side.

This view from the other side shows how the attacker uses his legs to control the defender's shoulders and upper body.

The attacker rolls or turns onto his right side as shown. As he does, the attacker uses his legs and the action of his turning action to roll the defender over his head.

The attacker rolls the defender over his head and onto his back.

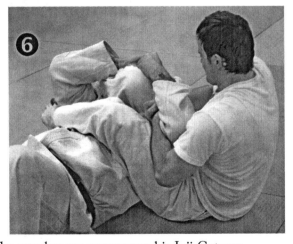

The attacker can now secure his Juji Gatame.

## HEAD ROLL JUJI GATAME WHEN OPPONENT POPS UP IN A RODEO RIDE

In some cases, if the defender (on bottom) is being controlled in a rodeo ride, he may try to post up and onto his feet. This photo shows the attacker controlling his opponent with the rodeo ride.

The attacker posts up high as shown in an attempt to get the attacker off of his back.

The attacker moves his body to his left (to the defender's right shoulder) and posts on the top of his head. As he does this, the attacker positions his left bent knee so that it will be placed on the back of the defender's head and neck. The attacker uses his right arm to hook and trap the defender's right arm. The attacker may use his left hand to post onto the mat for stability if necessary.

The attacker hooks his left foot and lower leg on the back of the defender's head as shown. As he does this, the attacker uses both of his hands and arms to hook and trap the defender's right arm. The attacker starts to turn into the direction of the defender's lower body.

The attacker continues to turn onto his left side, forcing the defender to roll forward over his head.

The attacker rolls the defender over as shown.

The attacker rolls the defender over his head and onto his back and secures his Juji Gatame.

## "NO HEAD" ROLL WITH LEG ASSIST INTO JUJI GATAME

This "no head" variation of Juji Gatame includes the action of the attacker grabbing the defender's leg or pant leg to assist the rolling action. The attacker is applying a belly-down Juji Gatame as shown.

The attacker quickly sits through and onto his left side and hip. As he does this, the attacker uses his right hand to grab the defender's near (right) pant leg.

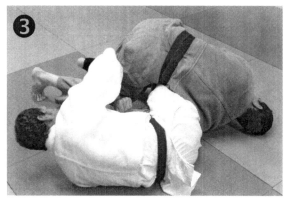

The attacker uses his right hand to grab the defender's pant leg and starts to lift and drag the defender's right leg over the attacker's head and body.

The attacker uses his right hand to drag the defender's right leg over the attacker as shown. This is being done while the attacker uses his legs to complete the "no head" variation of Juji Gatame to roll the defender over his head.

The attacker rolls the defender over and onto his back.

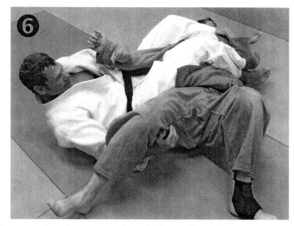

The attacker has completed the roll and can now apply Juji Gatame.

# HEAD ROLL JUJI GATAME FROM A SEATED RODEO RIDE

Sometimes, the attacker (behind his opponent) will use the rodeo ride to control his opponent and the grappler will end up in this seated position. Look at how the attacker uses both of his feet and legs to hook in and control the defender's hips and lower body. The attacker uses both hands to reach under his opponent's armpits and grab the lapels.

The attacker shifts his body to his left as he moves his left foot and leg across the front of his opponent at the belt line. The attacker uses his left foot to hook onto the defender's right hip to serve as an anchor. Look at how the attacker uses his left hand to hook up and under the defender's left shoulder.

The attacker rolls to his left side. As he does this, he swings his right leg up and onto the back of the defender's head and neck.

This view from the back shows how the attacker is positioned on his left side as he moves his right leg up and onto the back of his opponent's neck and head. The attacker is rolling to his left front direction.

The attacker continues to roll to his left front direction as he swings his right leg up and on the back of the defender's head.

This photo shows how the attacker rolls to his left front and forces the defender to bend forward and roll directly over his head.

The attacker's forceful rolling action makes the defender roll as well.

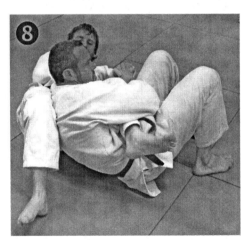

The attacker has rolled his opponent over his head and onto his back. The attacker's right leg is still on the back of the defender and is about to be swung over the defender's head.

The attacker swings his right leg over the defender's head and puts the defender in the leg press, ready to have Juji Gatame applied.

## SNAP DOWN TO HEAD ROLL JUJI GATAME

The grapplers are engaged in standing action. This variation of Juji Gatame is useful when an opponent is bent over in a crouch or defensive posture.

The attacker (left) uses his hands to snap the defender down to the mat as shown.

Immediately after snapping his opponent to the mat, the attacker moves to his right and to the defender's left.

The attacker uses his left hand to start to trap the defender's right arm as he continues to exert control with his leg on the back of the defender's head.

The attacker climbs up and onto the defender as shown.

The attacker starts to sit through onto his left hip to initiate the head roll Juji Gatame.

The attacker positions himself so his body is across the back of the defender's shoulders. The attacker posts his head on the mat as he moves his left leg over the defender's back and onto the back of his head.

The attacker sits though onto his left hip as he rolls his opponent over his head.

The attacker rolls the defender over his head and onto his back.

The attacker immediately secures his Juji Gatame.

## JUDO SWITCH TO HEAD ROLL JUJI GATAME

This is a "go behind" move used in many grappling and wrestling situations. The attacker is on his elbows and knees on the bottom with his opponent riding him from the top.

The attacker uses both of his hands and arms to grab the defender's left leg immediately above his knee. The left side of the attacker's head is planted firmly on the left hip of the defender.

The attacker moves to his left and around to the back of his opponent.

The attacker moves to behind his opponent as shown.

The attacker has now moved around his opponent and behind him, controlling him with a ride. The attacker uses his left hand to grab the defender's left wrist for control.

The attacker uses his left leg to hook in the left side of his opponent as the attacker moves up and on top of the defender.

The attacker moves his body across the back of his opponent to be positioned as shown in this photo. Look at how the attacker posts on the top of his head at the defender's left shoulder area.

The attacker places his right foot and leg on the back of his opponent's head and neck. As he does this, the attacker starts to sit through so that the will be on his right side. Look at how the attacker has used his left foot to anchor onto the defender's right hip and upper leg.

The attacker continues to sit through onto his right side, rolling his opponent over his head.

The attacker rolls the defender over and onto his back and applies Juji Gatame.

## HEAD ROLL JUJI GATAME FROM KNEELING

The attacker (on his knee) is in a bad position with his opponent dominating him from a standing position. The attacker makes sure to come up onto his right foot as shown.

This view shows how the attacker is positioned so that his right foot is on the outside of the defender's left foot. This extreme angle is necessary to allow the attacker room to swing to his left and across the front of his opponent.

### ▰▰▰ TECHNICAL TIP ▰▰▰

**The attacker should "stay round" when applying head roll Juji Gatame. By staying round, with the body curled up and compact, the attacker has greater ability to control his opponent's movement.**

The attacker swings his left leg across the front of the defender. This action makes the attacker roll onto his left side as shown. As he does this, the attacker jams his left foot into the defender's right hip. At this point, the attacker swings his right foot and leg over the defender's left shoulder and head.

The attacker rolls onto his left side and swings his right leg over the head of his opponent.

The attacker swings his right leg over his opponent and places it on the back of the defender's head. Doing this forces the defender to be driven forward as shown. Look at how the attacker is rolling forcefully over in the direction of his opponent's head.

The attacker completes his roll and as he does, he rolls his opponent over his head in a somersault.

The attacker continues to roll and swing his right leg over his opponent's head.

The attacker completes his roll and secures his Juji Gatame.

## HEAD ROLL JUJI GATAME FROM "WATSON JITSU" MOUNT POSITION

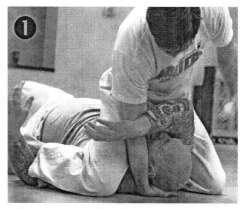

The attacker has control of his opponent in this mount position. Look at how the attacker's right leg traps the defender's left arm. The attacker uses his right hand to hook behind his opponent's neck and head.

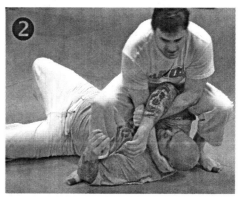

The attacker squats up slightly and as he does, he uses his left arm to hook and scoop up on the defender's right arm.

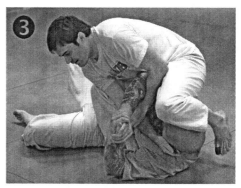

The attacker quickly turns to his right and moves his left leg onto the back of his opponent's head. As he does this, the attacker uses his right hand to lift his opponent's head off of the mat.

The attacker places his left leg and foot on the back of his opponent's head as he uses his right hand to post on the mat for stability. The attacker continues to use his left hand to hook and trap the defender's right arm.

The attacker rolls forward and onto the top of his head for stability.

The attacker rolls onto his left hip. Doing this forces the defender to somersault over his head.

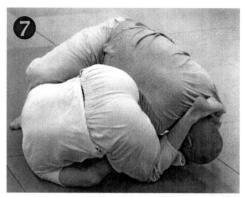

The attacker continues to roll onto his left knee and then to his side. As he does this, the attacker continues to hook and trap his opponent's right arm.

The attacker sits through, forcing the defender to roll over his head. If needed, the attacker may use his right hand and arm to grab the defender's leg to assist in dragging the leg over.

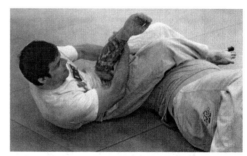

The attacker rolls his opponent over his head and onto his back, ready to secure Juji Gatame.

## RUSSIAN DRAG INTO HEAD ROLL JUJI GATAME

The attacker is on his back as the defender steps up on his left foot in an effort to pass the bottom grappler's guard (or even back away to get out of the situation). The attacker uses his right hand and arm to reach under the defender's left foot and leg as shown.

The attacker uses his right arm to hook the defender's left ankle or lower leg and pulls the left leg out straight as shown.

As he does this, the attacker rolls to his right hip and uses his left hand and arm to trap the defender's right arm. The attacker swings his left bent leg up toward the defender's head.

The attacker continues to roll to his right hip and side and places his left shin on the back of the defender's head. As he does this, the attacker continues to use his left hand and arm to trap the defender's right arm.

The attacker continues to roll to his right side as he wedges his left shin and foot on the back of the defender's head and neck as shown. This action forces the defender to roll in the direction of the defender's head.

The attacker continues to roll, applying the head roll Juji Gatame.

The attacker rolls the defender over the defender's head. In this situation, the attacker will use his right hand and arm to hook the defender's left leg to assist in rolling the defender over.

The attacker uses his right arm to hook and grab the defender's left leg to assist the head roll action taking place.

The attacker rolls the defender over the defender's head, continuing to use the arm hook on the defender's left leg for more control.

The attacker rolls the defender over with the head roll Juji Gatame and secures the armlock.

## HEAD ROLL JUJI GATAME FROM A TOP TRIANGLE

This could be included in the chapter on combinations, but it provides an interesting application using the head roll Juji Gatame, so it was included in this chapter. There are some combinations using Sankaku Jime (Triangle Choke) with Juji Gatame in that chapter.

The attacker is pinning his opponent with a vertical pin or mount position, but the defender is fighting hard to escape.

This photo (taken later) shows the initial position of the attacker. The attacker has started his triangle choke from this position with his left foot and leg over the left shoulder of the defender. As he does this, the attacker starts to trap the defender's right arm. (There will be more on this position and technique later in this book in the chapter on combinations.)

The attacker moves his upper body to his left as he uses both of his hands and arms to scoop and trap the defender's left arm. Look at how the attacker keeps his left leg placed over the defender's left shoulder.

The attacker forms a triangle with his legs on his opponent as shown here.

The attacker starts to roll to his right (in the direction of the defender's head) after the attacker firmly secures the triangle hold with his legs.

The attacker rolls to his right, and as he does, continues to trap the defender's left arm. The rolling action of the attacker forces the defender to roll over his head as shown.

The attacker rolls the defender over his head as shown in this photo.

The attacker rolls the defender over and onto his back with the triangle choke firmly in place.

The attacker controls the situation with the leg press and triangle hold with his legs. As he does this, the attacker starts to lever his opponent's left arm.

In this sequence (taken during a local freestyle judo event), the defender shrimps into the attacker in an effort to escape. The attacker continues to control the action with his strong triangle choke.

The attacker turns the defender onto his back again and aggressively levers the defender's left arm out straight.

The defender resists, but the attacker's lever is strong. The attacker, at this point, has moved his right leg up so that he may have both of his legs over his opponent when applying the Juji Gatame.

**IMPORTANT:** This sequence of photos shows how important is it for the attacker to keep firm hold of the defender's arm and not give up on the attack. The attacker controls the position, and because of this, the attacker controls the entire situation.

The attacker moves his right leg back under his opponent's head and forms a triangle again with his legs as shown. As he does this, the attacker, stretches the defender's arm, arches his hips and secures the Juji Gatame.

## HEAD ROLL JUJI GATAME FROM THE BACK OR GUARD

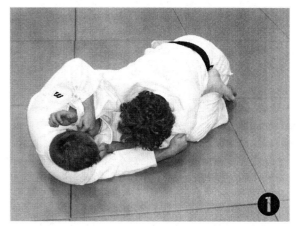

The attacker (in his back) rolls to his right hip as he uses his left arm to hook and trap the defender's right arm to the attacker's chest. The attacker anchors is right foot to the defender's left upper leg and hip.

The attacker continues to roll to his right hip and side as he moves his left leg over the defender's right side as shown. Look at how the attacker uses both hands and arms to hook, trap and straighten the defender's right arm.

The attacker continues to roll over his right side and swings his left foot and leg up and onto the back of his opponent.

The attacker places his left foot and leg on the back of his opponent's head and neck. The attacker has rolled over onto his front and is posting on the top of his head a shown.

The attacker now rolls onto his left hip and side as he uses his right hand to grab the defender's right leg to assist in rolling the defender over his head.

The attacker rolls the defender over the defender's head and onto his back. The attacker secures the Juji Gatame and gets the tap out.

## HEAD ROLL JUJI GATAME COUNTER TO A GUARD PASS

The attacker (on bottom) is fighting out of his guard position as shown. The opponent will attempt to control the bottom grappler's right knee in an effort to pass his guard. Sensing this, the bottom grappler uses both hands to initiate his trap of the top grappler's right arm.

As the top grappler moves over the bottom grappler's right upper leg to pass his guard, the bottom grappler uses both hands to further trap the top grappler's right arm. As he does this, the bottom grappler quickly rolls to his right side.

As the bottom grappler (the attacker) rolls to his right side, he continues to use both hands and arms to trap his opponent's right arm. The attacker swings his left leg up and over his opponent's back as shown.

The attacker continues to roll to his right, using both of his hands and arms to trap the defender's right arm. The attacker continues to drive his left leg and foot on the back of his opponent's head and neck. The attacker is posted on the top of his head.

IMPORTANT: As shown in this photo, the attacker's leg may not always be placed precisely on the back of his opponent's head and neck. Here the attacker's left shin is driving hard onto the defender's upper back. That's okay, because it works.

The attacker rolls onto his left side as shown. Look at how the attacker uses his legs to control the defender, rolling the defender over his head.

The attacker rolls the defender over his head and onto his back and applies Juji Gatame.

## JUJI GATAME FROM THE SIDE

Sometimes, the attacker may be positioned so that he is on his side with his legs controlling his opponent as shown here. Possibly, the bottom grappler moved to this position from his back or guard position, or maybe the bottom grappler had a good ride from the top position but lost it. Possibly, the grapplers ended up in this position from a scramble. In any event, the attacker is lying on his side as shown in this photo.

The attacker is lying on his left side with his legs hooked around his opponent. The attacker immediately uses his hands to hook his opponent's left arm.

The attacker uses both hands to hook and trap the defender's left arm as shown.

As he does this, the attacker rolls onto his left side (in the direction of the defender's head) and starts to post on the top of his head. Look at how the attacker is starting to move his right leg up.

The attacker moves his right leg up and over the defender's back and jams his shin in the back of the defender's head as shown. The attacker has now rolled onto his head as shown. The attacker continues to use both hands and arms to hook, trap and lever the defender's left arm.

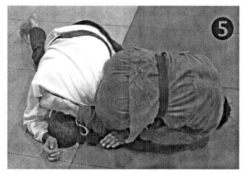

The attacker rolls onto his right side as he continues to trap and lever the defender's left arm. Look at how the defender is starting to roll over his head.

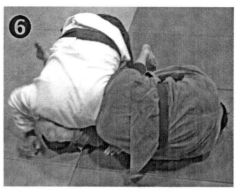

The attacker continues to roll and rolls the defender over his head as shown. All the while, the attacker uses both arms to lever the defender's left arm out straight.

The attacker rolls the defender over his head.

The attacker rolls the defender over his head and onto his back in the leg press position.

The attacker controls his opponent in the leg press and continues to lever his opponent's arms loose.

The attacker secures his Juji Gatame.

## HEAD ROLL JUJI GATAME WHEN OPPONENT MOVES AWAY WHEN ATTACKER INITIALLY ATTEMPTS A SPINNING JUJI GATAME

Sometimes, the top grappler (when fighting in the guard position) will attempt to back away from the bottom grappler in an effort to escape or pass the bottom grappler's guard. As the top grappler moves away from the bottom grappler, the bottom grappler rolls to his left side. As he does this, the bottom grappler (the attacker) starts to move his right knee and leg up toward the top grappler's head.

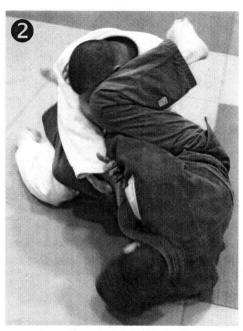

As the attacker rolls onto his left side, he places his right knee and shin on his opponent's head as shown. Look at how the attacker (on bottom) has places his left leg across the belt line of the top grappler.

The attacker continues to roll to his left side as he starts to apply the head roll Juji Gatame on his opponent with his right shin placed on his opponent's head.

The attacker continues to roll to his left side with his right shin jammed on the back and side of his opponent's head. This forces the defender to roll over as shown.

The attacker continues to forcefully roll over onto his back, forcing his opponent to roll over as well.

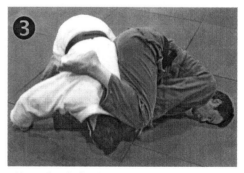

As he finishes his roll, the attacker applies his Juji Gatame.

## HEAD ROLL JUJI GATAME COUNTER TO A TOE HOLD

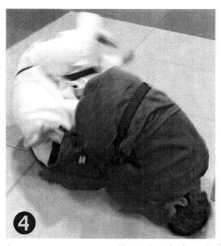

If the top grappler backs out of the guard to apply a toehold, the bottom grappler starts to roll to his left side (toward the action of the toehold).

The bottom grappler (the attacker) continues to roll to his left side. This does two things; it eases the pressure of the toehold and starts the bottom grappler into a good roll to initiate his Juji Gatame. Look at how the attacker starts to use his hands to grab and trap the top grappler's left arm. The bottom grappler starts to move his right leg up and over his opponent's back.

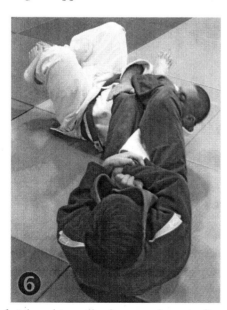

As he rolls to his left, the attacker continues to trap his opponent's left arm and places his right bent leg onto his opponent's upper back.

The attacker continues to roll as shown in this photo.

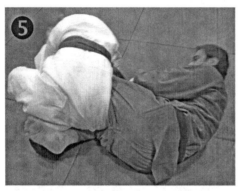

The attacker continues to roll through and places his right shin on the back of his opponent's head and neck. At this point, if the attacker has trapped and levered the defender's arm well enough, the attacker may be able to pull the defender's arm out straight apply Juji Gatame from this position.

The attacker continues to roll through, forcing his opponent to roll over his head as shown.

The attacker rolls his opponent over his head an onto his back and applies Juji Gatame.

### ▰▰▰ TECHNICAL TIP ▰▰▰

**When countering an opponent's submission technique, keep your cool, work methodically, but first get out of trouble. Your first instinct must be to either ease the pressure that your opponent is applying on you or escape the situation or position. After that is accomplished, immediately look to how you can counter or reverse the situation.**

## SPIN OUT THE BACK DOOR AND HEAD ROLL JUJI GATAME COUTNER TO A STACK

The bottom grappler is applying a spinning Juji Gatame and if the top grappler "stacks" the bottom grappler onto the bottom grappler's upper back or head, he will be better able to extract his right arm free (in this photo). **IMPORTANT:** This move is also called "going out the back door" and is seen in other parts of this book as well.

As the top grappler stacks the bottom grappler onto his upper back in an effort to escape, the bottom grappler starts to spin to his right and under the top grappler.

The bottom grappler (the attacker) continues to spin on his shoulders to his right and, as he does, reaches with his right hand and hooks his hand and arm on the shin or lower leg of the defender as shown. The attacker uses his left hand and arm to trap the defender's right arm to the attacker's chest.

The attacker continues to spin so that his head is now under his opponent's body as shown.

The attacker continues to spin under his opponent as shown. This spinning action starts to roll the defender over his head. Look at how the attacker uses his left arm to trap his opponent's right arm. In this case, the attacker uses a thigh grab with his left hand on his right upper leg to trap the defender's right arm. At this point, the attacker uses his right hand to grab his opponent's pant leg. If the defender has shorts on, the attacker can use his right hand to push upward onto the defender's right leg to assist in rolling him over.

The attacker continues to spin under the defender, rolling the defender over his head as shown.

This view shows how the attacker uses his feet and legs to control his opponent as the attacker uses the "no head" variation of the head roll Juji Gatame.

The attacker continues to spin, using his right hand to grab and control the defender's pant leg, pulling his legs over to assist in the rolling action.

The attacker rolls the defender over his head and onto his back as shown.

The attacker immediately secures his Juji Gatame.

The head roll is one of the most popular, and effective, applications of Juji Gatame. There certainly are other variations of head roll Juji Gatame, but what has been presented here will give you an edge over your opponents. Take what is shown, become adept in the skills of the technique and then modify it to make it your own.

Let's now turn our attention to the last (but not least) of the four primary applications of Juji Gatame: the hip roll Juji Gatame.

# HIP ROLL JUJI GATAME

## "SPEED HAS ITS PLACE ON THE GROUND BUT CONTROL IS FAR MORE CRUCIAL." NEIL ADAMS, WORLD JUDO CHAMPION

## HIP ROLL JUJI GATAME: AN INTRODUCTION

The hip roll is the fourth of the basic applications of Juji Gatame. Whenever the attacker rolls toward the direction of his opponent's hip as he applies Juji Gatame, the attacker is doing the hip roll Juji Gatame. By rolling (in this case, rolling toward the opponent's hip), the attacker builds momentum, gains control and is better able to apply power when applying Juji Gatame. By rolling or spinning (as in spinning Juji Gatame), the attacker increases the ballistic effect of the armlock as it is being applied.

Whether an athlete does a hip roll or head roll is often a matter of opportunity as much as it is preference. A good Juji Gatame exponent will train in all four basic applications of Juji Gatame and be prepared to use any of them as necessary. That being said, we all have preferences and some people simply like doing hip roll Juji Gatame while others prefer the head roll, spin or back roll. The bottom line is that however you control, roll or set your opponent up, do it so that it will be successful. Study the fundamentals, become proficient at them, and drill on them, ensuring that they become instinctive behavior. After that, mold the technique so that it works for you and works for you on a regular basis against opposition that is fit, skilled and motivated.

As with the head roll Juji Gatame, it is essential for the attacker to control the position, be precise in his movements and methodically roll the defender into the armlock. An important rule to keep in mind when working for any type of submission technique (in this case, Juji Gatame) is to "take your time, but do it in a hurry." In other words, methodically go from one move to another, always gaining more control over your opponent; but don't dawdle. Be efficient in your movements. Be workmanlike and get the job done; in this case, the job is stretching your opponent's arm.

### ▰▰▰ TECHNICAL TIP ▰▰▰

**When rolling, turning or spinning an opponent into Juji Gatame, the attacker increases the ballistic effect of the armlock. The rolling, spinning and turning actions are not done to be fancy or impressive, they are functional methods of gaining control over an opponent. No opponent will simply stay there and let you lock his arm; you have to move and control him in such a way that he is forced to submit to you.**

## ATTACKER ROLLS IN THE DIRECTION OF OPPONENT'S HIP

What marks the hip roll entry different from the head roll, back roll or spinning Juji Gatame applications is that the attacker rolls toward his opponent's hip, usually doing a shoulder roll as he does. This photo shows how the attacker rolls in the direction of the defender's hip.

## ATTACKER ROLLS OVER HIS SHOULDER IN THE DIRECTION OF OPPONENT'S HIP

The ability of the attacker to roll over his shoulder is important when doing the hip roll Juji Gatame. The attacker rolls over his left shoulder and in the direction of his opponent's left hip in this photo.

The attacker's shoulder roll into the direction of his opponent's left hip creates the momentum required to take the opponent from a stable position to an unstable position. Look at how the attacker uses his right leg to hook the defender's head, forcing the defender to roll as well.

As he completes his shoulder roll, the attacker uses his legs to force his opponent to roll over and onto his back.

## ATTACKER STAYS ROUND AND ROLL AND CONTROL

It is vital for the attacker to "stay round" and roll for control. Do not elongate your body if you are attempting to roll or turn an opponent over onto his back. By staying round, the attacker is better able to stay compact and control the rolling action, which builds momentum and power into the movement.

## ATTACKER HOOKS DEFENDER'S HEAD WITH HIS LEG AS HE ROLLS HIM OVER

By hooking the defender's head with his leg as shown here, the attacker forces the defender to roll over along with the attacker. The old saying, "where the head goes, the body follows" is certainly true.

## ATTACKER TRAPS HIS OPPONENT'S ARM AS HE ROLLS (ROLL AND CONTROL)

By trapping the defender's arm in the early stages of the attack and trapping it in more firmly as he rolls, the attacker will be better able to lever and stretch his opponent's arm to secure the Juji Gatame. This trapping action, along with the ballistic action of the attacker's roll, places the defender onto his back and in the leg press position at the finish of the roll. In some cases, the attacker may trap the defender's arm so well that the defender will tap out during the roll.

## ATTACKER STARTS THE ROLL FROM THE "L" POSITION

In the same way the attacker would start his head roll Juji Gatame, the most efficient way to initiate the head roll is for the attacker to position his body in the shape on an upside down "L."

## ATTACKER POSTS ON TOP OF HIS HEAD FOR STABILITY AND FOR A BETTER VIEW OF THE ACTION

The attacker posts on the top of his head in order to better stabilize his body as he works to gain further control over his opponent. By posting on the top of his head before he starts his roll, the attacker has the option to roll over either shoulder in either direction. The attacker also has a good view of his opponent as well as the surrounding area.

These fundamental skills and positions done correctly and efficiently will insure a high ratio of success when applying the hip roll Juji Gatame. By working to have technically sound movements based on efficient body mechanics and movement, an athlete will be better able to apply Juji Gatame under the pressure of a real fight or match against a fit, resisting and motivated opponent. Let's now examine and analyze some of the many variations of hip roll Juji Gatame.

## HIP ROLL JUJI GATAME: BASIC ENTRY

for control. The attacker leans forward and posts on the top of his head over the defender's right shoulder and arm as shown.

The defender is on his elbows and knees. The attacker is positioned to the right of the defender's body as shown.

The attacker drives his left leg under the defender's head. The attacker is posted on the top of his head for stability. The attacker uses both of his arms to hook and trap the defender's right arm to the attacker's chest.

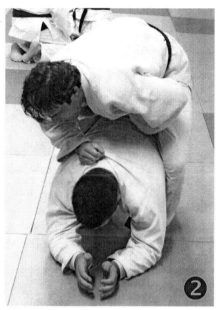

The attacker moves his body behind the defender's body, creating some momentum to help the attacker roll his opponent over. As he does this, the attacker jams his right foot and leg into the right side of the defender.

The attacker starts to roll over his right shoulder and into the direction of the defender's right hip.

The attacker leans over his opponent and as he does, he slides his right foot and leg under the defender's body

As he rolls over his right shoulder, the attacker uses his left leg to tightly hook the defender's head, forcing the defender to roll as well. The attacker continues to use both arms to trap the defender's right arm to the attacker's chest throughout the roll.

The attacker continues to roll, forcing the defender to roll as well.

The attacker completes his shoulder roll, coming up onto his buttocks to insure that he is as close as possible to his opponent in the leg press.

The attacker rolls back, levering the defender's right arm out straight, securing the Juji Gatame.

### TECHNICAL TIP

**From a tactical standpoint, hip roll Juji Gatame is good to apply when an opponent is on all fours with his arms extended in the previous sequence. By being higher off the mat because of the extended arms, the defender (unwittingly) gives the attacker more room to roll and in the direction of the defender's hip. This is one of the key reasons why it is not advisable to extend your arms if you are on all fours. The old adage that a "straight arm is easer to lock with Juji Gatame than a bent arm" is certainly true in this situation.**

## HIP ROLL JUJI GATAME WHEN DEFENDER POPS UP FROM A RODEO RIDE

The attacker (on top) uses a rodeo ride to control his opponent.

The attacker pops up onto his hands and feet in an attempt to shake the top grappler off of his back.

The attacker moves to his right, and over the defender's right shoulder. As he does, the attacker uses his left hand to reach and post on the mat for stability. The attacker uses his right arm to hook and trap the defender's right arm to the attacker's chest.

The attacker leans forward, posting on the top of his head for stability.

The attacker swings his left foot and leg under the defenders' head, hooking it. As he does this, the attacker starts to roll over his right shoulder and in the direction of the defender's right hip.

The attacker rolls over his right shoulder, using his left leg to hook the defender's head, forcing the defender to roll as well. The attacker uses both arms to trap the defender's right arm to the attacker's chest as the attacker rolls over his right shoulder.

The attacker completes his shoulder roll and immediately applies Juji Gatame.

## HIP ROLL JUJI GATAME FROM A JUDO SWITCH (GO BEHIND)

The bottom grappler is being controlled by the top grappler, who may be working to set the bottom man up for a triangle choke from the top position (or any other attack from this position).

The attacker (the bottom grappler) pops his head out from the middle of the top grappler's legs. As he does this, the attacker moves his head so that it is placed on the left side of the defender's hip. The attacker uses his hands and arms to grab and trap the defender's left upper leg, using a square grip to cinch in the defender's left leg in tight. The attacker has the left side of his head placed firmly on the defender's left hip.

The attacker uses his head as the pivot point and moves to his right, and to the left of the defender.

The attacker continues to move to his right and behind the defender as shown.

The attacker has now completed his judo switch and has moved behind his opponent in a ride position.

The attacker continues his attack quickly by digging his left foot and leg into the left hip and upper leg of the defender as shown.

As he does this, the attacker uses his left hand to grab the defender's left forearm or wrist. In a "no gi" situation, the attacker can do a wrist ride to control the defender's left forearm and wrist. Look at how the attacker has now climbed up on his opponent's back. The attacker starts to move his head to his left and over the defender's left shoulder.

The attacker leans forward, using his right hand to reach and post onto the mat for stability. The attacker uses his left hand and arm to hook and trap the defender's left arm to the attacker's chest.

The attacker immediately uses his right leg to hook under the defender's head as shown. The attacker starts to roll over his left shoulder.

The attacker rolls over his left shoulder, hooking the defender's head tightly with his right leg as he rolls.

The attacker rolls over his left shoulder, forcing the defender to roll over and onto his back as shown.

The attacker completes his shoulder roll and uses both arms to trap the defender's left arm to the attacker's chest.

The attacker rolls back, levers the defender's left arm and gets the tap out.

## HIP ROLL JUJI GATAME FROM OPPONENT'S LEG GRAB

A practical way to apply hip roll Juji Gatame is when an opponent grabs the attacker's leg from the bottom as shown here. In many situations, the bottom grappler will attempt to grab and control the top grappler's leg in an effort to break the top grappler down or initiate a go-behind or switch move (as was presented previously). The bottom grappler uses his arms to grab the top grappler's right leg as shown. The attacker's head is still positioned between the defender's legs.

The attacker (the top grappler) quickly turns to his right, pivoting off of his right knee, which is placed on the mat. As he does this, the attacker swings his left foot and leg over the defender's back and places his left foot under the defender's left hip and leg. At the same time, the attacker starts to use both hands and arms to hook and trap the defender's left arm.

The attacker rolls forward and onto the top of his head for stability, using both of his arms to trap the defender's left arm tightly to the attacker's chest.

The attacker rolls over his left shoulder, in the direction of the defender's left hip. The attacker uses his right leg to hook under the defender's head for control. The attacker continues to use his arms to trap the defender's left arm to the attacker's chest during the roll.

The attacker completes his shoulder roll and secures his Juji Gatame.

# SNAP DOWN TO HIP ROLL JUJI GATAME

This application is very similar to the snap down and head roll entry into Juji Gatame seen in the chapter on head roll Juji Gatame. It's also similar to the snap down and step over entry seen in the chapter on transitions.

The attacker has a lapel and sleeve grip on his opponent, who is bent over in a low crouch or defensive posture.

The attacker quickly moves backward and as he does, uses his hands to jerk downward on the defender's jacket, snapping the defender downward to the mat.

The attacker immediately moves to his left and to the right of the defender.

The attacker swings his left leg over the defender's back, getting on the defender's back.

The attacker sinks both of his feet and legs into the defender's hips and upper legs. As he does this, the attacker uses his left hand and arm to hook under the defender's left upper arm.

The attacker moves his head and body to his left, allowing him to hook his right foot and leg under the defender's head as shown. Look at how the attacker has placed his right hand on the mat for stability, allowing the attacker to safely post on the top of his head. The attacker is stable and controlling the position.

The attacker rolls over his left shoulder, in the direction of the defender's left hip. Look at how the attacker uses his right leg to hook the defender's head, forcing the defender to roll over as well.

The attacker completes his shoulder roll, rolling the defender over and onto the defender's back. The attacker immediately secures Juji Gatame.

## KNEE JAM HIP ROLL JUJI GATAME

The unique aspect of this application is that the attacker places the knee that does not hook his opponent's head on the defender's back instead of driving it under the defender's body and anchoring his foot on the defender's hip.

The defender is balled up tightly on elbows and knees. The attacker is positioned at the left of the defender.

The attacker places his right shin on the defender's lower back. As he does this, the attacker uses his left hand and arm to hook under the defender's right arm and shoulder. As he does this, the attacker starts to dive forward over the defender's body.

The attacker rolls over his opponent and posts on the top of his head.

This shows how the attacker places his right leg on his opponent's back as he posts on the top of his head.

The attacker hooks his left foot and leg under the defender's head, using his left hand and arm to hook and trap the defender's right arm.

This shows the attacker's position as he prepares to roll the defender over.

The attacker rolls over his right shoulder, in the direction of the defender's right hip. The attacker's right knee is jammed into the defender's right armpit as the attacker uses his left foot and leg to hook and control the defender's head, forcing him to roll over his right side. The attacker traps the defender's right arm to the attacker's chest as he rolls.

The attacker completes his shoulder roll, keeping his right shin jammed in the right side of the defender and his left leg hooked over the defender's head, pinning it The attacker will now roll back and apply Juji Gatame.

## ARM HOOK HIP ROLL JUJI GATAME

This variation of Juji Gatame shows why it's not a good idea for the defender to be in the "parterre" position on the mat with his arms extended. Extended arms give an opponent a better chance to hook and control them. The attacker stands at the left side of the defender, who is on all fours on the mat as shown.

The attacker uses his left foot and leg to step over and hook the defender's left extended arm. As he does this, the attacker moves his right foot and leg over the defender's buttocks and lower back and hooks it in the defender's right hip and upper leg area.

The attacker uses his right arm to hook the defender's right shoulder and upper arm in an uppercut movement, scooping and hooking it tightly.

This shows how the attacker uses his right foot and leg to hook and control the defender's right upper leg and hip. Look at how the attacker uses his right hand and arm to hook and control the defender's right upper arm. The attacker leans forward into the direction of the defender's right shoulder and arm.

As the attacker rolls over his right shoulder, he uses his left foot and leg to hook the defender's left upper arm

and shoulder. Look at how the attacker points the toes of his left foot to maximize the control he has over his opponent's left arm and shoulder as he rolls.

The attacker continues to roll over his right shoulder. Look at how the attacker continues to use his left foot and leg to hook and control the defender's left shoulder and arm. As he rolls, the attacker uses both hands and arms to hook and trap the defender's right arm to the attacker's chest.

The attacker continues to roll over his right shoulder, forcing his opponent to roll over with him. Look at how the attacker uses his legs to force the opponent to roll over with him. This shows how the attacker uses his left leg to powerfully hook and manipulate the defender's left upper arm, forcing the defender to roll over with the attacker.

The attacker completes his shoulder roll, rolling his opponent over and onto his back and controlling the defender with the leg press.

This photo shows how the attacker uses his left foot and leg to hook and control the defender's left shoulder and upper arm. The attacker does not have to move his left foot and leg over the defender's head to control him, so the attacker uses his left leg to trap the defender's left shoulder. The attacker's right leg is placed across the defender's torso, controlling it.

As he completes his shoulder roll, the attacker rolls back and secures his Juji Gatame.

## HUNGARIAN ROLL INTO JUJI GATAME

This entry for hip roll Juji Gatame is named the way it is because I first saw this move performed by a Hungarian athlete in a judo tournament in Europe years ago. This entry goes by other names as well.

The defender is on his elbows and knees. The attacker is positioned and standing at the right side of the defender.

The attacker quickly swings his left foot and leg over the defender's torso, hooking it as deeply as possible under the defender's body. As he does this, the attacker uses his right hand and arm to hook under the defender's left shoulder and arm. The attacker uses his left hand and arm to hook under the defender's left upper leg as shown. As he does this, the attacker dives forward, directly over his head.

As he does a somersault over the defender's body, the attacker uses both hands and arms to hook his opponent's left arm and leg in more tightly.

The attacker rolls directly forward, over his head.

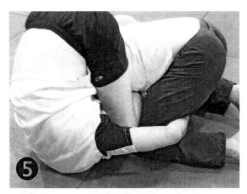

This shows how the attacker uses his left arm to hook the defender's left leg as the attacker rolls directly over his head in a somersault.

The attacker uses his right leg as a pendulum to help whip his body directly forward. This action really helps in forcing the defender to roll as well.

The defender completes his somersault, rolling the defender over with him. Look at how the attacker's left leg is across the defender's torso. Look at how the attacker uses his right arm to hook the defender's left arm and how the attacker uses his left hand and arm to hook the defender's left upper leg. The attacker starts to swing his right leg up and over the defender's head to pin it to the mat.

The attacker swings his right leg over the defender's head and quickly uses both hands and arms to hook and trap the defender's left arm to the attacker's body. The attacker rolls back and applies Juji Gatame.

## BELT AND NELSON INTO HIP ROLL JUJI GATAME WHEN DEFENDER IS ON ALL FOURS

The attacker is positioned at the top and front of the defender, who is on his elbows and knees as shown. The attacker uses his right hand to grab (palm down) the defender's belt at the middle of his back.

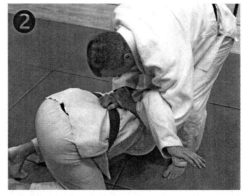

The attacker uses his left hand and arm to reach under the defender's right shoulder and upper arm. The attacker uses his left hand to grab his right wrist and starts to use his left forearm to lift upward, forcing the defender's right shoulder higher off the mat. The attacker places his left foot at the top of the defender's right shoulder area.

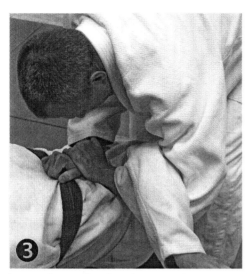

This shows how firmly the attacker controls the defender's right shoulder in the belt and nelson hold. This belt and nelson hold isolates and totally controls the defender's right shoulder and side.

The attacker swings his right leg over the defender's body as shown as he uses his left hand to trap the defender's right arm.

As the attacker swings his right leg over, he shoots it deeply under the defender's torso and rolls over his right shoulder as shown. The attacker continues to use his left

hand and arm to trap the defender's right arm to the attacker's chest.

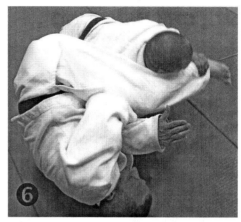

The attacker rolls over his right shoulder and uses his left leg to hook under the defender's head, forcing the defender to roll as well.

The attacker continues his shoulder roll, bringing his opponent over with him and onto his back.

As he completes his shoulder roll, the attacker secures Juji Gatame.

## BELT AND NELSON INTO HIP ROLL JUJI GATAME WHEN DEFENDER IS FLAT ON HIS FRONT ("CHICKEN JUDO")

The attacker is positioned as the top of his opponent who is lying on his front as shown. The attacker uses his right hand (palm down) to grab the defender's belt. As he does this, the attacker uses his left hand to hook under the defender's right shoulder. Look at how the attacker is positioned in front of, and above, the defender's right shoulder.

This shows how the attacker uses his right hand to grab (palm down) the defender's belt and uses his left hand and arm to hook under the defender's right shoulder and upper arm.

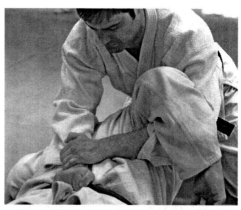

The attacker uses his left hand to grab his right wrist. Doing this traps the defender's right shoulder and arm tightly.

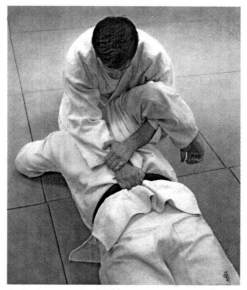

This shows how the attacker uses the belt and nelson to trap the defender's right shoulder and arm.

The attacker moves to his right, over the defender's head.

This shows how the attacker moves to his right, trapping the defender's head with the attacker's left foot and leg and the attacker's right knee, which is placed on the mat.

The attacker uses his right foot to step over the defender.

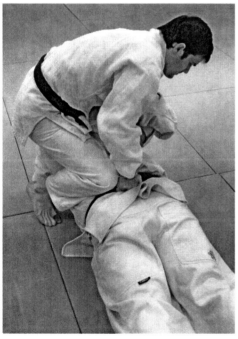

The attacker continues to move to his right and behind the defender's back as shown. Look at how the attacker jams his right shin and knee in the defender's back. The attacker uses his left hand to trap the defender's right arm to the attacker's chest.

The attacker starts to roll over his right shoulder in the direction of the defender's right hip.

The attacker continues to roll over his right shoulder, rolling the defender over with him. Look at how the attacker uses his left leg to hook, control and force the defender to roll.

Changing to the front view, this shows how the attacker uses his arms to trap the defender's right arm tightly to the attacker's chest during the roll.

The attacker completes his shoulder roll, rolling his opponent over with him.

As he finishes his shoulder roll, the attacker quickly secures Juji Gatame.

### ▬▬ TECHNICAL TIP ▬▬

**This variation of hip roll Juji Gatame is successful because the last thing the defender, who is lying on his front in a defensive position, thinks the attacker will do is to roll him over in this way.**

## SCOOP AND ROLL HIP ROLL JUJI GATAME

This application is a bit different from the belt and nelson entry in that the attacker does not grab or control his opponent's belt. Instead, the attacker uses his arm to hook and scoop the attacker's arm and shoulder to roll him over.

The defender is flat on his front with the attacker positioned at the top of the defender's body. He uses his left hand and arm to hook under the defender's right shoulder.

The attacker uses his left arm to hook and scoop the defender's right shoulder up off of the mat. As he does this, the attacker moves slightly to his right with his right knee on the mat as shown. The attacker steps up onto his left foot as shown. Look at how the attacker's right knee (on the mat) and left foot trap the defender's head. The attacker turns his body to his left as he uses both of his hands and arms to hook the defender's right arm to the attacker's chest.

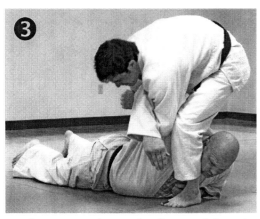

The attacker moves his right foot and leg over the defender's back.

The attacker rolls over his right shoulder and in the direction of the defender's right hip. This shows how the attacker rolls and uses both hands to trap the defender's right arm.

The attacker uses his left leg to hook the defender's head, forcing the defender to roll. The attacker's right leg is placed across the defender's torso. The strong hooking and controlling action of the attacker's legs helps greatly in forcing the defender to roll over onto his back.

The attacker completes his shoulder roll, controlling his opponent, and immediately secures his Juji Gatame.

## HIP ROLL JUJI GATAME WHEN OPPONENT IS FLAT ON FRONT IN DEFENSIVE POSITION ("CHICKEN JUDO")

The defender is lying on his front in a defensive position. The attacker positions his body with his right leg placed over the defender's back with his right foot jammed in the defender's right ribcage area. The attacker uses his right hand to grab his opponent's belt and his left hand to grab the defender's collar.

This closer view shows how the attacker's body is seated on the defender. Look at how the attacker is facing directly to the defender's right side.

The attacker uses his hands to pull and jerk the defender up off of the mat and onto the defender's left side, exposing the defender's front. The attacker moves his right foot and leg so that it traps the defender's torso as shown.

As he does this, the attacker moves his left foot and leg over the defender's head. The attacker uses his left arm to trap the defender's right arm to the attacker's chest.

The attacker starts to roll over his right shoulder in the direction of the defender's right hip.

This shows how the attacker rolls over his right shoulder in the direction of the defender's right hip.

The attacker continues to roll over his right shoulder, forcing his opponent to roll over with him.

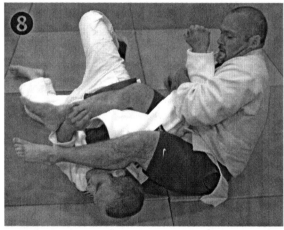

The attacker completes his shoulder roll and rolls the defender over and onto his back in the leg press position.

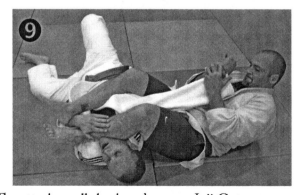

The attacker rolls back and secures Juji Gatame.

## KNEE JAM HIP ROLL FROM A KEYLOCK

The attacker controls his opponent by establishing a keylock on the defender's right arm. The top grappler starts his attack from the top position near the defender's head.

**IMPORTANT:** The attacker can also use the judo keylock (using the defender's jacket or belt to trap his hand and arm) if he chooses. The important aspect of this keylock control is that it allows the attacker more time and opportunity to apply a submission technique because of the control it gives to the attacker.

The attacker secures his keylock on the defender's right arm and pulls the defender's right elbow and upper arm to the attacker's chest to control it. As he does this, the attacker brings the defender's right arm up off of the mat, exposing the defender's entire right shoulder area.

The attacker moves his right foot and leg around and behind the defender's head, jamming his right shin against the left rear side of the defender. Look at how the attacker's right knee is placed at about the defender's right hip. As he does this, the attacker turns to his left, continuing to trap the defender's right arm to the attacker's chest.

The attacker starts to roll over his right shoulder. Look at how the attacker jams his right knee in the defender's right side.

The attacker jams his right leg on his opponent's right side and hip as the attacker continues to roll over his right shoulder.

This photo shows the attacker rolling over his right shoulder.

The attacker rolls over his right shoulder, rolling the defender over with him. As he does this, the attacker moves his left leg over the defender's head, hooking it and driving the defender's head over.

The attacker completes his roll, securing his Juji Gatame.

## HIP ROLL JUJI GATAME FROM "WATSON JITSU" MOUNT

The attacker controls his opponent with a high mount with his right leg trapping the defender's left arm as shown.

The attacker quickly steps up with his left foot as he uses his left hand to start to trap the defender's right arm. The attacker continues to use his right leg and knee to trap the defender's left arm to the mat.

The attacker squats up onto his right foot as he turns to his right. The attacker's right leg is now across the defender's torso. The attacker uses his left arm to further trap the defender's right arm tighter to the attacker's chest. The attacker starts to move his left foot and leg over the defender's head.

The attacker moves his left leg over the defender's head as he starts to roll over his right shoulder.

The attacker rolls over his right shoulder as he continues to use his left arm to trap the defender's right arm. The attacker uses his left leg to hook and control the defender's head during the roll.

The attacker rolls over his right shoulder, rolling the defender with him.

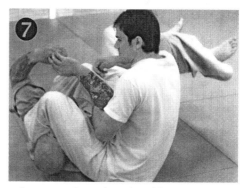

The attacker completes his shoulder roll. Look at how the attacker's left leg traps the defender's head tightly as the attacker sits up onto his buttocks with his crotch close to the defender's right shoulder. The attacker continues to use his left arm to trap his opponent's right arm.

The attacker rolls back to secure Juji Gatame.

The hip roll Juji Gatame is an adaptable and versatile application that can be easily adapted to the person doing it as well as to the circumstances in which it is applied. The common feature is in its name; the attacker rolls into the direction of the defender's hip. While not every variation of hip roll Juji Gatame may have been presented in this chapter, there were quite a few that covered a variety of situations and positions. As with every other variation of Juji Gatame seen in this book, take what has been presented here and make it work for you.

The next chapter examines trapping an opponent's arm and then levering the arm straight in order to apply Juji Gatame. These skills are vital to having an aggressive, functional and effective Juji Gatame.

# TRAPS AND LEVERS: CONTROLLING AN OPPONENT'S ARM AND PRYING THE ARM STRAIGHT

**"IT'S ALWAYS A GOOD DAY WHEN YOU CAN STRETCH A GUY'S ARM." DERRICK DARLING**

## LEVERS TO PRY AN OPPONENT'S ARM STRAIGHT

What may be an awkward term for some people, "levering" the defender's arm so that the attacker is able to secure his Juji Gatame is simply prying, pulling, yanking or wrenching the defender's arm loose and stretching it to get the submission. I first heard the term "lever" from Neil Adams. Previous to that, I simply called it "prying" the arm free. But, as Neil pointed out to me, you may do more than simply pry the arm free. You may hook, tug, pull, wrench, twist, pry, yank, crank or jerk an opponent's arm out straight to apply Juji Gatame. The word "lever" describes all of these actions and they are not simply limited to "prying" the arm free. Okay, this may be nothing more than an exercise in semantics, and some people may say that this is splitting hairs. But, if a master of Juji Gatame like Neil Adams calls it a "lever" then it's good enough for me.

But, before you lever an opponent's arm, you have to trap it first.

## TRAPPING THE ARM

In the chapter on Core Skills, "trapping" the arm was discussed. Trapping, catching, hooking, scooping, hugging, holding or in other words, securing and controlling an opponent's arm to the attacker's upper body, chest and torso is necessary before the arm can be levered and stretched.

I'm going to restate what was written in the chapter on Core Skills (with some additional commentary) because it's worth repeating here. Trapping an opponent's arm to your chest or torso allows you to use the weight of your body to roll or arch back and straighten it. You are using the weight of your body and not simply your arm strength to stretch his elbow. Trap your opponent's arm as quickly as possible and make it part of your initial movement. You may have already established a leg press position or followed through after a throw or takedown to a shoulder sit position, or you may have trapped your opponent's arm as you have rolled him or turned him onto his back or side. In any event, make sure to trap his arm as soon as you possibly can.

A key rule in trapping an opponent's arm is to use your arms to hook it. It's not a good idea to grab an opponent's arm with your hands and try to use the strength of your hands and arms to pry his arm out and straighten it. By hooking your opponent's arm with your arm or arms, you latch his arm tighter to your chest, torso or body and are able to use the weight of your body to roll back and lever his arm out straight.

## ▬▬ TECHNICAL TIP ▬▬

**The purpose of trapping an opponent's arm is to isolate it so the attacker can more easily lever (straighten, extend or stretch) the defender's arm to apply Juji Gatame. In many situations, the defender is grasping his hands together, holding his arms together, grabbing some part of his (or the attacker's) sleeve, jacket or uniform or grabbing onto some part of his body (including arms and legs) or some part of the attacker's body in an effort to prevent the attacker from loosening his grip and stretching his arm out straight. The purpose of a lever is to loosen an opponent's grip and straighten his arm out so the attacker can apply Juji Gatame.**

## SOME BASIC SKILLS ON TRAPPING THE OPPONENT'S ARM

Here are some fundamentals on how to effectively trap an opponent's arm. In most situations, the action of trapping an opponent's arm leads directly to the next logical step of levering his arm and ultimately stretching it to secure the Juji Gatame. Keep these basic skills in mind and make it a point to use them to get the best results when applying Juji Gatame.

## ATTACKER TRAPS OPPONENT'S ARM TO HIS CHEST

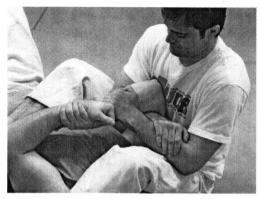

When trapping your opponent's arm, make sure to trap it high enough on your torso (at your chest level) so that your opponent is unable to pull his arm back and get his elbow lower than your crotch. His elbow must not be lower than the pivot point of your fulcrum at your pubic bone, otherwise, he will be able to extract his arm free and all your hard work will be for nothing. Look at how the attacker is using his arm to hook his opponent's arm. The attacker, whenever possible, should hook the defender's arm and the attacker should not simply grab the defender's arms with his hands.

## ATTACKER MAY LOWER HIS CHEST TO HIS OPPONENT'S UPPER ARM

Also keep in mind that the attacker may need to lower his chest to his opponent's arm to help in trapping it tighter. Don't simply try to pull his arm to your chest by using the strength of your arms and hands. You may have to meet it halfway by moving your chest to his arm and then letting the weight of your body straighten his arm as you roll back when applying the Juji Gatame.

## HOOK AND TRAP ELBOW TO ELBOW

The ideal situation when trapping an opponent's arm is for the attacker to hook his opponent's elbow with his elbow. This photo shows the attacker using his right arm to hook his opponent's right arm as the attacker applies a thigh lever. By hooking elbow to elbow, the attacker traps the defender's arm tightly and low at the elbow joint for maximum control of the defender's arm. Look at how the defender's right elbow is pressed firmly against the attacker's chest isolating the defender's right arm and making it easier to lever it straight and stretch it when applying Juji Gatame.

## TRAPPING THE OPPONENT'S ARM TO ATTACKER'S CHEST OR TORSO

The attacker uses his right arm to hook the defender's arm tightly to his chest. Look at how the defender's elbow is firmly pressed against the attacker's chest, totally isolating it and allowing the attacker to control it more.

## THE ANATOMY OF TRAPPING AN ARM: ALL PART OF A SEQUENCE OF EVENTS CONTROLLING AN OPPONENT

Here is how trapping an opponent's arm and levering it loose works effectively to secure the Juji Gatame.

The trap starts. The attacker uses his left hand and arm to hook the defender's right arm.
**IMPORTANT:** If possible, make the trapping action of the opponent's arm part of the roll, set up or breakdown. The sooner and more firmly you are able to trap your opponent's arm, the better chance you have of levering his arm out straight and securing Juji Gatame.

### ▬▬ TECHNICAL TIP ▬▬

**While it's not always this simple, think of trapping an opponent's arm the first step in a sequence of events that build on each other: Trap→ Lever→ Stretch.**

The trap continues with the attacker using his arms to hook and hold the defender's arm to his torso. The attacker starts the roll back to stretch the arm and secure the armlock by using the weight of his body (with the defender's arm trapped and attacked to the attacker's body) to straighten the defender's arm.

The sequence is successful. The attacker has successfully rolled back with his opponent's left arm firmly trapped to his body and has extended the arm to get the submission.

## TRAPPING FOR TIME

Sometimes, the attacker will trap his opponent's arm and immediately lever it out straight to secure the Juji Gatame. The trap is part of the roll, turn or breakdown from a groundfighting position or follow-through after a throw or takedown and the defender offers little, if any resistance, having been caught by surprise. The whole action happens quickly with the trap and lever coming in an immediate sequence of events.

However, there are other times when the attacker successfully traps the defender's arm, but the defender is able to actively resist having his arms pulled apart and one of them straightened into a Juji Gatame. In this instance, the attacker must do everything he can to keep the defender's arm trapped and maintain as much control in a leg press or other controlling position or ride as possible. The attacker must now work methodically in an effort to lever the defender's arm and stretch it for the tap out. This is what I call "Trapping for Time." This photo shows the defender on bottom grasping his hands and arms together as tightly as possible to keep the attacker from prying them apart and securing the Juji Gatame. The attacker is effectively trapping the defender's left arm to his torso and chest by grabbing his own lapel with his right hand as he quickly and methodically attempts to control and manipulate the defender in the leg press position. Look at how the attacker is using his left hand, working at the defender's hip area, to control the bottom man's movement.

Trapping the defender's arms to the attacker's upper body is an important aspect of controlling the defender in a leg press, shoulder sit or other controlling position. It may take several seconds or minutes to lever the defender's arm free and it is vital that that the attacker control the trapped arm all the while he is attempting to pry his opponent's hands and arms apart and straighten the arm to secure the Juji Gatame.

## ▮▮ TECHNICAL TIP ▮▮

The attacker needs two things to secure his Juji Gatame: time and opportunity. Time gives the attacker the opportunity to lever and pry his opponent's arm free to secure the armlock. By "trapping for time" the attacker successfully rides his opponent (in the leg press for instance), thus controlling the time. By trapping for time and ultimately controlling how much time he has, the attacker can create the opportunity necessary for a successful Juji Gatame.

## TRAPPING THE ARM

Trap your opponent's arm as quickly as possible. You will usually trap the arm you intend to stretch, but this may not always be the case. However, it usually is. The attacker hooks the defender's arm, latches onto it and immediately traps it to his chest as shown in this photo. As you can see, the attacker is in the shoulder sit position, and trapping his opponent's arm is part of the entire controlling position.
**IMPORTANT:** You have to trap your opponent's arm before you can lock it. If you don't have control of your opponent's arm, he has a better chance of pulling it free and escaping.

## TRAPPING THE ARM: AN INTEGRAL PART OF THE ARMLOCK

This sequence of a Spinning Juji Gatame shows how the attacker has the defender's arm trapped as quickly as possible in the entire process of the attack.

The attacker (on bottom) immediately uses his left hand to trap his opponent's right arm to his chest and torso as he starts his spin into the armlock. The attacker uses his left arm to hook the defender's right arm and, if possible, the attacker will add to the control of the trap by grabbing the defender's right forearm in addition to hooking it.

As the attacker rolls his opponent over onto his back, look at how he continues to use his left arm to scoop and trap the defender's left arm to his chest. **IMPORTANT:** The attacker makes sure that the trapped arm's is as high on his chest as possible so the defender's elbow is not below the attacker's fulcrum point on his pubic bone.

The attacker uses both of his arms to literally hug his opponent's right arm to his chest. Making sure that the defender's right arm is firmly attached to his chest, the attacker will immediately roll back to secure the Juji Gatame, using the weight of his body to help straighten the defender's right arm.

The attacker has rolled back with the defender's right arm completely straight and secured the armlock. Look at how the attacker keeps his arms hugging tightly to the defender's stretched arm.

## TRAPPING THE ARM: THE ARM HOOK OR HUG-EFFECTIVE, QUICK AND USED OFTEN

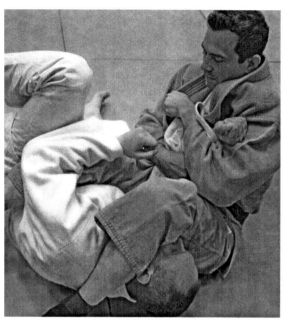

As seen in the previous sequence, the attacker crosses his arms, hooking the defender's right arm and hugs it to his chest. This is a common, and effective, way of trapping the arm. It is quick and leaves little room for the defender to extract his arm.

## TRAP AS YOU ROLL

In many situations, the attacker can trap the defender's arm as the attacker rolls or turns his opponent. This has been mentioned before (and will be mentioned again), as it is an important element in controlling your opponent's arm to apply Juji Gatame. Make it a point to practice hooking, scooping or hugging the defender's arm every time you work out or drill on Juji Gatame. This photo shows how the attacker hooks and traps the defender's arm to his chest as he rolls him.

## TRAPPING THE ARM: SCOOPING WITH THE HANDS

## TRAPPING THE ARM: THE ONE ARM TRAP

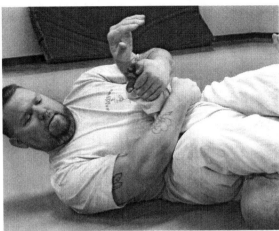

Sometimes it may not be possible to immediately hug or hook your opponent's arm with both of your arms and, in this case, you can use both of your hands to scoop and hook his arm as you pull it to your chest. Think of your hands as meat hooks so that you don't grab and try to use the strength of your hands and arms. (Your opponent may be stronger than you!) This initial scooping action allows the attacker's arm to slide in deeper, making for a more effective hooking action to trap the defender's arm. While this is not an ideal situation because the attacker is only using the strength of his hands and arms (the defender may be stronger), it is still better than losing the defender's arm and not securing the Juji Gatame.

### ◼◼◼◼ TECHNICAL TIP ◼◼◼◼

**When trapping the opponent's arm: trap and attack. Do not get overly concerned with securing your opponent's arm perfectly. By hooking his arm to your chest or torso, you have a good initial control of your opponent. Do not attempt to manipulate your opponent's hand so that the thumb is pointing up perfectly. It doesn't have to be perfect, the arm simply has to be trapped before you can control it further. After you trap (and control) your opponent's arm, you will be able to move it or manipulate it into a better position to lock it.**

Sometimes you may only be able to trap your opponent's arm with one arm, while your other arm is performing another task to secure control over his body. This photo shows how the attacker has rolled his opponent over and onto his back using his left hand to grab and control the defender's left leg and using his right hand to trap the defender's left arm to the attacker's chest.

In this case, hug his arm to your chest at firmly as possible using your bent arm to hook your opponent's arm to your chest. This photo shows the attacker using his right arm to hook his opponent's left arm, trapping it as he uses his left hand and arm to post on the mat for added stability while he executes a head roll Juji Gatame. This photo also shows how important trapping your opponent's arm is in the actual execution of Juji Gatame.

## TRAPPING THE ARM: ATTACKER GRABS HIS OWN LAPEL OR JACKET

The attacker will often grab his lapel (or other part of the jacket, belt or uniform) when controlling his opponent in the leg press. Doing this isolates the defender's arm and gives the attacker more time and opportunity to lever the defender's arm free and stretch it out with a Juji Gatame.

## TRAPPING THE ARM: KEYLOCK GRIP

Using a keylock is a strong method of trapping an opponent's arm, isolating it with a lot of control before levering the arm loose to apply Juji Gatame.

## TRAPPING THE ARM: GRAB YOUR OWN SHOULDER

Sometimes, the attacker may grab his own shoulder to trap his opponent's arm to his chest as shown here.

## TRAPPING THE ARM: ATTACKER GRABS HIS SLEEVE OR ARM

The attacker is using his right hand to grab his left sleeve at about the biceps area. The jacket provides a good handle to grab when controlling an opponent in the leg press as shown here.

In a no gi situation, the attacker can grab and hook onto his upper arm as shown here.

## TRAPPING THE ARM: GRAB YOUR THIGH

Sometimes, especially when the attacker controls his opponent in a leg press, the attacker may choose to grab his thigh to hold the defender's arm in place for an extended period. By grabbing his own thigh in this way, the attacker "anchors" or "locks" his hooking arm to the defender's arm as shown in this photo. When trapping for time, this thigh grab works well in keeping the defender from escaping.

## TRAP ARMS WITH PISTOL GRIP

In some situations, out of necessity or personal preference, the attacker may choose to grab his opponent's sleeves or wrists rather than hooking them to trap them. Grabbing your opponent's sleeves and trapping one or both of his arms to your chest is a viable way of controlling him. Using a "pistol grip" where the attacker cinches the end of his opponent's sleeves is a strong way of trapping his arms.

## SOME BASIC SKILLS ON LEVERING AN OPPONENT'S ARM

A "lever" is how we refer to the act of straightening the opponent's arm in order to apply Juji Gatame. One of the most interesting things about the entire subject of Juji Gatame is levering the opponent's arm so that it is extended, giving the attacker the opportunity to secure the armlock. Presented here are some of the most common levers used in all combat sports.

Before we get into the specific levers, there are some basic skills that apply to all levers, so here they are.

## ATTACKER HOOKS WITH HIS ELBOWS AND HUGS OPPONENT'S ARM TO HIS BODY

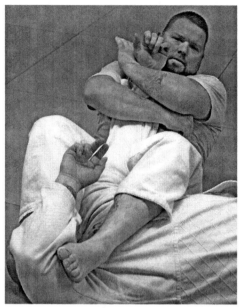

The attacker uses his arms to hook his opponent's arm to his body. Hooking with the elbows is fast, efficient and firmly traps the defender's arm to the attacker's body.

## HOOK LOW AND HIGH

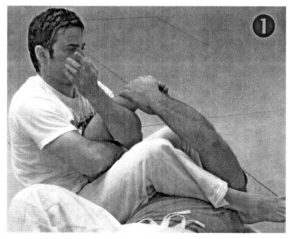

The attacker uses (in this photo) his right arm to hook and trap the defender's right elbow to the attacker's chest. The attacker initially hooks the elbow to his chest or torso, which is lower than the defender's upper arm, because doing this traps the defender's arm more tightly to the attacker's chest. The attacker immediately uses his left arm to hook and control the defender's forearm or wrist area in order to better pry the opponent's grip loose. This "low and high" control of the defender's arm

isolates his arm and gives the attacker a better trap and more control to lever the defender's arm our straight.

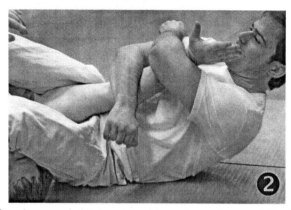

This low and high trapping action, along with the attacker's use of the weight of his body to roll back, loosens the defender's hand grip and extends the defender's arm.

## ATTACKER HOOKS OPPONENT'S ARM WITH THE PALM UP

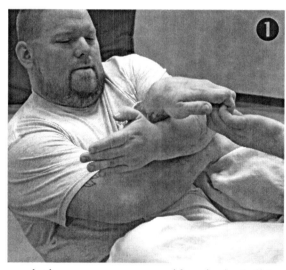

In much the same way you would curl a barbell in the weight room, it is a good idea to have your palms up when levering the defender's arm loose. The attacker will often (in order to slide his hand between the defender's grasped hands and arms) have his palm open as shown here. This allows the attacker to slide his hand through the defender's grasped hands and arms.

The attacker uses a "low and high" arm hook to trap the defender's right arm to the attacker's chest. As he does this, he starts to roll onto his back, using the weight of his body to straighten the defender's right arm.

The attacker traps the defender's right arm, rolls onto his back and fully extends and straightens the defender's right arm to apply Juji Gatame.

## ATTACKER CAN LEVER OPPONENT'S ARM FROM ANY POSITION

The defender does not have to be flat on his back in the classic "belly up" position with the attacker controlling him in a leg press for the attacker to lever his arm loose. The attacker can, and should, attempt to lever his opponent's arm out straight in any position that occurs.

### ▐ TECHNICAL TIP ▐

**The attacker should always "go fishing" for his opponent's arm. Think of your hands and arms as hooks and your opponent's arm as the fish, waiting for you to hook and catch his arm.**

Sometimes, the attacker may make a fist with his hand in an effort to exert more power into the movement. But notice that the attacker's right hand is palm up even with his clinched fist.

## ATTACKER USES HIS BODY WEIGHT TO EXTEND AND STRETCH HIS OPPONENT'S ARM

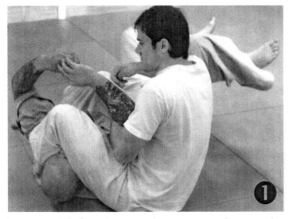

It is essential for the attacker to use the weight of his body to add more pressure in order to loosen the defender's grip. If the attacker attempts to use only the strength of his hands and arms to pry the opponent's grip loose, he may lose that battle, as the defender may be stronger. This photo shows how the attacker has just rolled his opponent over onto his back and immediately uses his left arm to hook the defender's right elbow, trapping it to the attacker's chest. The attacker is sitting on his buttocks.

## ATTACKER LEVERS OPPONENT'S ARM WHERE IT IS WEAKEST

This was discussed earlier in this book in the chapter on Core Skills, but should be mentioned here as well. The attacker traps his opponent's right arm and to lever it loose, the attacker starts to roll in the direction of his opponent's head. This puts a lot of pressure of the defender's right shoulder. **IMPORTANT:** The shoulder is one of the least stable joints in the body, so it is important to target the shoulder as much as possible when attacking with Juji Gatame. Cranking on an opponent's shoulder will help a lot in levering his arm.

The attacker has rolled to his right and toward his opponent's head, targeting in on the shoulder. The attacker starts to lever the defender's right arm.

The attacker has successfully levered the defender's right arm and the attacker rolls to his right to fully stretch the defender's arm out straight to apply Juji Gatame.

## SPECIFIC LEVERS AND SUBMISSION TECHNIQUES FROM THE LEG PRESS POSITION

Presented on the following pages are a variety of levers and methods of extending, straightening and stretching an opponent's arm. Also included are some other armlocks and chokes that the attacker can apply from the leg press position, and while these are not all Juji Gatame, they are useful when controlling an opponent from the leg press position.

## HOOK AND HUG ARM LEVER

This lever is one of the most common and often used. It's simple, direct and often gets the job done. While there may be other more complicated ways to lever an opponent's arm loose, this is one that proves simple skills aren't simply for simpletons.

After rolling or placing the defender into a vulnerable position, the attacker quickly uses both arms (at the same time) to hook the defender's arm. The attacker makes sure to hook with his elbows so that he can hug the defender's arm to the attacker's chest.

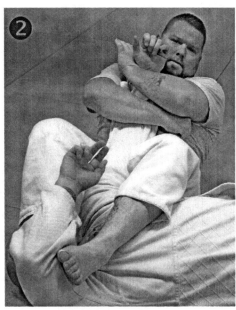

The attacker hugs the defender's arm to his chest as he continues to hook. This firmly traps the defender's arm to the attacker's chest. The attacker uses the weight of his body to roll back and stretch his opponent's arm straight.

## DOUBLE UPPERCUT ARM LEVER

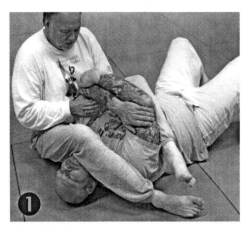

The attacker has his opponent in the leg press.

### TECHNICAL TIP

**In the same movement as actually punching, the attacker can lever his opponent's arm loose. Often, the ballistic effect of the attacker hooking the defender's arm's forcefully in the same way a boxer would deliver an uppercut punch to his opponent will quickly, and effectively, jerk or pull the defender's hands and arms apart.**

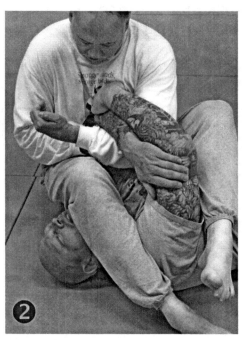

The attacker slides his left hand (look at how it is palm up) between the defender's arms. Look at how the attacker lowers his body so that the defender's left upper arm and elbow are firmly trapped to the defender's chest. The attacker uses his left hand and arm in a hard, punching motion similar to a boxer's uppercut punch.

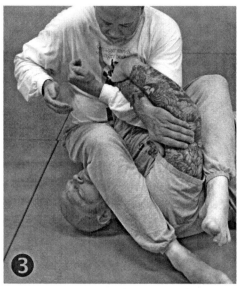

The attacker starts to drive his right hand through the defender's arms in the same motion a boxer would use an uppercut punch.

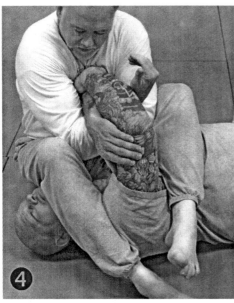

The attacker drives his right hand through the defender's arms as shown. Look at how firmly the defender's arms are trapped to the attacker's chest.

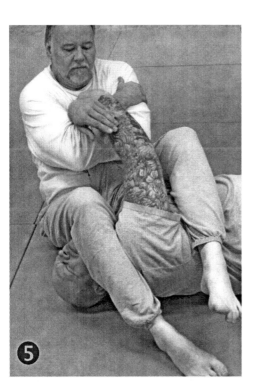

The attacker uses his right hand to grab his own left upper arm, trapping the defender's left arm firmly to the attacker's chest. The attacker uses the weight of his body to roll back. This action levers the defender's right arm loose.

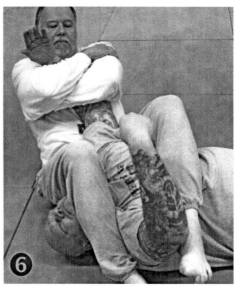

The attacker rolls back, extending and straightening the defender's left arm.

## HOOK AND UPPERCUT ARM LEVER

This is similar to the previous lever, but in this method, the attacker uses his left arm to trap the defender's left arm to the attacker's chest rather than using a hard uppercut motion to start to lever it free.

The attacker firmly traps the defender's left arm to the attacker's chest and quickly uses his right hand (palm up) to hook under the defender's left wrist and forearm. Look at how the attacker is using the "low and high" method to lever the defender's arm.

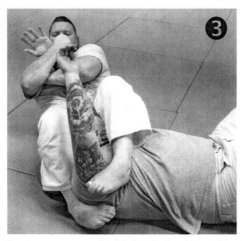

The defender separates the defender's grasp of his hands, traps the defender's left arm to his chest and uses the weight of his body to roll back and apply Juji Gatame.

### TECHNICAL TIP

Notice that in all situations, the attacker is controlling his opponent with a leg press and uses his feet and legs to "accordion" or squeeze the defender's shoulders together. By crunching the defender's shoulders together, the attacker weakens the defender's shoulders, and as a result, weakens the defender's grasp of his hands and arms, allowing the attacker to more easily lever the defender's arm free.

## HUG AND UPPERCUT ARM LEVER

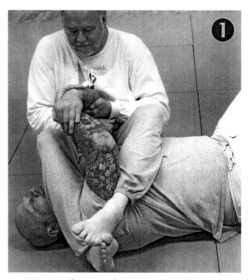

This is quite similar to the previous lever, but in this situation, the defender may be stronger than the attacker, so the attacker will have to use the weight of his body more efficiently to lever the defender's arm free. This photo shows the attacker controlling his opponent with the leg press.

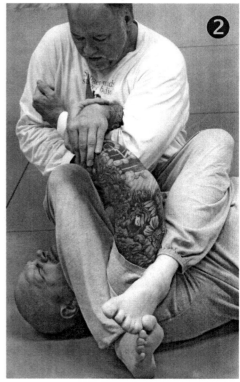

The attacker slides his left hand and arm between the defender's arms.

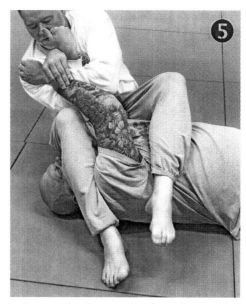

Because the attacker is stronger than the attacker in this situation, the attacker rolls to his right hip and side and into the direction of the defender's head. By doing this, the attacker keys in on the weakest part of the defender's body at this point, the shoulder.

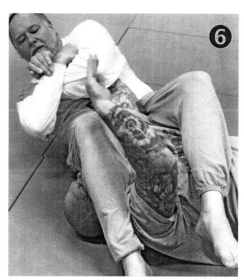

The attacker levers the defender's arm free and will apply Juji Gatame.

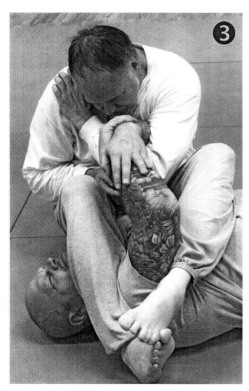

The attacker uses his left arm to hook and tightly hug the defender's left arm to the attacker's chest. Look at how the attacker curls his body forward so that the defender's left upper arm is more firmly trapped to his chest.

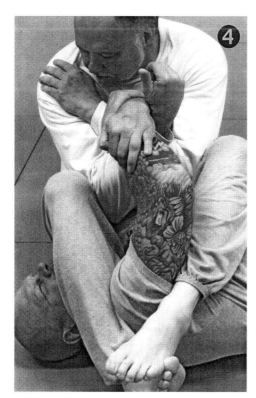

The attacker uses his right hand to slide between the defender's arms as shown.

## BENT ARM LEVER TO JUJI GATAME

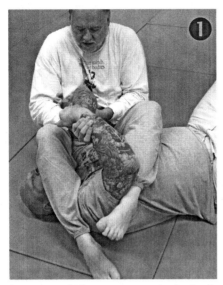

The attacker controls his opponent with the leg press.

The attacker uses his right arm to hook the defender's left upper arm and elbow firmly to the attacker's torso. The attacker slides his left hand directly under the defender's left wrist area.

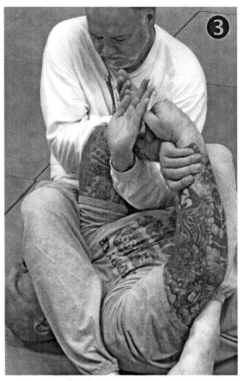

The attacker quickly moves his right elbow from its initial position so that it is now located between the attacker's torso and the defender's left forearm and elbow. The attacker will now grasp his hands together.

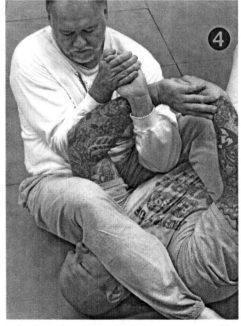

The attacker's right elbow and forearm are wedged onto the defender's left elbow and forearm. The attacker grasps his hands together. Look at how the attacker is using a "square" grip to lock his hands together firmly. The attacker uses his right arm to push forward against the defender's left elbow. The attacker uses his left hand to pull the defender's left forearm and wrist toward the attacker's body. This forces the defender to release his grasp and starts to crank the defender's arm.

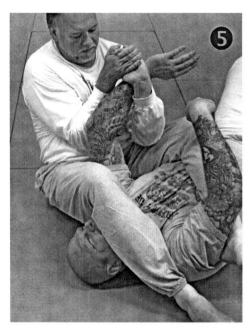

The attacker continues to crank the defender's arm much in the same way he would apply a bent armlock. This may be enough pressure on the defender's left elbow to force him to tap out, but if it isn't, the attacker will quickly apply his Juji Gatame.

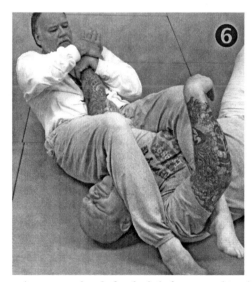

The attacker traps the defender's left arm to his chest to apply Juji Gatame.

## THIGH GRAB LEVER AND UPPER CUT

By grabbing his right thigh with his left hand (as shown in this photo), the attacker can firmly secure and trap the defender's left arm to the attacker's body. This thigh grab also provides a strong fulcrum to pry the defender's arm loose.

The attacker securely uses his left hand and arm to grab his right thigh or upper leg and traps the defender's left arm. The attacker slides his right hand and arm between the defender's arms as shown.

The attacker uses his right arm to hook in an uppercut movement as he rolls to his right side. As he does this, the attacker uses his left hand, which is grabbing and anchored on his right upper leg or thigh, as a fulcrum to lever the defender's left arm loose.

The attacker traps the defender's left arm to his chest, rolls onto his back and secures Juji Gatame.

## ARCH AND TILT THIGH GRAB LEVER

This is similar to the thigh grab, but in this variation, the attacker arches his hips off of the mat to add more pressure to lever the defender's arm loose. The attacker controls his opponent with a leg press and uses his right hand to grab onto his left upper leg or hip as shown. As he does this, the attacker turns to his left and uses his left hand to post onto the mat for stability.

The attacker turns further to his left in a twisting motion as he continues to use his right hand to hold and anchor onto his left thigh. This movement wrenches the defender's right shoulder and arm in the direction of the defender's head as shown.

The attacker does this twisting motion quickly and with a lot of force to lever the defender's right arm free.

The attacker quickly uses his left hand and arm to scoop and hook under the defender's right forearm and wrist. Look at how the attacker continues to use his right hand to grab his left thigh. The attacker rolls to his left side (in the direction of the defender's head).

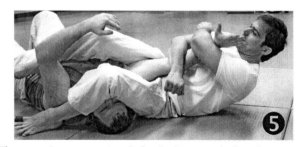

The attacker traps the defender's extended right arm to the attacker's chest as the attacker rolls onto his back to fully straighten the defender's stretched arm. This photo shows how the attacker uses the "low and high" trapping movement to control the defender's arm.

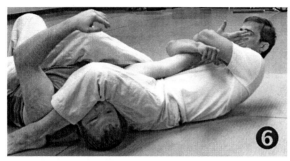

The attacker gets the tap out with his Juji Gatame.

## ARM AND LEG HOOK LEVER

The attacker controls his opponent with a leg press.

This photo shows a different angle. The attacker rolls to his left side, and as he does, he uses his left hand and arm to hook the defender's left leg. Look at how the attacker uses his right hand to hook the defender's left arm and trap it to the attacker's body. The defender often will attempt to sit up onto his buttocks in an effort to escape. If he does, the attacker uses his right leg and foot to hook around the defender's head as shown.

The attacker (if necessary) uses his right foot and leg to forcefully hook the defender's head, driving it back down to the mat. As he does this, the attacker grasps his hands together, firmly controlling the defender's left leg and left arm. The attacker has rolled onto his left side.

The attacker arches back, driving his hips forward and as he does, he extends the defender's trapped left arm as well as the defender's trapped left leg.

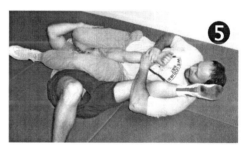

The attacker applies Juji Gatame from this position. The defender does not need to let go of his grasp in order to apply pressure.

This view shows how the attacker controls the defender's left arm and leg.

## LAPEL GRAB AND UPPER CUT LEVER

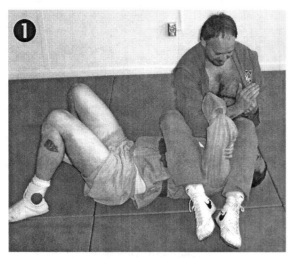

The attacker controls his opponent with a leg press. As he does, the attacker slides his right hand (the hand that is close to the defender's belt line) between the defender's arms as shown.

The attacker uses his right hand to grab the left lapel of his jacket. The attacker uses this hold to trap the defender's right arm to the attacker's chest.

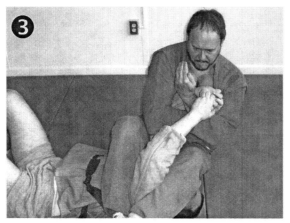

The attacker quickly uses his left hand to scoop or uppercut at the defender's right forearm and wrist area.

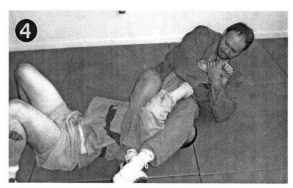

The attacker rolls to his left side (the side close to the defender's head) as he continues to uppercut with his left hand and arm.

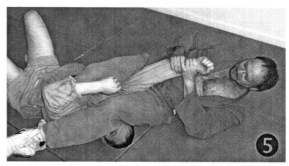

The attacker levers the defender's right arm loose and applies Juji Gatame.

## THIGH GRAB AND HEAD TRIANGLE LEVER

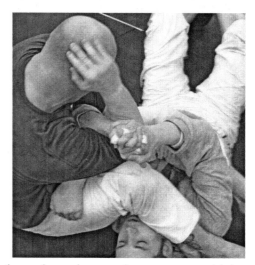

This shows how the attacker can use a thigh grab to trap the defender's left arm at the elbow as the attacker grabs behind his head or neck to trap the defender's left forearm or wrist. This is a strong method of trapping the arm, especially in "no gi" grappling situations.

# TRIANGLE AND HEAD GRAB LEVER

The attacker controls his opponent with the leg press and as he does, he slides his left hand and arm under his opponent's left arm.

The attacker uses his left hand to grab his right biceps or upper arm and as he does, the attacker reaches behind his head or neck and grabs it.

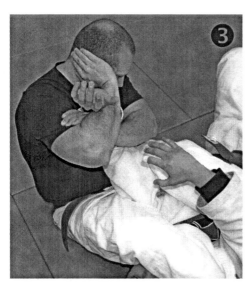

This view shows how the attacker traps the defender's left arm with his triangle grip. The attacker uses the weight of his body to roll back to lever the defender's arm.

The attacker rolls back and further traps the defender's extended left arm as shown.

The attacker secures his Juji Gatame.

# TRIANGLE LEVER WITH A FOOT KICK LEVER

This shows how different traps and levers can be used together. In this situation, the attacker is using the triangle trap along with a foot kick to lever the defender's arm loose to apply the Juji Gatame.

## ARM TRIANGLE LEVER

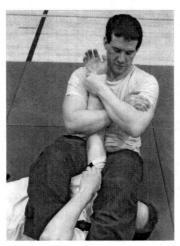

The attacker may keep his arm triangle trap on the defender's arm as shown. It doesn't matter how the attacker finishes the armlock as long as he keeps control of the defender's stretched arm and gets the tap out.

## THE ATTACKER KICKS OR PUSHES WITH HIS FOOT/FEET TO LEVER OPPONENT'S ARM

A common, simple and effective method of loosening the opponent's grip and straightening out his arm is for the attacker to use one (or both) feet to push or kick against the defender's arms, elbows or other parts of his body. This photo shows the attacker using his left foot to push on the inside of the defender's right elbow to loosen the defender's grip and straighten his arm.

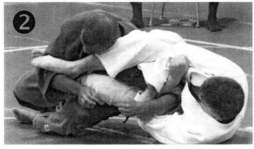

The attacker continues to use his right foot to push on the inside of the defender's right arm. This action has pulled the defender's grasped hands apart and the defender's left arm is starting to straighten.

## LEG KICK LEVER (LEG NEAREST DEFENDER'S HEAD)

The attacker controls his opponent with a leg press.

The attacker uses the foot that is close to the defender's head (in this photo, the right foot) to kick or push on the defender's biceps or inside the defender's elbow joint. The attacker kicks the defender's left arm downward in the direction of the defender's belt line. As he does this, the attacker rolls to the hip or side close to the defender's head (in this case, the right hip). This foot kicking downward and the weight of the attacker's body rolling upward (to the defender's head area) create a strong levering action.

The attacker levers the defender's left arm loose and applies Juji Gatame.

## LEG KICK LEVER (LEG NEAREST DEFENDER'S BELT LINE)

## BOTH LEGS KICK LEVER

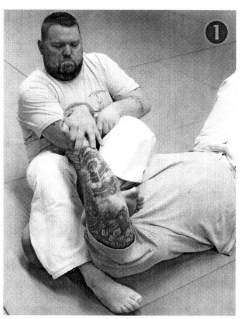

In this variation, the attacker uses both legs to kick or push against the defender's right elbow or biceps. In order to maintain a good leg press for control, the attacker may use one foot to wedge into the inside of the defender's right arm initially.

In this variation, the attacker controls his opponent with the leg press and uses his left foot to kick or push on the inside of the defender's right arm or at the defender's right biceps area.

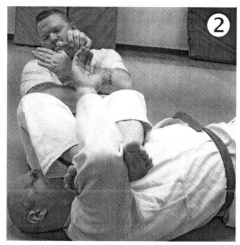

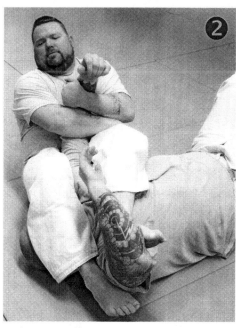

The attacker now uses the other foot to wedge into the elbow joint (or biceps area) of the defender as shown. As he does this, the attacker kicks or forcefully pushes with both feet against the defender's right arm.

The attacker uses his arms to hook and trap the defender's left arm to the attacker's body as the attacker kicks the defender's arms apart and applies Juji Gatame.

The attacker levers the defender's left arm loose and applies Juji Gatame.

## ATTACKER PUSHES ON DEFENDER'S HIP OR BODY TO LEVER HIS ARM

Sometimes, the attacker uses one or both feet to push on his opponent's hip (or other part of the defender's body) in order to lever the defender's arm. This photo taken at the AAU Freestyle Judo Nationals shows how the attacker uses his feet to manipulate and push the defender's hips in an effort to lever the defender's arm loose.

## LEG WEDGE LEVER

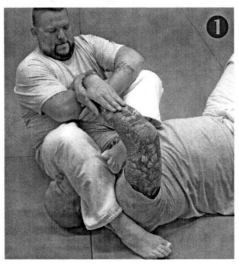

The attacker controls his opponent with the leg press and as he does, he uses his left foot and leg (the foot and leg close to the defender's belt line or hip area) to slide between the defender's arms as shown.

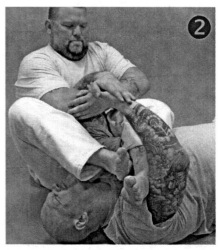

The attacker wedges his left foot and lower leg on the inside of the defender's left elbow and biceps area. As he does this, the attacker uses his right foot to push or kick against his left ankle. This action forces the defender to loosen his grip.

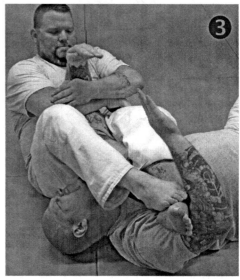

The attacker levers the defender's left arm loose and applies Juji Gatame.

This photo taken at the AAU Freestyle Judo Nationals shows how the attacker uses the leg wedge to lever his opponent's arm loose.

# KEYLOCK LEVER

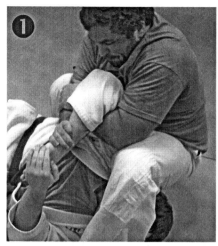

The attacker traps his opponent's arm to his chest with a keylock as shown here.

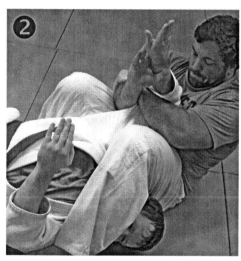

The attacker applies pressure with his hand on the defender's right forearm to loosen the defender's grasping hands. As he does this, the attacker rolls onto his back.

The attacker levers the defender's right arm loose and secures Juji Gatame.

# FAR ARM DRAG LEVER

The attacker controls his opponent with a leg press. The attacker uses both of his feet and legs to "accordion" or squeezes the defender's shoulders together. This weakens the defender's shoulders and upper body. As he does this, the attacker uses both hands to grab onto the defender's far arm (in this case, the defender's left arm) and pull or scoop the defender's left arm in, squeezing the defender's arms together.

This shows how the attacker uses both of his hands and arms to grab the defender's left elbow and pull the defender's arms together.

As he scoops the defender's arms in toward him, the attacker quickly uses his left arm to hook the defender's right (near) arm to the attacker's chest.

The attacker quickly uses his right hand to let go of the defender's left elbow and now uses both of his hands and arms to trap the defender's right arm to the attacker's chest. The attacker rolls back and applies Juji Gatame.

## HANDSHAKE LEVER

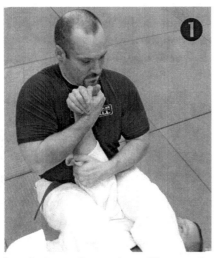

This is a simple, but effective lever. The attacker uses his right hand to grab the defender's right hand the same way he may shake hands. The attacker uses his left hand to trap the defender's right elbow to the attacker's body.

The attacker traps the defender's right arm to his body and rolls onto his back to apply Juji Gatame.

## ARM SLICER WITH LEG PRESSURE

The attacker controls his opponent with the leg press. The attacker uses his right arm to hook under the defender's right arm, trapping it to the attacker's chest. The attacker uses his right hand to grab his left forearm and his left hand to grab the defender's right forearm.

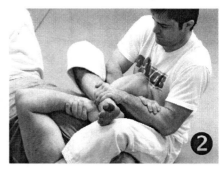

The attacker moves his right leg up and over onto the defender's near (left) arm as shown. The attacker uses his left hand to secure his right foot in place as necessary. At this point, the attacker applies downward pressure with his right foot on the defender's right forearm.

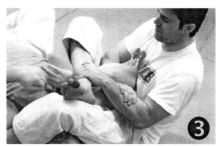

The downward pressure of the attacker's right leg causes pain in the defender's right bent arm. This will make the defender tap out.

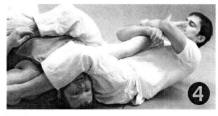

If the defender does not tap out from the bent arm lock that the attacker put on him, the attacker can quickly use his arms to hook and stretch the defender's right arm and secure Juji Gatame.

# TRIANGLE ARMLOCK AND LEVER

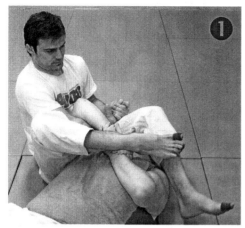

This is similar to the previous lever, but the attacker doesn't "slice" the defender's near arm as previously. The attacker controls his opponent with the leg press and uses his right arm to hook under the defender's right arm. As he does this, the attacker moves his right leg up and over onto the defender's grasped hands.

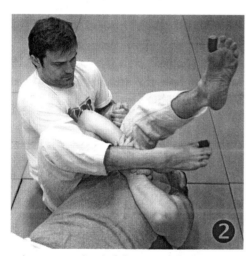

The attacker moves his left leg up and over on top of his right foot.

The attacker has now formed a triangle with his legs.

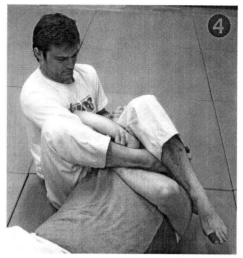

The attacker applies pressure down onto the defender's arms with the leg triangle.

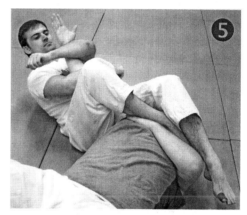

This causes the defender to loosen his grasp and levers the defender's right arm as shown.

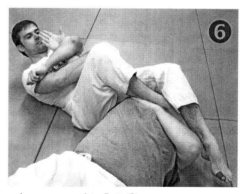

The attacker secures his Juji Gatame.

## TRIANGLE BENT ARMLOCK

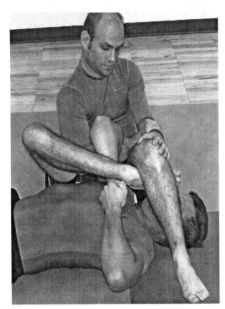

Sometimes, the attacker may choose to use his leg triangle to clamp down tightly on his opponent's near arm (in this photo, the right arm) and apply a bent armlock from this position.

## HENGES HANGER FROM LEG PRESS TO CHOKE TO JUJI GATAME

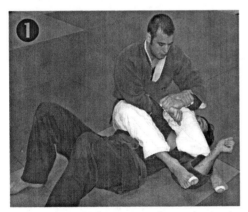

The attacker controls his opponent with the leg press. As he does this, the attacker uses his right arm to hook under the defender's right arm. The attacker then uses his right hand to grab his left wrist.

The attacker slides his left arm under the head of the defender as shown.

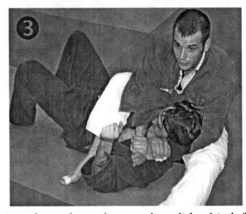

This view shows how the attacker slides his left hand under the defender's head and neck.

The attacker can apply a choke on his opponent by leaning back and using his left knee and leg to drive upward. Doing this, the attacker chokes the defender.

If the choke does not work, the attacker can roll to his right side. As he does this, the attacker starts to move his right leg over the defender's head.

The attacker stays on his left side and applies Juji Gatame from this position.

## BENT WRIST LOCK TO JUJI GATAME

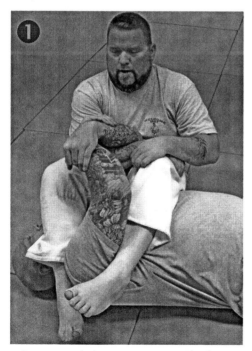

The attacker controls his opponent in the leg press.

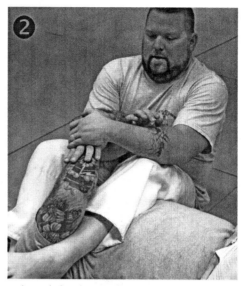

The attacker slides his right arm under the defender's left arm as shown. As he does this, the attacker places his left hand on the attacker's left hand.

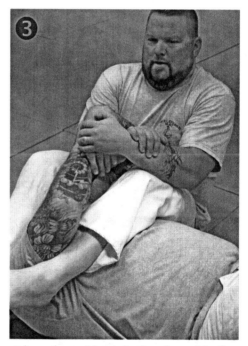

The attacker places his right hand on his forearm as shown. As he does this, the attacker uses his left hand to pull in on the defender's hand.

This photo shows how the attacker uses his left hand on top of the defender's left hand to create a wristlock. This creates pain in the defender's wrist and causes him to loosen his grip.

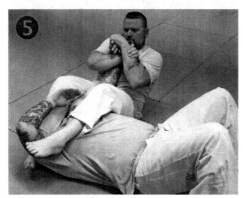

The attacker can apply this wristlock on his opponent and get the tap out.

If the defender chooses, he can use this wristlock to lever the defender's left arm loose and apply Juji Gatame.

While there are more variations of how to lever an opponent's arm or apply another submission technique from the leg press position, the skills presented in this chapter can give you some food for thought. But most of all, everything shown in this chapter has been (and continues to be) successfully used in all levels of competition in all combat sports. Realistically, you will have several levers that you prefer, and by making it a point to practice on them on a regular basis, they will become second nature to you and be part of your arsenal of skills.

The next chapter examines combinations. These are combinations to and from Juji Gatame and include a variety of armlocks, chokes, leglocks and pins.

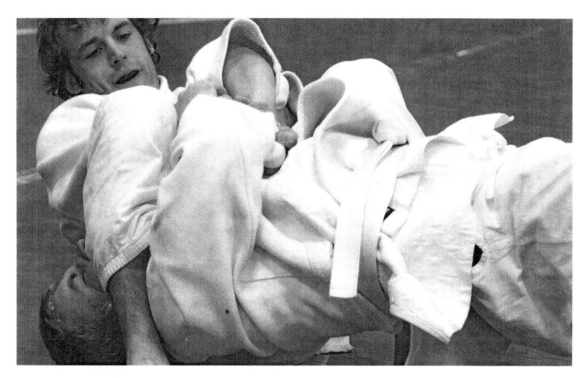

# COMBINATIONS USING JUJI GATAME

**"ONCE YOU GET THAT ARM, THERE'S NO LETTING GO OF IT." BECKY SCOTT, WORLD SAMBO CHAMPION**

## COMBINATIONS: LINKING SKILLS TOGETHER

What are often called "combinations" are any techniques that are linked together, often in a sequential or logical manner, with the end result of producing a victory over an opponent. This chapter examines combination skills that include Juji Gatame. In some cases, Juji Gatame is the end result and in other cases, Juji Gatame is the initial attack in the combination of attacks leading to an opponent's submission.

Quite a few combinations are presented in this chapter, but not every combination can possibly be included. New combinations are constantly being seen in all levels of competition. Please take what is presented in this chapter and expand on it so that new, innovative (but above all, effective and functional) combinations involving Juji Gatame will be developed. In other words, make it work for you.

Any combination of techniques can be used. In some cases, Juji Gatame may be the only technique used and in these instances, Juji Gatame is linked together with another Juji Gatame from a different position or angle.

Another consideration is that, in some situations, techniques that may seem totally unrelated might link together well, creating a functional and effective combination. Use your imagination when training and keep an open mind for what may work.

## TWO BASIC COMBINATION TYPES

While anything could be possible when two athletes are engaged in any combat sport, there are usually two basic types of combinations used. 1) In some combinations, the attacker actually attempts an initial technique with the purpose of getting the win, but because of the opponent's defensive move or escape (or even a change in position), the attacker has to try a follow-up technique to secure the win. 2) In other cases, the attacker purposely sets his opponent up with an initial move, which lures or forces the opponent to move into the desired, winning technique.

Again, it should be emphasized that almost anything is possible, but more often than not, combinations result from these two basic situations.

## SOME BASICS ON POSITION WHEN DOING COMBINATIONS

The attacker has three primary duties when doing a combination: 1) Attacker must establish initial position over the opponent; 2) Attacker must change position without losing control of opponent; 3) Establish a new position to secure the winning technique, or secure the winning technique or hold immediately.

Sometimes, as in number 3, the attacker's change from his initial position may put him in an ideal position so that he can immediately secure the winning move. In other cases, the attacker may have to quickly establish a new position that will enable him to secure the winning move. Remember a very important saying, "Control the position and then get the submission."

Presented here are some basic considerations when performing combinations.

## KEEP IT SIMPLE

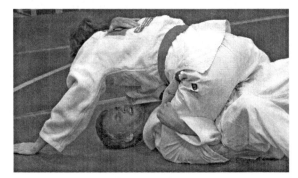

When working a combination from one move to another (or even to another), don't get fancy. Keep things simple and get the job done. The attacker should make sure to keep his movements compact and close to the body, never giving up the dominant position.

## DON'T GIVE UP CONTROL

When moving from one technique to another, never give up control of the position. If you do have to give up some control, always dominate your opponent. The attacker should logically link one technique to another, while maintaining control of the position.

## MAKE THINGS UNCOMFORTABLE

By keeping constant pressure and making things as unpleasant as possible for an opponent, the attacker has a better chance of maintaining control of the position and making things so bad for the defender, that the defender is thinking more of how to survive than thinking of how to escape (or fight back).

## EVERYTHING IS A HANDLE

Every part of both grappler's bodies and uniforms are handles. The attacker should grab, hook, pull, push or manipulate anything that will help him gain more control and secure the Juji Gatame.

## JUJI GATAME TO JUJI GATAME

One of the best combinations: don't let go of the opponent's arm and keep rolling and turning him.

Maybe it's not exactly a "combination" but one of the most effective ways to stretch an opponent's arm is to not let go of it. As the defender rolls, turns or moves in any way to try to defend or escape, the attacker's best option usually is to continue to trap his opponent's arm as tight as possible and keep trying to secure the Juji Gatame. In many situations, if the attacker keeps hold of the defender's arm as they roll, the Juji Gatame will be successful. This shows the attacker rolling his opponent with a spinning Juji Gatame as his initial attack.

The defender resists, but the attacker continues to roll and use his hands and arms to hook and trap the defender's left arm as the roll continues.

The defender sits up in an attempt to escape. As he does, the attacker stays round, continues to roll and continues to trap the defender's left arm.

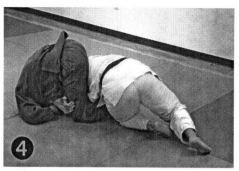

The defender continues to resist with the attacker relentlessly staying with him and continually holding onto the defender's left arm, all the while attempting to stretch it to secure his Juji Gatame.

The momentum of the defender's forward movement allows the attacker to roll as shown.

The attacker never lets go of his opponent's left arm, using his right hand (grabbing his left upper leg and thigh to tighten the hold) to trap the arm. The attacker rolls the defender over in a head roll Juji Gatame. Look at how the continued trapping and pulling on the defender's arm has pulled the left arm loose.

By continuing to trap and control the defender's left arm, the attacker can stretch the defender's arm from any position. This may not be "perfect" in the sense that the defender is not flat on his back and controlled in a leg press, but the attacker sees the opening to secure Juji Gatame and will take it.

The attacker levers and stretches the defender's left arm out straight, securing his Juji Gatame from this side position.

**IMPORTANT:** This sequence shows that if the attacker keeps a firm grip of his opponent's arm and continues to roll, turn or break his opponent down, the odds are quite good that the attacker will be successful in securing his Juji Gatame. Don't let go of his arm and keep rolling him.

### TECHNICAL TIP

A combination is comprised of any techniques that are linked together in a sequence. The purpose is for the attacker to constantly exert more and more control over his opponent until the opponent is beaten.

## JUJI GATAME LEG PRESS TO TATE SHIHO GATAME (VERTICAL 4 CORNER HOLD) OR MOUNT POSITION

Often, the simplest things get the best results. Moving from a Juji Gatame to a pin or controlling position may be the best thing to do in many situations. In this case, the attacker controls his opponent with the leg press and is trying to lever the defender's arm loose to secure Juji Gatame.

The attacker realizes that the defender is offering too much resistance so the attacker decides to control his opponent with a pin. The attacker uses his right arm to hook the defender's right arm as the attacker uses his left hand to push up, lifting his left hip off of the mat.

The attacker spins to his left as he uses his left hand to stabilize his body. Look at how the attacker swings his left leg away from the defender's head and turns his body to his left. Look at the position of the attacker's right leg with the knee on the mat. Doing this puts the attacker in a good position to pin his opponent.

The attacker now straddles his opponent as shown. Look at the positions of the attacker's legs. The attacker continues to use his right arm to hook and trap his opponent's right arm as the attacker lowers his body.

The attacker pulls his left leg back so that it rests on the left knee. The attacker now pins his opponent with Tate Shiho Gatame (Vertical 4-Corner Hold) or can control his opponent with a Mount.

### ▰▰▰ TECHNICAL TIP ▰▰▰

In some combat sports (such as judo), the attacker can switch from the leg press position and hold his opponent for time and win by a pin. In other combat sports, the attacker can control his opponent from this position and when he senses the time is right, can work to apply a submission technique.

## JUJI GATAME LEG PRESS TO VERTICAL HOLD OR MOUNT AND ON TO THE BENT ARMLOCK (UDE GARAMI)

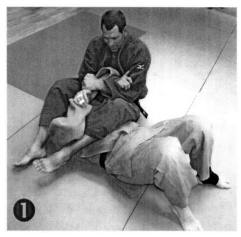

The attacker controls his opponent with the leg press.

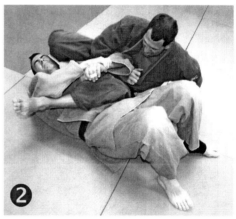

The bottom grappler offers a strong defense and the attacker realizes he may not secure Juji Gatame. The attacker swings his right leg back and away from the defender's head while using his left hand to post on the mat for stability and rolls to his left hip.

The attacker uses his left hand to push his body up off the mat and starts to sit up and onto the defender's torso.

The attacker sits up on his opponent, pinning him with a Vertical Pin or Mount.

As the attacker controls his opponent, he uses his left hand to grab the defender's right arm. The attacker extends his right arm and posts onto the mat for stability.

The attacker uses his left hand to push the defender's right upper arm to the mat. As he does this, the attacker moves his right hand over and starts to grab his opponent's left wrist.

The attacker uses his hands to form a keylock or "figure 4" on the defender's bent right arm. This forms the Ude Garami (Bent Armlock or Arm Entanglement) and the attacker applies pressure to get the submission.

## VERTICAL HOLD OR MOUNT TO STRADDLE PIN AND THEN TO JUJI GATAME

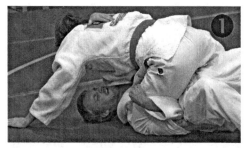

The attacker holds his opponent down with a Vertical Pin (or Mount) as shown here.

The attacker shifts his pinning position so that it is now an Uki Gatame (Straddle Hold). The attacker moves his right foot and lower leg under his opponent's head. The attacker leans to his right side, using his right hand and arm to post out onto the mat for stability. The attacker positions his left knee at the defender's right side as shown. The attacker can continue his pin from this position, but he will go for Juji Gatame. Look at how the attacker uses his left arm to trap the defender's left arm.

The attacker moves to his right side, withdrawing his left leg from the right side of his opponent's body. The attacker leans on his right hip, using his right hand posted on the mat to stabilize his body. The attacker is shifting his position so that he can control his opponent with the leg press and secure Juji Gatame.

The attacker has shifted his position so that he is now controlling his opponent with the leg press. The attacker has placed his right foot and leg over the defender's head. The attacker has his left shin placed in the defender's left side. The attacker now attempts to lever the defender's left arm loose to apply Juji Gatame.

The attacker continues to lever the defender's left arm loose and eventually secures the Juji Gatame for the win.

## JUJI GATAME LEG PRESS TO STRADDLE HOLD (UKI GATAME) TO VERTICAL PIN OF MOUNT LEADING TO JUJI GATAME

The attacker controls his opponent with this variation of the leg press. This might have taken place if the attacker has rolled the defender over onto his back and used his

right hand and arm to hook and control the defender during the roll.

The defender offers resistance and the attacker is unable to lever the defender's arm loose to apply Juji Gatame.

The attacker shifts his weight to his right hip and places his right hand on the mat for stability. As he does this, the attacker starts to move his left knee toward his opponent's head as shown.

The attacker pushes upward, allowing his body to shift to the right better. As he does this, the attacker jams his right foot under the left shoulder of his opponent and continues to move his left leg as shown so that it will be bent at the knee. The attacker uses his left hand and arm to trap the defender's right arm.

The attacker places his left knee on the mat and straddles his opponent as shown. The attacker has control with Uki Gatame (Straddle Pin or Hold) and firmly traps the defender's right arm with both of his arms.

If the attacker loses control with his Straddle Pin, he shifts to the Vertical Pin or Mount position. From here, the attacker might attempt to strangle his opponent with a Juji Jime (Cross Choke) or simply continue to pin his opponent.

If the choke is not successful or if the attacker chooses to switch to Juji Gatame, he comes up on his left knee as shown as he jams his right foot under his opponent's

left shoulder. As he does this, the attacker uses his left arm to hook and trap the defender's right arm to the attacker's chest.

The attacker quickly swings his left leg over his opponent's head and ends up sitting on his buttocks at the defender's right side near his shoulder.

The attacker uses both arms to hook, hug and trap the defender's right arm to the attacker's chest.

The attacker rolls back, levers the defender's right arm out straight and secures Juji Gatame.

## SPINNING JUJI GATAME TO STRADDLE PIN AND ON TO JUJI GATAME

The attacker does a spinning Juji Gatame.

The attacker spins his opponent over and onto his back. As he does this, the attacker continues to use his left arm to trap the defender's right arm to the attacker's chest. The attacker uses his right hand to grab between his opponent's legs, holding the defender's left leg.

The attacker shifts his body so that he is on his right hip and sitting on his opponent's torso at about the belt line. The attacker jams his left knee under the defender's head as shown. The attacker moves and places his right

foot under his opponent's left shoulder as shown. All the while, the attacker continues to use his left arm to trap his opponent's right arm.

The defender, realizing he is being pinned with Uki Gatame (Straddle Hold), may attempt to escape by turning his body away from the attacker as shown. As he does this, the attacker leans to his right and swings his left leg over the defender's head. The attacker uses his left arm to continue to trap the defender's right arm.

The attacker swings his left leg over his opponent's head, trapping the defender's right arm and levering the right arm to secure the Juji Gatame.

## NORTH SOUTH PIN (KAMI SHIHO GATAME) TO JUJI GATAME

The attacker holds his opponent with the North-South Pin (Kami Shiho Gatame-Upper Four Corner Hold). The attacker uses both arms to reach under his opponent's arms, holding the defender's belt as shown.

The attacker sits up slightly and uses both of his knees to trap his opponent's head, keeping control of the defender. As he does this, the attacker uses his right arm to hook under the defender's right upper arm as shown. The attacker pushes his opponent over onto the defender's left side.

To secure the position even tighter, the attacker forms a keylock with his hands on the defender's right arm as shown. Look at how the attacker uses his knees to trap the defender's head and how the defender is lying on his left side.

The attacker alters his position so that he brings his right knee up as shown.

The attacker jumps into a low squat as shown. As he does this, the attacker traps the defender's right arm to the attacker's chest.

As he moves into a low squat, the attacker moves his left foot and leg over his opponent's head. At the same time, the attacker starts to lever the defender's right arm loose as shown. Look at how the attacker uses the shoulder sit position to control the defender.

The attacker continues to lever his opponent's right arm loose and rolls back.

The attacker rolls onto his back and applies Juji Gatame.

## HEAD ROLL JUJI GATAME WHEN ATTACKER ATTEMPTS TO BREAKDOWN OR TURN OPPONENT AND OPPONENT POSTS HIS LEG TO DEFEND

The attacker attempts to break his opponent down (turn the opponent over onto his back) with any move he wishes, but the Both Elbows Breakdown is used in

this sequence (and the following sequences as well). For more information on this breakdown and other breakdowns and pins, refer to GROUNDFIGHTING PINS AND BREAKDOWNS (Turtle Press).

The defender uses his right leg to post out to his right side, preventing the attacker from turning the defender over onto his back. As he does this, the attacker quickly moves his right leg over the defender's back and hips as shown. Look at how the attacker uses his left hand to post onto the mat for stability.

The attacker jams his right leg in and under the defender's body at about the belt line. As he does this, the attacker extends his body over the defender's upper body and uses his right arm to hook and trap the defender's right arm. The attacker continues to use his left hand to post onto the mat for stability as he places the top of his head on the mat near the defender's right arm as shown.

This view shows how the attacker positions his body. Look at how the attacker uses his right foot to anchor onto the defender's left upper leg and hip. The attacker uses his left leg to hook over the defender's head in preparation for doing the head roll Juji Gatame.

The attacker starts to roll to his left side, turning the defender over as he does.

The attacker continues with his head roll Juji Gatame, rolling the defender directly over the defender's head.

The attacker continues to roll the defender over his head as shown.

The attacker finishes the head roll Juji Gatame and starts to lever the defender's right arm out straight as the attacker rolls onto his back.

The attacker rolls back and secures his Juji Gatame.

# BACK ROLL JUJI GATAME WHEN ATTACKER ATTEMPTS TO BREAK HIS OPPONENT DOWN AND OPPONENT POSTS HIS LEG TO DEFEND

The attacker attempts to break his opponent down with the Both Arms Breakdown but the defender shoots his right leg to his right, posting it on the mat and preventing the attacker from turning the defender over.

The attacker quickly moves his left knee directly by the defender's left shoulder. As he does this, the attacker moves his right leg over the defender's body as shown.

The attacker jams his right foot and lower leg in the defender's right hip and upper leg. The attacker's left knee is still placed on the mat at the defender's left shoulder area. The attacker uses his arms and hands to grab and trap the defender's right arm.

The attacker leans and rolls to his left rear corner and onto his left buttocks as he uses his right leg and foot to lift the defender's right upper leg. As he does this, the attacker jams his left knee in hard against the defender's left shoulder. Doing this forces the defender to roll backward to his left shoulder as shown.

This view shows how the attacker uses his right leg and foot to lift the defender's right upper leg.

The attacker continues to roll the defender over backward and onto his left side as shown.

This shows how the attacker uses his left hand to post onto the mat for stability, allowing the attacker more strength and control of the entire movement. Look at how the attacker uses his right foot and leg to sweep or whip the defender's lower body over and his right arm to hook and trap the defender's right arm to the attacker's chest.

The attacker rolls the defender over backward and onto his back. As he does this, the attacker starts to swing his left leg over the defender's head.

The attacker rolls his opponent onto his back and controls him with the leg press. The attacker can now secure Juji Gatame.

## HIP ROLL JUJI GATAME WHEN OPPONENT ATTEMPTS TO BREAK HIS OPPONENT DOWN AND OPPONENT DEFENDS BY POSTING HIS LEG

The top grappler has attacked his opponent with a breakdown, but the defender shoots his right foot and leg out to his side, posting it on the mat to prevent the attacker from turning the defender onto his back. The attacker quickly swings his right leg over the back of the defender as shown.

The attacker places his right leg under the defender's body and across his belt line. As he does this, the attacker uses his left hand to post onto the mat for stability and places the top of his head on the mat by the defender's right shoulder as shown.

The attacker moves his left leg over then under the defender's head. The attacker rolls over his right shoulder and into the direction of the defender's right hip. The attacker is now doing a hip roll Juji Gatame.

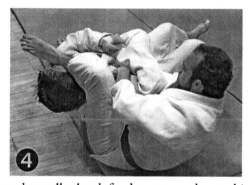

The attacker rolls the defender over and onto his back. As he does this, the attacker uses both of his arms to hook and trap the defender's right arm to the attacker's torso or chest.

The attacker completes the hip roll Juji Gatame and secures the armlock.

## JUJI GATAME LEG PRESS TO SIDE SANKAKU JIME (TRIANGLE CHOKE)

The attacker controls his opponent with the leg press.

The attacker moves his right foot and leg up and under the right upper arm and elbow of the defender.

The attacker slides his right foot and leg between the defender's chest and right arm.

The attacker uses his right leg to control the defender's upper body as he slides or moves his left leg up and over the defender as shown.

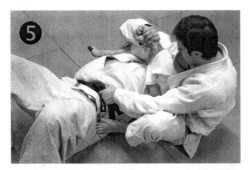

The attacker moves his left foot onto the left hip of the defender as shown. After he does this, the attacker uses his left hand to grab the defender's belt at about the left hip area. Look at how the attacker uses his right arm to trap the defender's left arm to the attacker's chest.

The attacker rolls to his left hip and side as he slides his left foot (that was on the defender's hip) under the defender's left shoulder and upper back. As he does this, the attacker slides his right foot and leg deep under the defender's right armpit area.

This view shows how the attacker slides his feet and legs to control the defender as described in the previous photo.

The attacker forms a triangle with his legs by placing the top of his right foot in the back of his left knee.

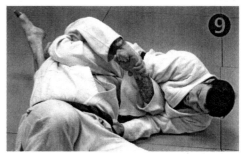

The attacker is lying on his left hip and side as he applies pressure with his legs using the Triangle Choke. The attacker continues to use his right arm to trap the defender's left arm to the attacker's chest.

The attacker continues to apply the Triangle Choke as he arches his back, driving his hips forward, and stretches the defender's left arm out to apply Juji Gatame. If the choke doesn't get him, the armlock will. This is what "double trouble" is all about.

## JUJI GATAME LEG PRESS TO SANKAKU JIME (TRIANGLE CHOKE)

The attacker controls his opponent with the leg press.

The attacker slides his left foot and leg up and then between the defender's chest and right arm.

This shows another view of how the attacker moves his left foot and leg through and between the defender's chest and right arm.

The attacker places the top of his left foot behind his right knee forming a triangle with his legs. As he does this, the attacker rolls back onto his left buttocks to apply pressure with the leg triangle.

This top view shows how the attacker uses his leg triangle as he rolls back onto his left buttocks, applying the choke.

To apply more pressure on the Triangle Choke, the attacker can roll further back and use the strength of his legs to apply pressure.

To make sure he gets the tap out, the attacker also applies Juji Gatame, getting the win by "double trouble."

## JUJI GATAME LEG PRESS TO LEG CHOKE AND ON TO JUJI GATAME

The top grappler controls his opponent with the leg press and slides his right foot and leg under the defender's right arm as shown. Look at how the attacker has moved his left leg so that it is placed under the defender's head (much like a pillow).

The attacker (on top) drives his right foot and leg through and across the top of the defender's chest as shown. The attacker uses his right hand and arm to hook and trap the defender's right arm.

The attacker uses his right hand to reach under the defender's head and grab his right ankle as shown.

The attacker slides his right hand under the defender's head and grabs his own left forearm. As he does this, the attacker uses his left hand to grab and pull his right ankle tight. This creates a strong choke.

If, for some reason, the defender does not tap out, the attacker continues to use his right arm to trap the defender's right arm and starts to move his left hand and arm to trap the defender's right arm as well.

The attacker continues to keep his legs hooked together as he starts to lever the defender's right arm out straight.

The attacker pulls the defender's arm out straight and rolls back.

The attacker rolls back, straightening the defender's right arm and securing the Juji Gatame.

## JUJI GATAME LEG PRESS TO REVERSE SANKAKU JIME (TRIANGLE CHOKE)

The attacker controls his opponent with the leg press. The attacker tries to lever the defender's left arm loose, but is unable to stretch it.

The attacker moves his right foot and leg up to start to slide it under the defender's right arm.

The attacker slides his right foot and leg over the defender's right shoulder and under his right arm as shown.

The attacker sits up higher and rolls to his right hip, using his right hand, which is posted on the mat for stability, to push him up.

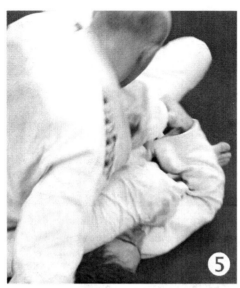

This shows how the attacker drives his right foot and leg in deep over the defender's right shoulder and under his right arm.

The attacker pops up off the mat so that his right hip does not touch the mat.

The attacker continues to drive his right foot through as he leans forward as shown.

The attacker places the top of his right foot on the back of his left knee to form a triangle with his legs.

The attacker applies pressure with his legs as he moves to his left, using his right hand to push off of the mat to help elevate his body, adding to the pressure of the Triangle Choke.

## JUJI GATAME LEG PRESS TO A NOOSE CHOKE

The attacker (on top) controls his opponent with the leg press. For some reason, he is unable to lever the defender's right arm straight. The attacker slides his right arm under the defender's right arm. The attacker uses his right hand to grab the top of his left forearm. As he does this, the attacker uses his left hand to grab the defender's left forearm or wrist.

The attacker withdraws his left leg so that it is now under the head of the defender.

The attacker releases his grip with his left hand on his opponent's left wrist and slides his left forearm and arm under the defender's head, moving his right forearm directly onto the trachea of the defender's throat. Look at how the attacker's hand is palm up.

This shows another application of this choke where the attacker's bottom (anchor) hand is facing palm down and grabbing the defender's left wrist.

## AROUND THE WORLD: JUJI GATAME FROM ONE SIDE TO JUJI GATAME ON THE OTHER SIDE

The defender (on bottom) starts his escape by shrimping into the top grappler and stealing his right shoulder and arm back from the attacker's attempt to lever his arm from the leg press.

The attacker uses his left hand and arm to hook the defender's right arm as the defender turns into the attacker in his effort to escape the initial Juji Gatame.

The attacker switches hands and uses his right hand to grab the defender's left upper arm and shoulder as the attacker uses his left hand to post onto the mat for stability. The attacker starts to push off the mat with his left hand

The attacker quickly swings his right leg over and forward as he pushes off of the mat as shown. Look at how the attacker turns to his left as he uses his right arm to trap the defender's left arm.

The attacker moves around so that he has spun around to the opposite side from his initial position.

The attacker continues to spin around and starts to swing his right leg around as he uses his right arm to further trap the defender's left arm tighter.

The attacker swings his right leg over his opponent's head so that he is now on the opposite side from where he started. This spinning action from one side to the other creates a lot of momentum into the action of the Juji Gatame attack.

The attacker rolls back to apply his Juji Gatame.

## HIP ROLL JUJI GATAME WHEN DEFENDER ROLLS AWAY TO ESCAPE

The bottom grappler turns away to escape the top grappler's Juji Gatame, or may have been taken to the mat and managed to turn away and pull his right arm free from the attacker's grasp.

The attacker crouches low as he uses his left foot and leg to step over the defender's head and uses his right shin to jam in the defender's right side. The attacker uses both hands and arms to hook and trap the defender's right arm.

The attacker places his left hand on the mat for stability as he starts to roll over his right shoulder in the direction of his opponent's hip. The attacker keeps his right shin jammed on his opponent's back and right side.

The attacker continues his shoulder roll and forces the defender to roll over as well.

The attacker completes his shoulder roll and secures his Juji Gatame.

## AROUND THE WORLD: JUJI GATAME FROM ONE SIDE TO JUJI GATAME FROM THE OTHER SIDE WITH LEG SCISSORS CONTROL OF OPPONENT'S HEAD

The defender shrimps into the attacker (on top) in an effort to escape from Juji Gatame.

The attacker uses both arms to hook the defender's left arm as shown. Doing this stabilizes and controls the situation and prevents the defender from shrimping in any more.

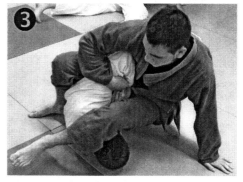

The attacker places his left hand on the mat for stability as he pushes up and off the mat.

The attacker places the top of his left foot on the back of the defender's head. The attacker moves his right knee over his opponent and places it on the mat as shown.

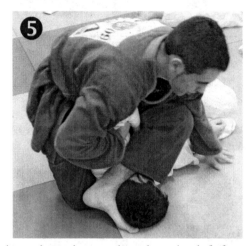

This shows how the attacker places his left foot on the back of his opponent's head for control. This isolates the defender's head and prevents him from turning in or away to escape.

The attacker swings his right foot and leg over his opponent's head and starts to roll onto his back.

As he rolls back, the attacker uses his legs to trap his opponent's head as shown.

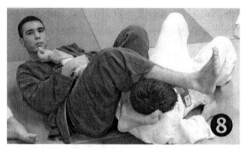

The attacker levers his opponent's left arm out straight as he controls the defender's head with his leg scissors.

## SERIOUS DOUBLE TROUBLE FOR THE DEFENDER: ROLLING KATA HA JIME (SINGLE WING CHOKE) TO JUJI GATAME

When World Sambo Champion Becky Scott competed in judo, she used this with great success. The attacker approaches his opponent from the right side. The attacker uses his left foot and leg to step over his opponent as the attacker uses his left hand and arm to hook the inside of the defender's left arm as shown. As he does this, the attacker uses his right hand to grab the left lapel of the defender to initiate a lapel choke.

The attacker rolls over his opponent as shown, and as he does, the attacker places the back of his left hand on the back of the defender's head and neck. The rolling action of the attacker tightens the lapel choke on the defender.

The attacker rolls over the defender as shown here.

The attacker rolls over his opponent and rolls the defender over as well. The Kata Ha Jime (Single Wing Choke) is in effect.

The attacker makes sure to continue to roll so that he ends the position by sitting in his buttocks as shown here. The choke is a powerful one, but if for some reason it does not work, the attacker is in good position to apply Juji Gatame.

If the choke is not effective (it usually is, but for some reason, it may not work), the attacker kicks his right leg over the defender's head, pinning it to the mat. The attacker controls his opponent with the leg press as shown. By initially winging the defender's left arm, the attacker is in excellent position to secure the Juji Gatame.

The attacker traps the defender's left arm with both of his arms as shown.

The attacker rolls back and secures Juji Gatame.

### TECHNICAL TIP

**The old saying "one thing leads to another" is certainly true in grappling or fighting sports. One thing really does lead to another such as a choke to an armlock, a pin to an armlock, a leglock to an armlock (or the reverse) or an armlock to an armlock, especially if the attacker controls the position.**

## SINGLE WING CHOKE FROM BEHIND OPPONENT IN RODEO RIDE TO JUJI GATAME

Sometimes, the attacker has established a rodeo ride and is working to strangle his opponent with Kata Ha Jime (Single Wing Choke) as shown. The attacker is making a real attempt to choke his opponent but the opponent offers effective resistance and starts to escape from the choke.

The attacker realizes that he is losing control of the choke, so he rolls to his left side and mostly onto his left hip, making sure to use his left hand to continue to control the defender's left shoulder and arm. As he does this, the attacker starts to swing his right leg up and over his opponent's right shoulder and head.

The attacker swings his right leg over his opponent's head. Look at how the attacker uses both arms to hook and trap the defender's left arm while rolling further over onto his left hip (making sure to stay off of his back; the attacker does not want to be flat on his back).

The attacker levers the defender's left arm out straight and secures his Juji Gatame.

## HIP ROLL JUJI GATAME TO HEAD ROLL JUJI GATAME

The attacker is on top and applying the hip roll Juji Gatame. Another situation is that the attacker, on top, is attempting to secure a belly-down Juji Gatame and wants to hook his left leg under the defender's head for control.

The bottom grappler uses his left hand to grab the attacker's left ankle or lower leg and pushes it out from under his head.

The attacker immediately places his left shin and foot on the back of his opponent's head and pushes down with his left leg on the defender's head as shown.

The attacker can now apply the head roll Juji Gatame.

The attacker rolls his opponent over his head and onto his back as shown.

As he finishes the head roll Juji Gatame, the attacker secures the armlock.

**IMPORTANT:** This combination may seem obvious, but it's important to have the wherewithal and ability to think to do it when the opportunity presents itself.

## HEAD ROLL JUJI GATAME TO HIP ROLL JUJI GATAME WHEN DEFENDER TRIES TO BACK OUT AND AWAY

The attacker is attempting to roll his opponent with the head roll Juji Gatame, but the defender moves away by backing away and to the direction of his lower body.

By backing away, the defender inadvertently often raises his body and head off the mat (even slightly) enough for the attacker to quickly slide his right leg under the head of the defender as shown.

The attacker now has enough room to hook his left leg under (or on) the defender's head and is now able to do the hip roll Juji Gatame by rolling over his left shoulder.

## HIP ROLL JUJI GATAME TO KICK OVER BENT ARMLOCK (UDE GARAMI OR OMO PLATA)

The attacker sets his opponent up by driving his right leg under the defender's right side as shown.

The attacker continues by extending himself over his opponent and setting him up for a hip roll Juji Gatame.

The attacker uses his right arm to trap the defender's right arm as the attacker jams his left leg under the defender's head as shown.

The defender backs out and away enough to disrupt the attack. The attacker immediately rolls to his right side.

The attacker sits through on his buttocks and as he does, he starts to use both hands to scoop and trap the defender's right arm. The attacker slides his right leg out from under the defender. The attacker's left leg is hooked over the defender's right shoulder and upper arm.

The attacker continues to sit through, pushing up off the mat with his left arm.

The attacker sits up onto his buttocks and uses his left leg to hook over the defender's right shoulder and upper arm. The attacker is spinning on his buttocks and to his left (toward his opponent). Look at how the attacker has trapped the defender's right arm between his legs.

The attacker continues to spin to his left and uses his left leg to trap the defender's right shoulder and upper arm. To apply pressure, the attacker uses his left leg and knee to push down on the defender's right shoulder and upper arm.

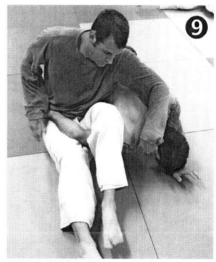

The attacker continues to spin to his left and doing this moves his legs to the right. This traps and bends the defender's right arm between the attacker's legs. The attacker uses his left leg to drive down on the defender's right upper arm and shoulder. There is a lot of pressure on the defender's right shoulder and arm at this point.

The attacker drives his left leg downward, putting a lot of pressure on the defender's left shoulder and bent arm.

## DOUBLE TROUBLE FROM THE BOTTOM: SANKAKU JIME (TRIANGLE CHOKE) APPLIED WITH JUJI GATAME

The attacker (on bottom) initiates Sankaku Jime (Triangle Choke) from this position.

The attacker starts to form a triangle with his legs by placing his right leg over his opponent's left shoulder. The attacker may use his left hand to grab his right ankle to help form the triangle.

The attacker swings his left leg up and over the top of his left foot to form the triangle.

The attacker, to get a strong angle to apply the choke, shrimps to his right and uses his right hand to grab the defender's left leg. Look at how the attacker uses his left hand to trap the defender's right arm.

This shows the sideways angle that the attacker has as he applies the Triangle Choke. This angle helps in providing a tight triangle. Look at how the attacker uses his right hand and arm to hook under the defender's left leg just above his knee. The attacker uses his left hand and arm to trap the defender's right arm to the attacker's torso.

Even though the choke is in effect, the attacker may choose to make sure of the tap out by using his left hand to lift up on the defender's left leg. The attacker uses his legs to drive the defender onto his right side.

The attacker rolls his opponent onto the defender's right side. As he does this, the attacker uses his hands and arms to trap the defender's right arm and levers it straight. The attacker continues to apply pressure with the Triangle Choke.

This shows how the attacker stretches his opponent's arm with Juji Gatame from the side as he applies the Triangle Choke. This is a classic "double trouble" situation that is hard to escape for the defender.

## SANKAKU JIME (TRIANGLE CHOKE) FROM THE GUARD INTO SPINNING JUJI GATAME

Sometimes, a Triangle Choke from the bottom doesn't work, so the attacker can quickly switch to a spinning Juji Gatame.

The bottom grappler attempts a Triangle Choke from this position, but the top grappler jams the bottom man's legs wide apart, stopping the attack.

The attacker (on bottom) quickly spins to his left and slides his left leg over the right shoulder of his opponent. As he does this, the attacker uses his right arm to start to trap the defender's left arm.

The attacker continues to spin to his left and swings his right leg up and over the defender's head as shown.

The bottom grappler continues to spin and starts to roll the defender over as shown.

The attacker continues with his spinning Juji Gatame, rolling the defender over and onto his back.

The attacker controls his opponent with the leg press and levers the defender's right arm straight.

The attacker rolls back and applies Juji Gatame.

## DOUBLE TROUBLE FROM THE BACK: SANKAKU JIME (TRIANGLE CHOKE) COMBINED WITH ARCHING JUJI GATAME

The attacker (on bottom) starts to form a Triangle Choke from this position.

The attacker sinks the triangle in tight.

The defender manages to pull back and loosen the effect of the Triangle Choke.

The attacker scoots his buttocks in close to the defender as he uses his left hand to trap the defender's right arm to the defender's chest.

The attacker quickly grabs with his left hand onto the defender's forearm, stretching the arm out straight. As he does this, the attacker arches his back and drives his hips upward. This pulling action with the arms and arching action of the hips created pressure on the defender's right elbow, getting the tap out.

## TOP POSITION (MOUNT OR VERTICAL PIN) TO DOUBLE TROUBLE: SANKAKU JIME (TRIANGLE CHOKE) AND JUJI GATAME

The top grappler controls his opponent with a Mount or Vertical Pin. Look at how the attacker's right knee is pinning the defender's left upper arm.

The attacker (on top) slides his right foot and leg over the defender's left shoulder and under the defender's head. As he does this, the attacker uses his left hand to grab behind the defender's head and pulls up on the defender's head. The attacker uses his left hand and arm to hook and trap the defender's right arm as shown.

The attacker uses his left hand to grab his right ankle (that is placed under the defender's head). As he does this, the attacker rolls backward onto his right hip, forcing the defender to be pulled up as well.

The attacker forms a leg triangle by placing his right foot on the inside of his left knee as shown. Look at how the attacker has also trapped the defender's right arm in the triangle.

The attacker uses his hands and arms to pull the defender's right arm and extend it so that it is straight. As he does this, the attacker applies pressure with the Triangle Choke, putting the defender in "double trouble" with the Triangle Choke and Juji Gatame from this position.

## DOUBLE TROUBLE ROLL FROM THE TOP TO SANKAKU JIME (TRIANGLE CHOKE) AND JUJI GATAME

The top grappler controls his opponent with a Mount or Vertical Pin as shown.

The attacker (on top) moves his right leg directly to the side, posting it on the mat as shown.

The attacker slides his right leg up and over the defender's left arm and shoulder, moving his right foot under the defender's head as shown.

The attacker places his right foot under the defender's head and uses his left hand and arm to trap the defender's right arm as the attacker uses his right hand to grab and hook the defender's head. The attacker uses his right hand to pull up on the defender's head.

The attacker uses his left hand to grab his right ankle, trapping the defender's head as shown. The attacker's left forearm is on the right side of the defender's neck and the attacker's right thigh is on the left side of the defender's neck. By pulling up with his left hand on his right ankle, the attacker creates a Leg Choke and may get the tap out at this point.

If the defender does not tap out, the attacker rolls to his right front corner, continuing to control the defender's head with this Leg Choke. As he rolls to his right, the attacker extends his left leg and starts to slide his right foot under the left knee of the attacker.

As he rolls to his right, the attacker forms a triangle with his legs as shown.

The attacker continues to roll, using his left arm to trap the defender's right arm. Look at how the attacker has a strong triangle with his legs as he rolls.

The attacker completes his roll, and as he does, uses his hands and arms to pull and extend the defender's right arm. The attacker continues to apply pressure with his leg triangle putting the defender in "double trouble" with a Juji Gatame and Triangle Choke from this bottom position.

## SPINNING JUJI GATAME, OPPONENT DEFENDS AND ATTACKER USES SANKAKU JIME (TRIANGLE CHOKE)

The attacker (on bottom) attempts a spinning Juji Gatame with the attacker using his left arm to trap the defender's left arm as shown.

The defender moves to his left, pulling his left arm loose and free, escaping the armlock.

The attacker stops spinning to his left.

By stopping his spin to his left, the attacker lures the defender back in between the attacker's leg and into his guard as shown. The attacker starts to move his right leg up and over the top grappler's left shoulder.

The attacker positions his legs so that he works a Sankaku Jime (Triangle Choke) from the bottom as shown.

To add pressure to the choke, the attacker spins to his right so that he is sideways relative to the defender's position.

## SPINNING JUJI GATAME TO KICK OVER UDE GARAMI (ARM ENTANGLEMENT OR OMO PLATA)

The attacker attempts a spinning Juji Gatame and uses his right hand and arm to trap the defender's left arm.

The defender pulls his left arm away and free as the attacker does the spinning Juji Gatame.

The defender's left arm is completely pulled free and out of trouble at this point.

The attacker continues to spin to his left and swings his left leg over the defender's right upper arm and shoulder. Look at how the attacker uses his left leg to hook and control the defender's head, driving it downward to the mat.

The attacker swings his left leg over the defender's upper right arm at about the shoulder area as shown. The attacker continues to spin and spins up to his buttocks.

The attacker spins up to his buttocks as he drives his left foot and leg over the defender's right shoulder and upper arm. The attacker moves into the position in this photo. As he does this, the attacker uses his right hand to grab the defender's right wrist.

This view shows how the attacker uses his right hand to grab the defender's right wrist. As he does this, the attacker presses his left knee and leg downward, pinning the defender's right shoulder onto the mat as shown. The attacker uses his left hand to grab onto the defender's body for stability. The attacker generates power form his hips as he drives forward.

This shows the leg position of the attacker as he dos the Kick-Over Ude Garami (Bent Armlock or Omo Plata).

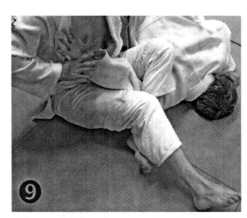

The attacker can also form a triangle with his legs to create pressure on the defender's right upper arm and shoulder.

## SPINNING JUJI GATAME, OPPONENT PULLS ARM FREE AND ATTACKER USES UDE GARAMI (ARM ENTANGLEMENT OR BENT ARMLOCK)

The attacker (bottom) attempts a spinning Juji Gatame, trying to use his left arm to trap the defender's left arm.

As the attacker does spinning Juji Gatame, the defender moves back and pulls his left arm away and free.

The attacker immediately slides his left hand and arm under the defender's left arm and uses his right hand and arm to pull the defender's left arm down to the attacker's chest. Look at how the attacker is positioned sideways relative to the defender.

The attacker moves his right hand and arm over the defender's right upper arm, using his right hand to hook the inside of the defender's right elbow. As he does this, the attacker uses his right hand to grab and manipulate the defender's right wrist and lower arm upward.

The attacker uses his right hand to grab his left wrist as the attacker uses his left hand to continue to push upward, bending the defender's arm. Look at how the attacker is forming a "figure 4" or Bent Armlock on the defender's right arm and using both of his feet to push downward on the defender. Specifically, look at how the attacker uses his right leg to push down on the defender's head, controlling it and pushing it downward to the mat.

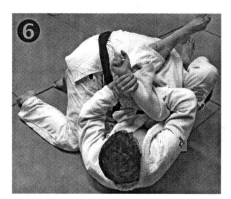

The attacker applies upward pressure with his hands as he uses his right elbow to hug the defender's right elbow, pulling the elbow low to the attacker's chest. The attacker cranks the defender's right hand upward and hugs the defender's right elbow downward, causing a lot of pain in the defender's right elbow and shoulder.

## SPINNING JUJI GATAME, OPPONENT PULLS HIS ARM FREE AND ATTACKER USES UDE GATAME (STRAIGHT ARMLOCK)

The attacker (bottom) starts to use spinning Juji Gatame.

As the attacker shrimps and spins to his left, he uses his right hand and arm to trap his opponent's left arm.

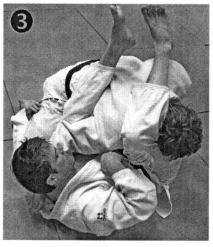

The defender pulls his left arm free, escaping the Juji Gatame attack. Often, the defender will have his right arm positioned across the attacker's chest and upper body. The defender may be thinking of using this arm to control the attacker (to set up a pin or side position).

The attacker quickly uses both hands and arms to attack the defender's right arm. The attacker starts to grasp his hands together at the defender's right elbow in a square grip.

The attacker grasps his hands together in a square grip making sure that the attacker's left forearm is placed on the back of the defender's extended right elbow. The attacker now has a firm Ude Gatame (Straight Armlock) applied.

This shows how the attacker uses both his hands and arms to trap and apply pressure on the defender's extended and straightened right arm. To add more pressure, the attacker can slide or drag his left forearm upward toward the attacker's head. Doing this creates more pain in the defender's extended right arm.

## BENT ARMLOCK FROM THE TOP TO JUJI GATAME

The attacker has taken his opponent to the mat or used a breakdown to set the opponent up so that the defender is on his right side as shown. The attacker is kneeling and actually sitting on the defender's head, using both knees to pinch the defender's head, trapping and isolating it. The attacker starts to apply Ude Garami (Bent Armlock).

The attacker secures and applies the Bent Armlock on the defender's left arm as shown.

Sometimes, the defender is strong enough to resist and pull his left arm in to ease the pressure from the Bent Armlock. In some cases, the defender will also turn to his right side in an attempt to escape.

If the Bent Armlock is not successful and the defender manages to escape and roll onto his right side (in this photo), the attacker quickly comes up from his knees to a squat and moves his right leg over the defender's head. Look at how the attacker is controlling the defender with a shoulder sit position. The attacker uses both hands and arms to hook and trap the defender's left arm to the attacker's chest.

The attacker rolls back, trapping and levering his opponent's left arm.

The attacker rolls back and applies Juji Gatame.

## DEFENDER ESCAPES FROM UDE GARAMI (BENT ARMLOCK) AND ATTACKER USES JUJI GATAME

The attacker has his opponent in an Ude Garami (Bent Armlock or Arm Entanglement). The attacker is applying the armlock from the defender's left side and on the defender's left arm as shown.

The defender slides his left arm under the attacker's right armpit and grabs his right forearm in an effort to escape from the Bent Armlock.

The attacker uses his right hand and arm to release his grip of the defender's right wrist and hook the defender's left upper arm as shown. The attacker rises up off of his opponent as he uses his left arm to hook and trap the defender's left arm more firmly.

The attacker continues his attack by using his right arm to hook and trap the defender's left arm as shown. As he does this, the attacker raises his body up higher, giving him more room to move into Juji Gatame.

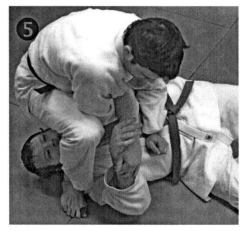

The attacker moves up so that he is now squatting. The attacker has his left shin jammed in the defender's left side and back area. The attacker moves his right foot and leg over the defender's head as shown.

The attacker is now controlling his opponent with a shoulder sit position. The attacker uses both hands to hook and trap the defender's left arm to the attacker's chest as shown.

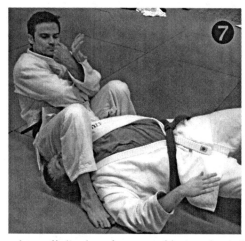

The attacker rolls back and traps and levers the defender's left arm loose, extending it as shown.

The attacker rolls back and secures Juji Gatame.

## ATTACKER JUMPS INTO UDE GATAME (STRAIGHT ARMLOCK) FROM HIS KNEES AND SWITCHES TO JUJI GATAME

The attacker is on his knee with his opponent standing over him.

The attacker swings his right foot upward, throwing his body into a spinning Juji Gatame attacker.

The attacker spins under his opponent in an attempt to secure Juji Gatame on the defender's right arm.

The defender pulls his right arm loose, but the attacker quickly switches to Ude Gatame (Straight Armlock) on the defender's left arm as shown.

The attacker continues to spin and rolls the defender onto his left side as shown. The attacker continues to use the Straight Armlock to get the tap out.

The attacker uses Ude Gatame (Straight Armlock) on his opponent's left arm. In this photo, the attacker is successful and will get the submission. Often, as shown here, the defender will have both of his arms compromised and extended as shown. Look at how the defender's right arm is trapped as well.

The defender may offer a good defense and pull his left arm back and out of the Straight Armlock. As he does this, the attacker quickly uses both of his hands to grab and slide onto the defender's extended right arm, securing a tight Juji Gatame. **IMPORTANT:** If the first attack (Ude Gatame) doesn't work, the attacker can immediately switch to Juji Gatame.

### ■ TECHNICAL TIP ■

**Always look for a way to win. Keep your wits about you and if an opportunity presents itself, take it to beat your opponent. Don't have blinders on or tunnel vision. If you need to make an adjustment to get better control of your opponent, make it and do what is necessary to win.**

## SPINNING JUJI GATAME, DEFENDER PULLS HIS ARM FREE AND ATTACKER USES A STRAIGHT LEGLOCK

For those who use leglocks or lower body submission techniques, this is a good example of how to use a leglock in combination with a Juji Gatame attempt.

The attacker (on bottom) sets his opponent up to start his spinning Juji Gatame.

The attacker spins to his left but his opponent offers a good defense and starts to move away as he pulls his left arm free from the attacker's grasp.

The defender pulls his left arm far enough away that the attacker loses control of it. The defender stands in an effort to pull the attacker up and off the mat.

The attacker continues to spin to his left and uses his left hand to reach and hook the defender's right ankle or lower leg as shown.

The attacker uses his left hand to firmly grab his opponent's right ankle. As he does this, the attacker starts to move his left foot and leg down, placing his left knee on the inside of his opponent's right upper leg as shown. Look at how the attacker uses his left foot to anchor and control the defender's right hip.

The attacker uses his left hand, which is grabbing his opponent's right ankle, to pull himself further to his left so that the attacker is sideways under his opponent as shown. At this point, the attacker starts to swing his right foot and leg over his opponent's head and upper body.

The attacker rolls onto his left side and shoulder as shown and uses both hands to hook and grab onto the defender's right lower leg.

The attacker continues to roll to his left side and shoulder as he "laces" his legs around his opponent's right leg as shown. Look at how the attacker places his right foot and leg on his opponent's right buttocks and upper leg area as the attacker uses his left foot and leg that is jammed in the defender's right hip to trap and "lace" the defender's right leg. The attacker's left knee is placed on the defender's right knee area (this is important). The attacker uses both hands to firmly hug the defender's right lower leg and ankle to the attacker's left shoulder and chest area.

The attacker has laced his opponent's right leg completely with the attacker's left knee and leg blocking the defender's right knee. The attacker arches his back and drives his hips into the defender's right leg as the attacker uses his hands and arms to hug and trap the defender's lower right leg. This action straightens the defender's right leg, "barring" it at the knee. Think of this leglock as the leg version of Juji Gatame.

As mentioned at the first of this chapter, there are many combinations using Juji Gatame. The combinations presented here were selected because they all work, but keep in mind that there are a lot of other combinations that also work so always be on the lookout for new ways to use Juji Gatame in combination with other techniques. As with every other technique seen in this book, take these skills and mold them so they work for you. Be creative and always be open to finding new ways to combines skills to beat your opponents, but always make sure to control the position so you can get the submission on your opponent.

Let's turn our attention to transitions where standing attacks are linked to ground attacks in the next chapter.

# TRANSITIONS TO JUJI GATAME FROM THROWS AND TAKEDOWNS

## "WHEN I WAS COMPETING, MY BIG GOAL WAS TO GET MY OPPONENT ON THE MAT, STRETCH HER ARM AND MAKE HER GIVE UP." ANNMARIA (BURNS) DEMARS, WORLD JUDO CHAMPION

## TRANSITIONS: THE VITAL LINK FROM STANDING TO THE GROUND

A fighter or grappler in any combat sport needs a balanced approach to standing and to the ground. Well-rounded fighters win fights and matches. While every successful athlete has a personal arsenal of skills that he or she does with a high level of skill, that same successful athlete is also well rounded. No one can be a master of every technique or of every situation, but we all can develop the skills necessary to move from one position to another with finesse and skill.

The ability to move from a standing attack to a ground attack is very much part of being a well-rounded grappler. While the rules of the various combat sports may differ in what is allowed and what is not allowed (example: in the sport of judo, the attacker must attempt to throw his opponent, while in many forms of submission grappling, the rules aren't so restrictive), the basic skill of following an opponent to the mat to secure Juji Gatame is always a good idea.

This is what this chapter is all about: effectively following through from a throw or takedown to Juji Gatame.

## CLOSE AND CONTROL THE SPACE

When following through from a throw, takedown (or any move that gets an opponent to the ground or mat), the attacker must close the space between his body and his opponent's body immediately. The attacker must get as close as possible as quickly as possible in order to secure the Juji Gatame (or any submission technique). This shows how the attacker has immediately followed through from this throwing technique and is starting to gain more control with a shoulder sit. This effectively closes the space between the attacker and the defender. By closing this space, the attacker also controls the space, which in turn controls the movement of his opponent more effectively.

## CONTROL THE POSITION, THEN GET THE SUBMISSION

By immediately closing the space between his body and his opponent's body, the attacker is better able to control the position that both the defender is in as well as the position that the attacker is in. By controlling the position, the attacker is better able to apply the finishing

submission technique. The attacker continues his follow through from his throwing technique to a shoulder sit position in addition to trapping the defender's arm to the attacker's chest. The attacker is now in great position to roll back and secure his Juji Gatame.

### ■ TECHNICAL TIP ■

**When following through from a standing attack to groundfighting, make the transition as fluid and smooth as possible. It takes a lot of practice to become fluid from standing to the ground, but it's worth the effort. One drill that is helpful is the "Spin and Stretch" drill presented earlier in this book in the chapter on exercises and drills.**

## THE CONCEPT OF "KIME"

Many years ago, the Japanese invented the concept of "kime" or (loosely translated) the concept of finishing an opponent effectively. This ties in directly to the previous concepts of the attacker closing and controlling the space and immediately controlling the position of his opponent after throwing or taking him to the ground.

The attacker throws his opponent to the mat (in this case, the attacker uses Tai Otoshi, the Body Drop Throw).

### ■ TECHNICAL TIP ■

**A major aspect of kime (finishing the opponent from a throw) is to make sure that the opponent lands hard. Think of a throw as a submission technique. Don't merely try to take an opponent down; throw him hard onto the mat or ground. As my good friend Fritz Goss said, "Throw him so hard, his teeth rattle." Odds are quite good that if his teeth rattle, everything else he has will be rattled as well, which makes it easier to control him on the ground and secure Juji Gatame.**

The attacker effectively finishes the throw by following through, making sure that the defender lands as hard as the attacker wants as well as where the attacker wants (in this case, the attacker wants his opponent to land primarily on his back and back/side in order to follow through with Juji Gatame).

## THE DIFFERENCE BETWEEN AND THROW AND A TAKEDOWN

Don't confuse a throw and a takedown. They have different purposes. Sure, both a throw and a takedown get an opponent from his feet (in a standing position) down to the ground or mat. But a throw can actually end a fight. If you've been around long enough, you might have seen someone knocked out cold from a hard throw in a judo or sambo match, or even in a MMA fight. There is no doubt that a throw can be considered a submission technique. (Remember, the main purpose of a "submission" technique is to make an opponent submit or quit fighting, which ends the fight.) Throwing an opponent hard onto the ground can certainly end a fight. The opponent may be thrown so hard, he gets knocked out or gives up. However, the opponent may not get knocked out or give up, so it is highly recommended to always finish an opponent off with a ground technique (such as Juji Gatame or any effective submission technique or pinning technique). Following through from a hard throw to a pin or submission technique is the "insurance" you may need to win the fight. This, in a nutshell, is the purpose of this chapter. The attacker should transition from standing to the ground, controlling the situation as much as possible in order to force the opponent to surrender (or, if he chooses not to surrender, pay the consequences for not surrendering).

A takedown does exactly that; it takes an opponent to the ground. The purpose of a takedown is to take an opponent to the ground or mat and finish him off with a submission hold or technique, controlling position or pin. A takedown can certainly be performed in such a way that it becomes a hard throwing technique, but a takedown's main purpose is to get an opponent down to the ground or mat in an effort to secure an effective finishing hold or gain a controlling position. I'm not disparaging takedowns in any way. Every grappler, no matter what form of sport combat he or she specializes in, should be adept at both throws and takedowns. But it is important to know the difference between the two because they have different functions.

A good rule of thumb is to always follow through to a submission technique after your throw or takedown.

## TAI OTOSHI (BODY DROP THROW) TO JUJI GATAME

This throw lends itself well to an immediate follow through to Juji Gatame, but most any throwing technique that throws the defender forward and over the attacker's body is good. This photo shows the attacker using Tai Otoshi to throw his opponent.

The attacker throws his opponent.

As the attacker finishes the throw, he makes sure to maintain a good hold onto his opponent, planting him on the mat with control

## ▰▰▰▰ TECHNICAL TIP ▰▰▰▰

**Juji Gatame can be used as a follow-up technique from just about any throw or takedown. In practice at the dojo or gym, experiment with how you can transition from different throws or takedowns into Juji Gatame.**

The attacker immediately places his left shin in the defender's left side and under his left shoulder. The attacker places his right foot and leg over the defender's head as shown. As he does this, the attacker squats low over his opponent, continuing to use his hands and arms to control the defender.

The attacker immediately uses his hands and arms to hook and trap the defender's left arm to the attacker's chest. As he does this, the attacker continues to squat low, staying round and rolls onto his back.

The attacker rolls back and as he does, arches his hips to provide more pressure on his opponent's extended left arm and elbow. This secures the Juji Gatame.

## KNEE DROP SEOI NAGE (SHOULDER THROW) TO JUJI GATAME

Doing a knee drop throw like this offers the attacker a high percentage throwing attack that gets points against his opponent, but just as important, gets his opponent down to the mat for Juji Gatame.

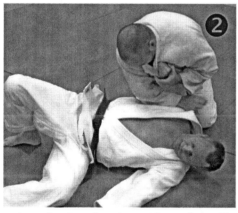

The attacker finishes his knee drop Seoi Nage and quickly uses his right hand to start to trap his opponent's right arm as shown. Look at how the attacker's body is immediately above the defender's right shoulder.

The attacker quickly pops up off of his knees and into a squat position immediately above the defender's

right shoulder. As he does this, the attacker uses both hands and arms to trap the defender's right arm to the attacker's torso.

The attacker quickly swings his left leg over the defender's head, making sure to clamp his knees together, trapping the defender's right arm and shoulder. Look at how the attacker keeps his right shin jammed in the defender's right side at about the ribcage area.

The attacker rolls back and applies Juji Gatame.

## SINGLE LEG TAKEDOWN TO JUJI GATAME

The attacker drives in with a single leg takedown.

As he throws or takes the defender down to the mat, the attacker makes sure to keep his body on the outside of the defender (in this case to the right side of the defender).

The attacker moves to his left and toward the defender's head. As he does, the attacker starts to squat low and uses his left hand to trap the defender's right arm to the attacker's chest.

As he squats low, the attacker jams his right shin in the right side of the defender at about the ribcage area. The attacker moves his left foot and leg over the defender's head. The attacker may have to use his right hand and arm to push the defender's right leg away, preventing the defender from shrimping into the attacker. Look at how the attacker uses his left hand and arm to hook and trap the defender's right arm to the attacker's chest. Look at the angle of the attacker's body relative to the defender. The attacker's body is facing toward the defender's lower body. Doing this allows the attacker to have a strong shoulder sit position over his opponent and enables him to trap the defender's right arm more tightly.

As he uses both hands and arms to trap the defender's right arm tightly to his chest, the attacker shifts his body to his left so that it is now facing sideways relative to the defender. Doing this tightens the attacker's trap on the defender's right arm and makes the entire hold tighter and more secure for the attacker. The attacker is now ready to roll back and lever the attacker's right arm out straight.

The attacker rolls onto his back, levering the defender's right arm straight and secures Juji Gatame.

## SPINNING JUJI GATAME FROM A THWARTED SINGLE LEG TAKEDOWN ATTACK

Not every leg grab, pick or throw will work for the attacker. If this is the case, this variation of spinning Juji Gatame will get an opponent's arm even if he hasn't been taken down first.

The athletes are in a standing position.

The attacker drops and sinks in his leg grab using his right hand to attack his opponent's right leg as shown.

The defender moves his right leg back, escaping the takedown.

The attacker immediately pulls his right arm back in and comes up off of his right knee to a semi-squat position as shown.

The attacker swings and rolls his body to his right (under his opponent) as he moves his right leg up and places his right foot at about the left hip of his opponent. As he does this, the attacker swings in and under his opponent, setting him up for the spinning Juji Gatame.

The attacker swings his left leg up and over the defender's head. As he does this, the attacker uses both of his hands and arms to trap the defender's right arm to the attacker's torso and chest.

The attacker executes a spinning Juji Gatame and rolls the defender over and onto his back as shown.

The attacker controls his opponent with the leg press, trapping the defender's right arm to the attacker's chest.

The attacker rolls back and secures his Juji Gatame.

**▮▮▮▮ TECHNICAL TIP ▮▮▮▮**

In a street fight or self-defense situation, Juji Gatame may not be a good choice as a ground technique. Even though Juji Gatame is a great submission technique in sport fighting, you could be vulnerable lying on your back or side in a street fight. Carefully consider your options and do what is necessary to protect yourself in a self-defense situation.

## SPIN AND STRETCH

This was shown in the chapter on exercises and drills, but is also a useful takedown or throwing technique if the defender is on his knees as shown with the attacker standing.

The attacker uses his right foot and leg to step across the defender's right side. Look at how the attacker places his right heel at on the outside of the defender's right knee. The attacker starts to spin his opponent to his right and to the defender's right side.

The attacker spins his opponent over and onto his back as shown.

As he does this, the attacker moves his right foot and leg in and jams his right shin in the defender's right ribcage area. Look at how the attacker uses his arms to finish his opponent and drive him onto the mat. The attacker uses his right arm to start to trap the defender's right arm.

The attacker immediately controls his opponent with a shoulder sit position as shown, using both hands to trap the defender's right arm to the attacker's body.

The attacker tightens his trap on the defender's right arm as he prepares to roll back. Look at how the attacker controls his opponent by squatting low and almost sitting on the defender's head as the attacker prepares to roll back.

The attacker rolls back, levering the defender's right arm out straight.

The attacker rolls back and secures his Juji Gatame.

## STANDING SPIN TO JUJI GATAME

This looks identical to the Tomoe Nage (Circle Throw) attack to Juji Gatame but it isn't. In this application, the attacker swings his body up and under his opponent and does not attempt to use Tomoe Nage.

Starting Position One: The attacker leads with his left foot as shown, and makes sure that his left foot is placed on the outside of his opponent's right foot.

Starting Position Two: The attacker and defender may be moving about the mat or as shown in this photo, the attacker leads with his left foot and drops back with his right foot to give himself more momentum to swing his right foot up to his opponent's left hip.

The attacker swings his right foot toward the outside of his opponent's left hip as shown. As he does this, the attacker spins off of his left foot. The attacker spins to his right as he extends his right leg as shown.

The attacker spins to his right and under the defender's body as shown.

The attacker continues to spin to his right and under his opponent. Look at how the attacker's head is moving toward his opponent's left leg and side as he spins.

The attacker spins completely under his opponent as shown. Look at how the attacker is sideways to his opponent.

The attacker quickly swings his left leg up and over his opponent's head. As he does this, the attacker uses his left hand and arm to start to trap the defender's right arm to the attacker's chest.

The attacker uses his left leg to hook and control the defender's head as shown. Doing this, along with the spinning action of the attacker, forces the defender to roll forward as shown. The attacker continues to use his left arm to trap the defender's right arm.

The attacker rolls his opponent over the defender's head.

The attacker spins and rolls his opponent over and onto his back. The attacker secures Juji Gatame.

## ATTACKER PULLS OPPONENT TO THE MAT INTO THE GUARD AND INTO SPINNING JUJI GATAME

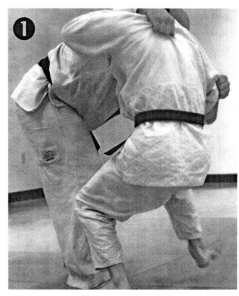

The attacker uses his hands and arms to pull his opponent and as he does this, the attacker swings under his opponent.

The attacker swings under his opponent, pulling the defender down with him as the attacker rolls onto his back.

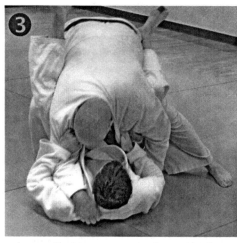

The attacker pulls his opponent down to the mat with him and has the defender between his legs as shown.

Before the defender has time to drop to his knees, the attacker shrimps and spins to his right, swinging his left leg up to start to hook it over the defender's head. Look at how the attacker places his right leg at his opponent's left side as the attacker spins.

The attacker spins in under his opponent and swings his left leg over the defender's head.

The attacker uses his left leg to hook over the defender's head as the attacker spins under him. All the while, the attacker uses both hands to hook and trap the defender's right arm to the attacker's chest.

Getting to the back view, the attacker's spinning action looks like this. Look at how, in the action of his spin, the attacker spins high on his shoulders, allowing him to spin faster and with more control.

**IMPORTANT:** When spinning under an opponent, the attacker does not want much of his back (or any part of his body) touching the mat. The less body contact to the mat, the better the attacker spins under his opponent.

The attacker continues to spin under his opponent and this forces the defender to roll over as shown.

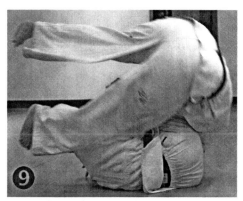

The attacker continues to spin and roll his opponent over.

The attacker has spun under his opponent and rolled the defender over and onto his back. The attacker secures his Juji Gatame.

## SPINNING TOMOE NAGE (CIRCLE THROW) TO JUJI GATAME

This is probably the standard, classic, approach used in judo for using Tomoe Nage (Circle Throw) as the set-up for Juji Gatame. There will be other ways to use Tome Nage to get an opponent to the mat on the following pages, but this is the method that is often used and used with a high ratio of success.

The athletes are standing facing each other.

The attacker places his right foot onto his opponent's left hip. As he does this, the attacker starts to shrimp and turn to his right.

The attacker shrimps and spins to his right and under his opponent as shown. The attacker uses his right foot, which is placed in his opponent's left hip, as the pivot point enabling him to swing under the defender.

The attacker spins under his opponent and makes sure to position his body so that his head is near his opponent's left leg and foot. Look at how the attacker's body is sideways and under his opponent.

The attacker swings his left leg up and over his opponent's head. As he does this, the attacker uses both of his arms to hook and trap the defender's right arm to the attacker's torso.

The attacker continues to spin under his opponent and uses his legs to help roll his opponent over and onto his back as shown.

The attacker applies Juji Gatame immediately.

## 2-ON-1 TOMOE NAGE TO JUJI GATAME

This variation works from the attacker's extreme stance at the defender's right side as shown in this photo. The attacker uses his left hand to grab his opponent's right

lapel (in no gi, the attacker can use his left hand to grab the defender's right arm or head). The attacker uses his left hand to grab low on the right sleeve of the defender. Look at how the attacker leads with his left foot and leg and the attacker is standing about a foot's length from the defender's right foot.

The attacker swings his right leg up and places his right foot on the defender's left hip. The attacker maintains his 2-on-1 grip on the defender's right arm.

The attacker spins to his right and under his opponent using his right foot (placed on the defender's left hip) as the pivot point.

The attacker continues to use his hands to maintain his 2-on-1 grip on the defender's right arm as the attacker spins to his right and under his opponent. Look at the position of the attacker's head close to the defender's left foot and leg.

As he spins under his opponent, the attacker swings his left leg up and over the defender's head.

The spinning action of the attacker and the control he exerts with his legs (look at how the attacker uses his left leg to hook over the defender's head) rolls the defender over. The attacker maintains his 2-on-1 grip onto his opponent's right arm.

The attacker completes his spinning action, rolling his opponent to the mat. The attacker can now secure his Juji Gatame.

# FOOT JAM ON OPPONENT'S HIP TO JUJI GATAME

This is a successful way to get an opponent to the mat and stretch his arm. The attacker (on the left in this photo) is positioned at the right front corner of the defender. The attacker swings his right leg up and places his right foot on the defender's left hip (look at how the attacker's right toes are pointing out and his right heel is pointing in toward the defender's crotch).

The attacker swings under the defender so that the attacker will land on his left hip. The attacker uses his right foot jammed in the defender's left hip as the anchor or pivot point as he swings under the defender. To help pull the defender down, the attacker uses his right hand (grabbing the defender's left lapel) to pull forward and down.

The attacker lands on his left side with his right foot still jammed in the defender's left hip. The attacker's right leg is straight. The attacker pulls the defender forward and down to the mat.

The attacker quickly swings his left leg up and over his opponent's head. The attacker continues to use his left hand and arm to hold and trap the defender's right arm during this entire movement. Doing this extends the defender's right arm. The attacker rolls to his right as he swings his left leg over the defender's head.

The attacker swings his left leg over his opponent's head and uses both hands to grab and trap the defender's extended right arm to the attacker's chest. The attacker rolls over his right hip to his right.

The attacker continues to use both hands to pull hard on the defender's extended (and straight) right arm.

Look at how the attacker has used his legs to control the defender. The attacker can arch his back and drive his hips forward and into the defender's straight right arm and get the tap out at this point.

If for some reason, the defender does not give up, the attacker continues to roll and rolls onto his left hip as shown. The attacker continues to use both his hands and arms to pull on the defender's straight right arm.

The attacker may use his right hand to grab the defender's right pant leg to start the action of rolling the defender over. The attacker sitting onto his left has also created strong momentum to force the defender to roll forward and over his head in a somersault.

The attacker uses his right hand to pull, drag and lift the defender's right pant leg to assist the head roll action.

The attacker has rolled his opponent over and onto his back and secures his Juji Gatame.

## INSIDE THIGH KICK (OR PUSH) TOMOE NAGE TO JUJI GATAME

This is the favored approach to Juji Gatame that some notable women athletes have used through the years, including World Judo Champion AnnMaria (Burns) DeMars and World Sambo Champion Becky Scott. Sandi (Quenelle) Harrelson, who has been a national champion in sambo and judo, was also a specialist in this set-up and demonstrates it here.

The attacker (on the left in this photo) stands with her left foot on the mat to the right of the defender's right foot. The attacker starts to swing her right foot and leg up to her opponent's left leg.

The attacker places her right foot on the inside of the defender's left thigh. Look at how the attacker is positioned in relation to the defender. The attacker uses her right hand to pull forward and down on the defender's left lapel.

The attacker swings down and onto her right hip and as she does this, she jams her right foot hard into the defender's left inner thigh.

The weight of the attacker's body and the action of her pulling with her right hand on the defender's left lapel

pulls the defender forward and down. The attacker uses her right foot to jam the defender's left inner thigh, forcing the defender's left leg to be pushed out (to the defender's left) as shown. The attacker uses her left hand to grab and trap the defender's right arm.

This action forces the defender to fall forward onto his front as shown. The defender's right arm is extended and straight at this point. The attacker immediately swings her left foot and leg over the defender's extended right arm, right shoulder and head.

The attacker hooks her left leg under her opponent's head as shown. As she does this, she arches her back, drives her hips forward and locks the extended and straight right arm of the defender.

This view shows how the attacker applies the belly-down Juji Gatame.

If, for some reason, the defender does not tap out, the attacker rolls backward, and as she does, hooks her left leg around the head of the defender. The attacker continues to uses both hands and arms to pull and trap the defender's extended and straightened arm. The defender might tap out at any point during this roll.

The attacker rolls across her back and hips, using her left leg to hook her opponent's head, forcing him to roll over as well. The attacker applies Juji Gatame from this position.

## LEG JAM (OR BELTLINE) TOMOE NAGE TO JUJI GATAME

The attacker (back to the camera) has a lapel and sleeve grip (in no gi it could be a head and arm tie-up). The attacker sets a fast tempo and moves to his right (and to the defender's left).

As the attacker moves to his right, he plants his left foot in the middle of his opponent's stance as shown. As he does this, the attacker spins to his right and swings his right leg up so that the attacker's right foot is placed on the defender's right hip as shown. The attacker's right leg is bent and his right lower leg is placed across the defender's belt line.

This view shows how the attacker spins to his right and under his opponent, placing his right foot on the opponent's right hip.

The attacker spins under his opponent and lands in this sideways position relative to his opponent. The attacker's right bent leg continues to be jammed across the front of the defender at the defender's belt line. The attacker uses his left hand to pull the defender's right arm down toward the attacker in an effort to trap it.

The attacker quickly swings his left foot and leg over his opponent's head as shown. The attacker uses his left leg to hook over the defender's head, forcing the defender to roll over onto his back.

The attacker rolls his opponent over and secures his Juji Gatame.

## TECHNICAL TIP

**In many cases, how we react to a situation determines success or failure. As the old saying goes; "You don't rise to the occasion, you rise to your level of training." By doing a lot of drill training, especially "situational" drill training where you are work in real-world situations, is essential to success in the fighting sports. However, situational drills are only useful if the people doing them are skilled in solid fundamentals first. In other words, be as skillful as possible in the fundamentals, and then make those fundamentals work for you in a real situation; initially in drill training, then on to free grappling (randori) and then in a real match or fight. World-class skill is simply applying fundamentals to their full potential.**

## SNAP-DOWN AND STEP-OVER TO HIP ROLL JUJI GATAME

Both grapplers are standing but the grappler on the right is bent over.

The attacker uses both of his hands to pull on the defender, and yank or snap the defender forward and down to the mat. A he does this, the attacker, places his left foot and leg on the right side of the defender's head as shown. The attacker spins his right leg over the defender's body as shown.

The attacker swings his right leg over the defender's body and places it over the defender's right arm and shoulder as shown.

The attacker uses his left arm to trap the defender's right arm and the attacker does a right shoulder roll as shown.

The attacker continues with the shoulder roll, forcing the defender to roll over as well.

The attacker completes the hip roll Juji Gatame and rolls the defender over and onto his back.

The attacker finishes the Juji Gatame.

## SNAP-DOWN TO HEAD ROLL JUJI GATAME

The grapplers are in a standing position, but the grappler on the right is bent over.

The attacker (on the left) uses his hands to pull his opponent forward and down to the mat. As he does this, the attacker moves to his left and to his opponent's right side.

The attacker swings his left leg over his opponent and gets onto the defender's back.

The attacker quickly uses his left arm to hook and trap the defender's right arm. As he does this, the attacker leans forward and uses his right hand to reach out and post onto the mat for stability.

The attacker moves his left leg across the defender's back. The attacker posts on the top of his head near the defender's right shoulder.

The attacker places his left foot on the back of the defender's head as shown. Look at how the attacker is now posted on the top of his head and sideways to his opponent.

The attacker jams his right foot into the defender's left upper leg and hip area. The attacker drives his left knee down and to his right so that the attacker will land on his right hip, forcing the defender to roll forward. At this point, the attacker uses both arms to hook the defender's right arm to the attacker's chest.

The attacker does a head roll Juji Gatame on the defender, forcing the defender to roll directly over his head as shown.

The attacker finishes the roll and secures his Juji Gatame.

## ▰▰▰▰ TECHNICAL TIP ▰▰▰▰

**Different combat sports have different rules. Make sure you know the rules of the sport you are fighting in to see what is considered "legal" in getting an opponent down to the mat.**

## FLYING JUJI GATAME

"Flying" armlocks are risky. However, they can (and do) work. It takes a lot of practice and steely nerves to attempt "flying" or "jumping" armlocks, but if you are inclined to try them, go for it.

The attacker (left in the photo) is positioned so that this left foot is on the outside and to his left of his opponent's right foot. The attacker's right foot and leg are back (this gives the attacker room to make his attack).

The attacker swings his right leg up with the intent of placing his right knee on his opponent's right hip and ribcage area. The attacker has already started to use his left hand to trap the defender's right arm. The attacker uses his left hand to grab over his opponent's right elbow and onto his upper arm.

The attacker jumps up, jamming the outside of his right knee on the opponent's right hip or ribcage area. As he does this, the attacker starts to spin to his right.

The attacker continues his spin to his right with his right knee jammed in the defender's right side. The attacker swings his left leg up and over his opponent's head.

The attacker swings to his right and under his opponent. As he does this, the attacker places his left leg and foot over his opponent's head.

The attacker continues to spin under his opponent, using his feet and legs to control the defender's roll. The attacker uses his hands and arms to trap the defender's right arm to the attacker's torso.

The attacker spins deeply under his opponent, rolling the defender forward as shown.

**IMPORTANT:** Think of this flying Juji Gatame as the same thing as a spinning Juji Gatame; only when doing the flying version, the attacker starts from a standing position. Technically, the flying Juji Gatame and the spinning Juji Gatame are quite similar.

The attacker continues to roll his opponent over and continues to use his hands and arms to trap his opponent's right arm during the roll.

The flying Juji Gatame is completed with the attacker ready to apply the armlock to finish his opponent.

### TECHNICAL TIP

**Don't underestimate flying or jumping Juji Gatame attacks. Even the most experienced athletes can get caught unaware and be a victim to one of these Juji Gatame variations.**

## JUMPING JUJI GATAME

This differs from the flying Juji Gatame in that the attacker jumps up and onto his opponent so that the attacker's legs are split as he jumps onto the defender. This photo shows the athletes at the starting position. The attacker is on the left in the photo.

The attacker jumps up and onto his opponent and throws his right leg past his opponent's left hip.

After initially jumping up and onto his opponent, the attacker swings his left leg over his opponent's head.

Doing this swings the attacker under his opponent and the momentum of this jumping and swinging movement will force the defender to roll forward.

As the attacker swings under his opponent, he uses his left leg to hook over the defender's head, controlling the rolling action of the opponent. Look at how close the attacker's head is to the defender's left leg and foot ,indicating that the attacker has swung very deep under his opponent, breaking the defender's balance forward.

The attacker continues his attack and rolls the defender over as shown.

The attacker completes his jumping Juji Gatame and works to secure the armlock.

## JUMPING HEAD ROLL JUJI GATAME

The start of this attack is similar to the previous one but the attacker uses the head roll Juji Gatame instead.

The attacker jumps up and onto his opponent, swinging his right leg past his opponent's left hip and side. The attacker quickly bends his left leg so that his left knee swings up and over the defender's right shoulder as shown.

As the attacker jumps onto his opponent, he swings and places his left leg and the top of his left foot on the back of the defender's head.

Look at how the attacker places his left foot and shin on the back of the defender's head as the attacker swings deeply under his opponent. The attacker's head is moving to his right and toward the direction of the defender's left leg.

The attacker swings and spins deeply under his opponent forcing the defender to start to roll forward. Look at how the attacker's left foot is jammed at the back of his opponent's head as the attacker rolls the defender forward.

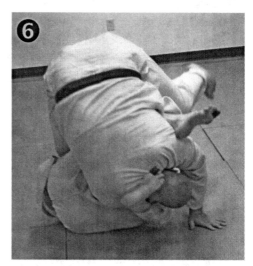

The attackers explosive jump and spinning action, along with his leg control of the defender, forces the defender to roll forward and over his head.

The attacker completes his head roll Juji Gatame and secures the armlock.

## HEAD ROLL JUJI GATAME COUNTER IF OPPONENT GETS YOU ON THE MAT WITH AN ANKLE PICK OR LEG GRAB TAKEDOWN

The hardest part of pulling off a move like this is to keep your composure, realize the situation you are in and have the ability to think to do it. We all are human and after being taken down, we react instinctively; work on this situation in practice so that if it does happen to you in a match or fight, you instinctively react in a way that will benefit you. In this photo, the grappler on his knees uses an ankle pick or leg grab (or any takedown) and the athlete on the right being taken down will be the attacker in this sequence of photos.

The grappler on top moves to the bottom grappler's left side in an effort to get to his side and control him.

The bottom grappler (the attacker) turns onto his left side (toward his opponent). Look at how the attacker uses his right hand to grab his opponent's left arm or

sleeve and how the attacker uses his left hand to grab his opponent's lapel (if in a no gi situation, the attacker will use his left hand to grab and hook his opponent's head). The attacker (on bottom) also shrimps out a bit and away from his opponent. Doing this, the attacker pulls his opponent forward and off balance and in the process of doing this, the bottom grappler gives himself some space between his body and his opponent's body.

The attacker rolls to his left hip and side as he now uses both hands to grab his opponent's left arm as shown. The attacker starts to move his right knee up toward his opponent's back.

The attacker continues to roll to his left side as he moves his right foot and leg up over his opponent's near shoulder (left shoulder in this photo). As he does this, the attacker uses his hands and arms to start to pull on his opponent's left arm in an effort to trap it to the attacker's chest.

The attacker continues to roll to his left as shown and traps his opponent's left arm with his arms.

The attacker continues to roll as shown. Look at how the attacker is using the head roll Juji Gatame with one modification: his left leg is not placed under his opponent's body. It is bent with the attacker's left foot jammed on the defender's left side as shown. This happens because the top grappler may have initially passed by the attacker's legs and the attacker was not able to drive his left leg under his opponent and anchor his foot as is usually done in a head roll Juji Gatame. If the attacker is initially able to slide his left foot under his opponent, it is a good idea to do so, but if not, use this variation.

The attacker continues his head roll Juji Gatame as shown. In this instance, the attacker uses his left hand to grab his opponent's left pant leg to assist in rolling the defender over his head.

The attacker completes his head roll Juji Gatame. You can see how the attacker uses his left hand to grab his opponent's left pant leg to assist in pulling him over.

The attacker completes his head roll Juji Gatame and will immediately secure the armlock.

## SPINNING JUJI GATAME COUNTER IF YOU'VE BEEN THROWN TO THE MAT BY YOUR OPPONENT

This is a last ditch attempt that may come in handy if your opponent has thrown you. In some sports such as judo, the referee may call Ippon and end the match, but if the referee calls a smaller score, you are still in the fight. In other combat sports, a throw doesn't always win the match and this variation of Juji Gatame may be the thing that snatches victory out of the jaws of defeat. I recommend that every grappler, no matter what combat sport he or she engages in, should practice this last-ditch counter Juji Gatame and make it something that you do whenever you get thrown. Just because you have been taken down or thrown does not mean that you are out of the fight. This photo shows how the top grappler has thrown the bottom grappler to the mat.

The bottom grappler (the attacker) immediately curls his body up and jams his right knee and shin in his opponent's torso at about the belt line. As he does this, the attacker slightly rolls to his right hip (the side close to his opponent). The attacker starts to swing his left leg up and over his opponent's head as shown.

The attacker swings his left foot and leg up and over his opponent and hooks his left leg over his opponent's head and neck. As he does this, the attacker uses both arms to hook and trap the opponent's right arm close to the attacker's chest. Look at how the bottom grappler is in good position to perform a spinning Juji Gatame.

The attacker does a spinning Juji Gatame, rolling his opponent over and onto his back as shown.

The attacker finishes the roll, taking his opponent over and onto his back and finishes with the Juji Gatame as shown. Look at how the attacker has kept his right shin jammed in his opponent's right side and how the attacker uses his left leg to control his opponent's head.

Juji Gatame is a good "insurance policy" after throwing or taking your opponent to the mat or ground. Just like a good insurance policy, an effective transition from a throw or takedown to Juji Gatame will pay off when you need it.

For those who have punching or kicking as part of their combat sport, I apologize for not including transitions from these skills to the ground. Hopefully, you will take what has been presented here and apply it to fit your particular needs.

The next chapter examines Juji Gatame from a variety of different finish positions, such as belly-down, with an opponent on one or both knees, and other positions that take place.

# JUJI GATAME FROM BELLY DOWN, ON THE KNEES AND OTHER FINISHING POSITIONS

## "IT DOESN'T MATTER WHERE HE IS. IF YOU WANT HIS ARM BAD ENOUGH, YOU'LL GET IT."
BILL WEST

## AN OPPONENT'S ARM CAN BE STRETCHED BY A JUJI GATAME IN ANY NUMBER OF POSITIONS

An incident that took place years ago at a national judo tournament illustrates what this chapter is about. After tapping out to Bill West (one of our Welcome Mat athletes who was an excellent technician in Juji Gatame) Bill's opponent asked him, "What did you do?" Bill's opponent commented that when Bill was trying to apply his Juji Gatame, the opponent thought he had defended himself sufficiently enough but found himself flat on his front and tapping out. He told Bill, "I relaxed because I thought I could wait until the referee said matte (the referee's command to stop the action) because you were out of position to get the armlock." This brief conversation tells a lot. First, if you are defending against Juji Gatame, never relax and never assume you or your opponent is out of position. Second, if you are the defender, never wait for the mat official to call a halt to the action or expect the referee to get you out of trouble. That's your job, not his. Third, if you're the attacker, do what Bill did; never let go of your opponent's arm and keep rolling him until you get him to tap out and the referee signals for you to stop.

Juji Gatame can be applied from almost any position that is seen in any form of sport (or real) personal combat. Neither the attacker nor defender has to be in the classic "belly up" position when applying Juji Gatame. While the entry into Juji Gatame might come from spinning, back roll, head roll or hip roll application, the end result could have the attacker or defender (or both) end up and finish the armlock in any variety of positions; again proving the versatility of Juji Gatame.

This chapter takes a close look at a variety of ways

that Juji Gatame can be applied when one or both grapplers are lying on the front, side, kneeling, squatting or any position that might take place in a fight or match. Obviously, not every position possible can be presented in one chapter, or even in one book, so use your imagination when practicing Juji Gatame, and remember, never let go of his arm!

## ▌▌▌▌ TECHNICAL TIP ▌▌▌▌

**Never let go of your opponent's arm, stay round and keep rolling and controlling him as much as possible until you force him to tap out to your Juji Gatame. In almost every case of catching an opponent in an odd position, the attacker has followed the cardinal rules of: 1) Never let go of his arm. 2) Keep rolling, stay round and continue to do everything possible to control the action. 3) Don't stop locking his arm until the referee tells you to stop.**

## SOME COMMON FINISH POSITIONS FOR JUJI GATAME

As mentioned previously, not every Juji Gatame is applied with the attacker and defender "belly up" or lying on their backs in what the Japanese call "aomuke" or in the face up position. A lot of effective Juji Gatame attacks end up in a lot of different positions. Some (but certainly not all) finish positions are presented here.

## ATTACKER IS BELLY DOWN

A common finish position is for both the attacker and defender to be "belly down" as shown here.

## ATTACKER IS BELLY DOWN WITH LEG AND FOOT ON THE BACK OF DEFENDER'S HEAD

Another "belly down" position is with the attacker using one foot and leg to drive down on the defender's head as shown here. Doing this, the attacker has another measure of control over his opponent.

## ATTACKER IS ON HIS SIDE AND HIP FACING THE DEFENDER'S LEGS AND LOWER BODY

Another common finish position for Juji Gatame

## ATTACKER IS ON SIDE WITH HIS FOOT AND LEG ON OPPONENT'S HEAD

The attacker is lying on his side and using a foot and leg to control his opponent's head as shown here.

## ATTACKER ON HIS SIDE AND HIP FACING SAME DIRECTION AS DEFENDER

Sometimes, the attacker is lying on his side and facing the same direction as his opponent.

## ATTACKER AND DEFENDER ARE "UPSIDE DOWN"

When the defender mounts a furious and aggressive defense, he may attempt to swing his legs over the attacker as shown here. In other cases, the attacker may secure his Juji Gatame as he rolls his opponent.

## DEFENDER IS ON BOTH KNEES

Sometimes, the attacker can finish his Juji Gatame when the defender is on both knees. In situations like this, the defender may have attempted to stand in an effort to pull the attacker up off the mat or simply may have tried to get on his knees and back away.

## DEFENDER IS ON ONE KNEE

In some instances, the defender may attempt to get onto one knee in an effort to pull the attacker off the mat or to avoid being rolled or turned onto his back.

## DEFENDER ON SIDE OR BUTTOCKS

In some situations, the defender may be caught when positioned on his buttocks or hips as shown here. These situations represent the many varied ways and positions that Juji Gatame can be effectively applied.

## BELLY DOWN JUJI GATAME FROM THE BOTTOM (GUARD) POSITION

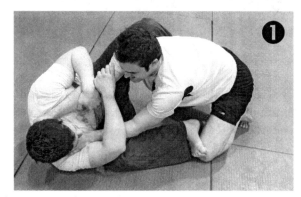

The attacker (bottom) rolls to his right hip and side as he uses both hands to grab his opponent's right arm. The attacker places his right foot on his opponent's left knee (very low to the mat).

---

The attacker pushes with his right foot and leg onto the defender's left knee. Doing this pushes the defender's left knee back. As he does this, the attacker rolls further onto his right side. This stretches the defender as shown.

The attacker quickly swings his left foot and leg over his opponent as shown. All the while, the attacker uses his left arm to trap the defender's right arm to the attacker's chest.

The attacker hooks his left foot and leg over his opponent's head as the attacker uses both hands to firmly trap the defender's right arm to the attacker's chest. The attacker continues to roll over his right side.

The attacker rolls over onto his front, using both hands and arms to pull hard on the defender's extended right arm. As he does this, the attacker arches his back and drives his hips forward onto the defender's straightened right arm to secure Juji Gatame.

## BELLY DOWN JUJI GATAME STARTING FROM TOP RIDE POSITION

The attacker (on top) controls his opponent with a rodeo ride as shown. The attacker uses his right arm to hook his opponent's right shoulder.

The attacker turns to his right, moving his body across the defender's back. The attacker places his left hand on the mat for stability as he moves.

The attacker leans over his opponent and places the top of his head on the mat for stability. As he does this, the attacker places his left leg under the defender's head as shown. Look at how the attacker is sideways across the defender's back.

The attacker uses his hands to form a keylock on the defender's right arm as shown. This traps the defender's arm firmly to the attacker's chest.

The attacker may have to use his feet and legs to push against the defender's arms to lever them apart.

This photo shows how the defender can use his hands to grab, push or pull the defender's feet in an effort to defend or escape the Juji Gatame.

The attacker may have to place his right leg on the mat so he can push off of it for additional power in kicking or pushing the defender's hands apart.

The attacker's buttocks are firmly placed at the defender's right shoulder the entire time to ensure that the attacker has good leverage for the armlock. At this point, the attacker has pulled the defender's hands apart and is starting to straighten the defender's right arm.

The attacker uses both feet to push or kick the defender's left shoulder and arm away as the attacker levers the defender's right arm straight.

The attacker arches his back and drives his hips forward and onto the defender's extended right arm to secure the belly down Juji Gatame.

## KNEE PUSH BELLY DOWN JUJI GATAME

The attacker is controlling the defender from this top position and using both arms to trap the defender's left arm to the attacker's chest. The attacker is posted on his head for stability as well as to see what he is doing.

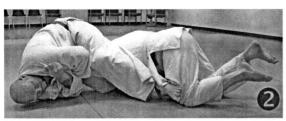

The attacker uses his left foot and leg to push the defender's left knee. As he does this, the attacker starts to drive forward with his hips, creating pressure on the defender's left arm. Look at how the attacker uses both of his arms to trap the defender's left arm.

The attacker continues to drive with his hips as he uses his left foot to push and extend the defender's left leg. This flattens the defender onto his front and secures the Juji Gatame for the attacker.

## ATTACKER "CRAWLS UP" OPPONENT AND DRAGS HIS ARM OUT TO SECURE BELLY DOWN JUJI GATAME

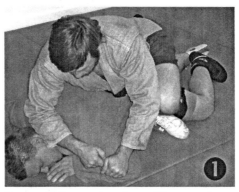

The defender is flat on his front. The attacker controls him with a ride and uses both hands to grab the defender's left elbow as shown.

The attacker slides his left hand and arm under the defender's left upper arm and shoulder.

The attacker moves up the defender's body getting close to the defender's left shoulder as shown.

The attacker moves to his left (away slightly from the defender) and as he does, the attacker uses his left arm to drag the defender's left arm out as shown.

The attacker swings his right foot and leg over the defender's head and places it under the defender's head as shown. Look at how the attacker moves to his left and a wider angle away from the defender. Doing this places the attacker sideways to the defender, weakening the defender's ability to protect his extended left arm.

The attacker is sideways to the defender as shown. The attacker uses both arms to hook and trap the defender's extended left arm to the attacker's chest. The attacker arches his back, driving his hips forward onto the straightened left arm of the defender, securing Juji Gatame.

## RUSSIAN DRAG WHEN DEFENDER IS ON ONE OR BOTH KNEES TO BELLY DOWN JUJI GATAME

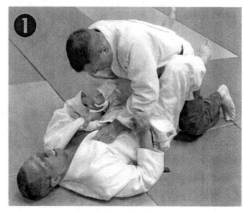

The attacker is on the bottom with the defender on his knees.

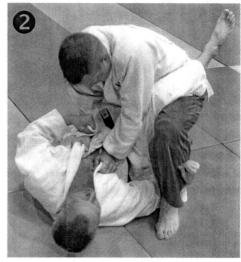

The defender moves up so that he is kneeling with his left knee up as shown. As the defender does this, the attacker uses his right hand to grab under the defender's left lower leg and hooking it with his left arm.

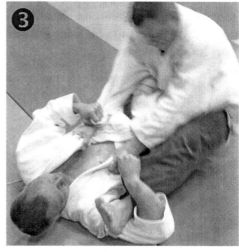

The attacker uses his right arm to hook and pull the

defender's left leg, straightening it as shown. This action forces the defender to fall back onto his left side.

The attacker has dragged the defender so that the defender is on his left side as shown. As he does this, the attacker starts to swing his left foot and leg over the defender's right shoulder and head. The attacker uses his left hand and arm to trap the defender's right arm to the attacker's torso. The attacker starts to roll to his right over his right side.

The attacker continues to roll to his right and slides his left foot and leg up and onto the back of the defender's head and neck.

The attacker continues to roll to his right, using both arms to trap and pull the defender's right arm to the attacker's chest as the attacker rolls. The attacker places his left shin on the back of the defender's head as shown. The attacker drives forward with his hips onto the defender's straightened right arm and secures Juji Gatame.

## RUSSIAN DRAG WHEN DEFENDER IS STANDING TO BELLY DOWN JUJI GATAME

The attacker is on his back and the defender is standing above him. The attacker uses his right hand and arm to reach and hook under the defender's left ankle or lower leg. The attacker uses his left hand and arm to trap the defender's right arm to the attacker's torso.

The attacker rolls to his right side and he uses his right arm to hook and pull on the defender's left ankle or lower leg. This forces the defender to fall to his left rear side.

The attacker jams his right leg firmly on the defender's left side at about the ribcage area as the attacker continues to use his right arm to hook and pull the defender's left lower leg. The attacker starts to swing his left foot and leg up and over.

The attacker continues to use his right arm to hook and pull the defender's left leg straight, forcing the defender to fall onto his left side. The attacker rolls over his right side and swings his left leg over the defender's right shoulder and head. Look at how the attacker uses his right arm to continue to hook and trap the defender's left lower leg.

The attacker places the top of his left foot on the back of the defender's head and neck as the attacker continues to roll to his right. Look at how the attacker uses his right arm to hook and trap the defender's left leg, straightening it. The attacker uses his right arm to trap the defender's right arm to the attacker's chest.

The attacker continues to roll to his right, using his arms to trap the defender's right arm and left leg. As he rolls to his right, the attacker arches his back and drives forward with his hips, placing pressure on the defender's extended right arm and extended left leg.

The attacker may roll to his right a bit more if more pressure is needed to get the tap out.

# JUDO SWITCH TO BELLY DOWN JUJI GATAME

This is quite similar to the Juji Gatame variation where the attacker "crawls up" his opponent who is flat on his front. This variation shows an effective set up where the attacker turns a defensive situation into an offensive one.

The attacker is on all fours with the defender on his knees as shown. The attacker uses both his hands and arms to grab and hug the defender's left leg immediately above the knee. The attacker places the left side of his head on the defender's left hip.

The attacker is on his knees as shown and moves to his right with the goal of getting behind his opponent.

The attacker continues to move around and behind his opponent as shown.

The attacker does the judo switch (go behind) and positions his body behind the defender. This often forces the defender to flatten out on his front as shown.

The attacker climbs onto his opponent's back and uses his left hand to slide and hook under the defender's left upper arm and shoulder.

The attacker moves up the defender's body getting close to the defender's left shoulder as shown.

The attacker moves to his left (away slightly from the defender) and as he does, the attacker uses his left arm to drag the defender's left arm out as shown.

The attacker swings his right foot and leg over the defender's head and places it under the defender's head as shown. Look at how the attacker moves to his left and a wider angle away from the defender. Doing this places the attacker sideways to the defender, weakening the defender's ability to protect his extended left arm.

The attacker is sideways to the defender as shown. The attacker uses both arms to hook and trap the defender's extended left arm to the attacker's chest. The attacker arches his back, driving his hips forward an onto the straightened left arm of the defender, securing Juji Gatame.

## BELLY DOWN JUJI GATAME WHEN DEFENDER SITS UP TO ESCAPE LEG PRESS

This is a classic example of how the attacker does not let go of his opponent's arm and keeps trying to secure the armlock. This sequence was photographed at the AAU Freestyle Judo Nationals with the attacker scoring with this Juji Gatame. This may not be the most aesthetically pleasing Juji Gatame, but it worked and as Shawn Watson once said, "It's only pretty if it works!"

The attacker controls his opponent with the leg press as shown. The defender manages to "steal" back his right arm and shoulder and is on his right side. The defender swings his left leg over to attempt to sit up to escape the armlock.

The attacker doesn't give up on the armlock and uses both hands and arms to lever and pull on his opponent's right arm to extend it.

The defender manages to sit up in his effort to escape the Juji Gatame. The attacker continues to lever the defender's right arm. The attacker starts to roll to his right side as the defender sits up on his buttocks.

The attacker rolls over his left side and onto his front as shown. All the while, the attacker uses both of his arms to pull on his opponent's right arm.

The attacker arches his back, driving his hips forward and onto the defender's straightened right arm, getting the tap out with this Juji Gatame.

### TECHNICAL TIP

The attacker must not give up on continuing to attack his opponent's arm. Keep pulling, prying, stretching and yanking. Be relentless, aggressive and uncompromising. Get your opponent's arm, don't let go and don't stop pulling it straight.

## UPSIDE DOWN JUJI GATAME WHEN DEFENDER SITS UP TO ESCAPE LEG PRESS

The defender manages to launch a good defense and pull his right arm back from the attacker. This situation happens often and proves that the attacker, by not giving up on the armlock and continuing to pull on his opponent's arm can get the tap out.

The defender manages to sit up onto his buttocks, but the attacker never lets go of the defender's left arm. Even though the attacker has been turned to his left side, he continues to pull on the defender's arm and applies Juji Gatame from this odd, almost compromised position.

## JUJI GATAME WITH ATTACKER ON HIS SIDE AND FACING DEFENDER'S LOWER BODY

This variation shows how the attacker, relentlessly pulling, prying and levering his opponent's arm, will eventually wear down and weaken his opponent, stretching the arm out straight and securing Juji Gatame.

The attacker has started a head roll Juji Gatame, but the defender has managed to flatten onto his front and roll away, escaping momentarily.

The attacker uses both arms to trap and lever his opponent's left arm. To add more leverage and pressure, the attacker rolls onto his right side. This forces the defender to arch up as shown.

The attacker continues a relentless pulling action on his opponent's left arm in an effort to lever it straight. As he does this, the attacker rolls onto his right hip and side.

The attacker rolls onto his right side, levering the defender's left arm.

The attacker is now lying on his right side. He levers his opponent's left arm out straight.

The attacker continues to roll onto his left side as he uses both hands to pull hard on his opponent's extended left arm, securing the Juji Gatame.

## TECHNICAL TIP

**The term "going out the back door" often refers to how the attacker reverses the initial direction of his movement to secure the same (or another) position or technique.**

## ATTACKER GOES OUT THE BACK DOOR

The attacker holds onto the opponent's arm and secures Juji Gatame as the opponent sits up to escape Juji Gatame.

The attacker is controlling his opponent with the leg press and attempting to lever the defender's arm. The defender starts to shrimp into the attacker in an effort to escape.

The defender turns into the attacker and starts to sit up to escape. The attacker continues to uses both hands to trap his opponent's right arm.

As the defender sits up and gets to his knees for a stable base, the attacker stays round and rolls onto his back right shoulder as shown.

The attacker continues to roll over his right shoulder and side as he uses both hands to lever the defender's right arm straight.

The attacker rolls over his right side, and as he does, arches his back driving his hips forward and onto the defender's extended right arm.

The attacker rolls over and onto his left side and hip as he secures Juji Gatame.

**IMPORTANT:** This shows how important it is for the attacker to stay round and continue to hold onto his opponent's arm.

## ATTACKER GOES OUT THE BACK DOOR

The attacker uses Juji Gatame off of his side when the defender stacks him.

The attacker starts his spinning Juji Gatame with the defender on both of his knees.

The defender starts to stand and shift his body to his right in the direction of the attacker's head. By doing this, the defender stops the spinning action of the attacker momentarily.

The defender stands and continues to move to his right. By doing this, the defender places the attacker high on his shoulders and upper back as shown. The attacker realizes this and starts to roll over his left shoulder (the shoulder close to his opponent). The attacker continues to use both hands to trap the defender's left arm to the attacker's chest.

The attacker continues to roll over his left shoulder and, if necessary, uses his left hand to block or push the defender's lower right leg for stability.

The attacker rolls backward over his left shoulder, all the while trapping the defender's left arm. As the attacker finishes his shoulder roll, he arches his back and drives his hips into his opponent's straightened arm to secure Juji Gatame.

## ATTACKER GOES OUT THE BACK DOOR

The attacker uses Juji Gatame from the side when the opponent attempts to kneel or stand.

The attacker attempts spinning Juji Gatame by spinning to his right as shown.

The defender comes up on one knee so that his left knee is now off the mat. As he does this, the defender moves to his right to stop the spinning action of the attacker. Doing this forces the attacker to be positioned up on the back of his shoulders and head as shown. Realizing this, the attacker continues to spin to his right across the back of his shoulders and starts to do a rear somersault. The attacker anchors his right foot onto his opponent's left upper leg as shown (doing this provides the attacker stability in his spinning movement).

The attacker continues to spin across the back of his shoulders and to use his left hand and arm to trap the defender's right arm to the attacker's chest.

The attacker spins through completely, ending up on his left hip as shown. As he does this, the attacker continues to use his left hand to trap the defender's right arm to the attacker's chest. Look at how the attacker uses his right leg and foot to anchor and control the defender's left leg and his right foot and leg to hook and control the defender's head. The attacker may use his right hand to grab the defender's right leg so the attacker can pull his body closer to the defender's legs, making the attacker's position more secure.

The attacker is now positioned on his left hip and side and applies Juji Gatame from this position.

## ATTACKER SPINS ON HIS SHOULDERS AND DOES JUJI GATAME FROM HIS SIDE AS A COUNTER TO DEFENDER'S STACK

The attacker (on bottom) attempts a spinning Juji Gatame but the defender moves away to avoid the attack. Sensing this, the attacker starts to roll to his left shoulder and spin under his opponent as shown.

The attacker spins completely across the back of his shoulders as shown, staying round as he spins under his opponent. The attacker uses his left hand to trap the defender's left arm to the attacker's chest.

This view from another angle shows how the attacker spins under the defender and uses his left hand to grab onto the defender's left knee for stability in the spinning action. Look at how the attacker uses his feet and legs to hook and control the defender's head, pulling the defender's upper body forward as well.

The attacker spins completely through ending up on his right hip as shown.

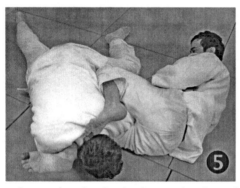

The attacker arches his back, driving his hips forward onto the extended left arm of the defender to secure Juji Gatame.

This view shows how the attacker finishes the spin and secures the Juji Gatame.

## JUJI GATAME WHEN OPPONENT PASSES ATTACKER'S GUARD

The top grappler moves to his left (to the bottom grappler's right) in an effort to get past the bottom man's legs. The bottom grappler (the attacker) quickly uses both arms to hook and trap the top grappler's right arm to the attacker's chest. The attacker (bottom) rolls onto his right side and as he does, he starts to swing his left foot and leg over the top grappler's right shoulder as shown. **IMPORTANT:** The bottom grappler must stay round as he rolls onto his right hip and side.

The attacker continues to roll onto his right hip and side and as he does, he places his left shin across the back of his opponent's shoulders and head as shown. The attacker's left foot and leg are extended in front and across the defender's belt line to serve as an anchor for the attacker's rolling movement.

The attacker rolls over onto his front, posting on the top of his head if possible. Look at how the attacker is starting to roll the top grappler forward, over his head.

The attacker continues to roll, forcing the defender to go forward onto his head as shown. The attacker maintains a firm trap with both of his arms on his opponent's right arm. **IMPORTANT:** If the defender does a somersault, rolling over his head, the attacker can follow through with ahead roll Juji Gatame to get the tap out.

The attacker finishes on his left hip and side, arching his back and driving his hips forward onto the defender's extended and straight right arm to secure Juji Gatame.

## JUJI GATAME WITH ANCHOR FOOT ON OPPONENT'S BACK AS A COUNTER TO OPPONENT'S GUARD PASS

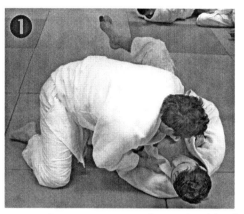

The top grappler is moving to his right (the bottom grappler's left) to pass the bottom grappler's guard and, in fact, the top grappler has moved past the bottom grappler's legs to successfully pass his guard. As this happens, the bottom grappler (the attacker) rolls to his left side and starts to move his right foot and leg up.

The attacker rolls to his left side (making sure to stay as round as possible) and uses his right arm to trap the to grappler's left arm. The attacker swings his right foot and leg up and over his opponent's left shoulder.

The attacker rolls onto his left shoulder, placing his right lower leg on the back of his opponent's head as shown.

The attacker rolls over his left shoulder and high on his upper back as he wedges his right shin on the back of his opponent's head. The attacker also jams his left shin on the defender's left side at about his ribcage area. The attacker continues to trap the defender's left arm.

This view from another angle shows how the attacker places his feet and legs. The attacker's right foot and shin are placed on the back of the defender's head and the attacker's left foot and shin are placed at the defender's left side.

The attacker continues to roll and rolls over as shown.

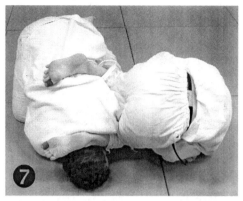

The attacker rolls over onto his right shoulder and side. This is why "staying round" is important as it gives the attacker the mobility to control his opponent.

The attacker rolls through and onto his right hip and side as shown. Look at how the attacker uses his feet and legs to control his opponent.

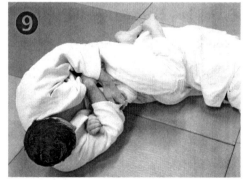

This view shows how the attacker uses both of his arms to trap his opponent's extended left arm and applies Juji Gatame from this position.

## LEG HOOK ON HEAD AND BELT LINE SPINNING JUJI GATAME TO BELLY DOWN JUJI GATAME WHEN OPPONENT TRIES TO BACK AWAY

The bottom grappler attempts to perform a spinning Juji Gatame or attack from the bottom. The top grappler moves back away from the bottom grappler to escape. As this happens, the bottom grappler (attacker) rolls to his left hip and starts to swing his right foot and leg up.

The attacker continues to roll to his left hip and swings his right foot and leg up over his opponent's head. As he does this, the attacker uses both arms to trap his opponent's left arm. The attacker places his left shin across the front of his opponent's midsection (belt line).

The attacker uses his left leg to hook and control his opponent's head as the attacker continues to jam his left

shin across the midsection of the defender. The attacker continues to roll over his left shoulder as shown.

The attacker continues to roll over his left shoulder and onto his front as shown. Look at the position of the attacker's legs and feet in controlling his opponent.

The attacker rolls through and onto his right hips and side as shown. As he does this, the attacker continues to trap and lever the defender's extended left arm. The defender may tap out at this point.

The attacker continues to roll through, adding pressure to the defender's compromised left shoulder and straightened left arm. The attacker arches his back, driving his hips forward and onto the defender's left arm to secure Juji Gatame from this position.

## BELLY DOWN OR JUJI GATAME FROM THE SIDE FROM THE SEATED RODEO RIDE

The attacker controls his opponent from behind with this seated rodeo ride.

The attacker shifts to his left hip and places his left foot on the defender's right hip as an anchor. As he does this, the attacker uses his left hand to hook up and under his opponent's left shoulder. Look at how the attacker moves to his left behind his opponent.

This view from the back shows how the attacker moves to his left so that he is sideways to his opponent.

This back view shows how the attacker rolls to his left hip and places his right shin on the back of his opponent's head. At this point, the attacker uses both arms to trap his opponent's left arm to the attacker's chest.

The attacker rolls to his left, forcing the defender to roll as well.

The attacker continues his roll, making sure to stay round and continually trapping and controlling the defender's left arm.

The attacker rolls over to his right hip and side as shown.

As the attacker finishes his roll, he arches his back and drives his hips forward placing pressure on the defender's straightened left arm.

This view shows how the attacker applies Juji Gatame from this position.

## ARCHING JUJI GATAME WHEN OPPONENT IS ON HIS KNEES

The attacker is fighting his opponent from the guard and the defender (on top) starts to stand. The bottom grappler uses his left leg to hook over his opponent's right shoulder and pulls the top grappler down to prevent him from standing.

The attacker (on bottom) uses both arms to hug and trap the defender's left arm to the attacker's chest. As he does this, the attacker starts to move his right leg over his opponent's left shoulder.

The attacker swings his right foot and leg over his opponent's head as the attacker spins to his left. The attacker also uses his left foot and leg to hook over the defender's head for control

The attacker arches his back, driving his hips forward onto the extended left arm of the defender, securing Juji Gatame from this position.

## KNEE JAM JUJI GATAME FROM THE SIDE WITH DEFENDER ON HIS KNEES

The attacker (on bottom) controls his opponent and has his right shin placed across the top grappler's belt line with the attacker's right knee on the defender's left hip and the attacker's right foot anchored on the defender's right hip.

The attacker rolls to his right side as he uses both of his hands and arms to trap the defender's right arm to the attacker's chest.

As the attacker continues to roll to his right side, he swings his left foot and leg over the defender's head as shown. The attacker's right shin is still placed across the defender's belt line.

This view shows how the attacker rolls to his right side and applies the Juji Gatame from this position.

If the defender attempts to pull his arm back or move away, the attacker arches his back, driving his hips forward and locking the defender's extended right arm.

**IMPORTANT:** While this is a simple variation of Juji Gatame, it works and is still a good for every grappler to have in his or her arsenal.

## SINGLE ARM LEG CROSS ARCHING JUJI GATAME

The attacker (on bottom) uses both hands and arms to trap his opponent's left arm.

The attacker moves his right leg up and over his opponent's left shoulder and arm.

The attacker wedges his right foot and lower leg under the defender's neck and on his throat. Look at how the

attacker's right leg is bent and placed over the defender's extended left upper arm. The attacker starts to arch his back, driving his hips up as he starts to use both arms to pull tighter on the defender's left arm.

The attacker quickly swings his left foot and leg up.

The attacker places his left foot and lower leg under the defender's chin. The attacker is crossing his legs, trapping his opponent's extended left arm as shown. As he does this, the attacker arches his back, driving his hips forward and locking the defender's straightened left arm.

## LEG TRIANGLE SINGLE ARM ARCHING JUJI GATAME FROM SIDE ANGLE

The bottom grappler (the attacker) uses both hands to grab and trap the top grappler's hands as shown.

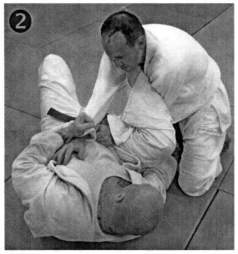

The attacker shrimps onto his right hip as he uses his right hand and arm to reach under his opponent's left leg to grab and control it. As he does this, the attacker places his right foot and shin under his opponent's neck.

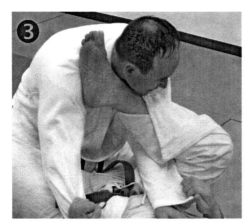

This shows how the attacker jams his right foot and shin under his opponent's head.

The attacker uses his left hand to trap the defender's right arm to the attacker's torso as the attacker moves his left leg up and over the defender's head to control it. As he does this, the attacker arches his back, driving his hips into the straightened right arm of the defender, locking it.

## ONE LEG HOOK OVER ARCHING JUJI GATAME

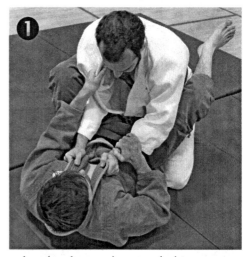

The attacker (on bottom) controls his opponent from the guard position.

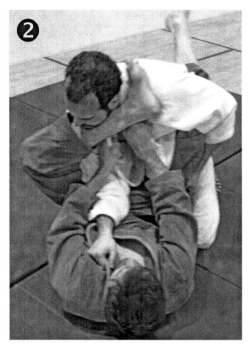

The attacker uses his left hand and arm to trap the defender's right arm to the attacker's chest as the attacker slides his left foot and leg up and over the defender's right shoulder, placing his left shin under the defender's neck as shown. The attacker uses his right foot and leg to hook around the defender's left side and back, controlling it.

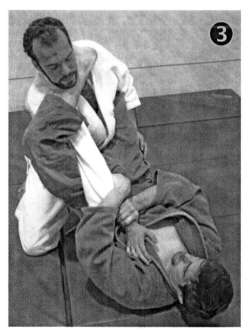

The attacker arches his back, driving his hips forward and locking the defender's extended, straightened right arm.

## SINGLE ARM LEG TRIANGLE ARCHING JUJI GATAME

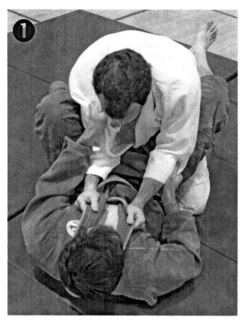

The attacker is the bottom grappler and is fighting his opponent from the guard.

The attacker moves his right foot and leg up and over the defender's left shoulder. As he does this, the attacker starts to move his left leg up as well.

The attacker slides his left foot and leg over his opponent's right arm (which the attacker has trapped to his chest). The attacker continues to swing his right foot and leg up.

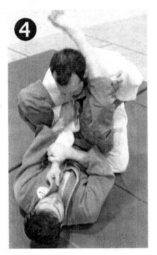

The attacker places his left foot and shin over his opponent's right shoulder and under his chin. The attacker places his right foot and leg over the top of his left foot and over his opponent's left shoulder, forming a triangle with his legs. At this point, the attacker uses both hands to trap his opponent's extended right arm,

With a strong leg triangle on his opponent, the attacker firmly traps the defender's right arm as he arches his back, driving his hips forward and onto the defender's straight right arm securing the Juji Gatame from here.

# DOUBLE ARM LEG CROSS OVER ARCHING JUJI GATAME

The bottom grappler (the attacker) uses both hands to grab both of his opponent's arms, trapping them to the attacker's chest.

The attacker moves his left foot and leg up as shown.

The attacker places his left foot and shin under his opponent's chin.

The attacker moves his right foot and leg up immediately after trapping his opponent's right upper arm with his left leg.

The attacker moves his right foot and leg up and over the defender's left shoulder and upper arm, trapping the opponent's left arm. Now, the attacker's crossed legs trap both of the defender's extended arms. The attacker arches his back, driving his hips forward against both of the straightened arms of the defender, locking them.

## DOUBLE ARM LEG TRIANGLE ARCHING JUJI GATAME

The attacker (on bottom) controls his opponent from the guard position as shown. The attacker uses both hands to reach over his opponent's arms and grabs his opponent's lapels, trapping both of the defender's arms.

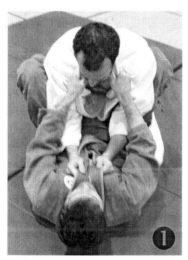

The attacker moves his left foot and lower leg over the defender's right shoulder and upper arm. As he does this, the attacker starts to move his right foot and leg up

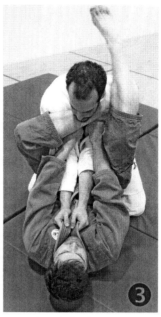

The attacker jams his left shin under his opponent's neck. As he does this, the attacker uses both hands and arms to pull his opponent's arms down to him, trapping them firmly to the attacker's torso. The attacker moves his right foot and leg up so the back of his right knee is to of his left foot creating a triangle with his leg as shown. This forms a tight trap on the defender's arms.

The attacker tightens the leg triangle as he arches his back, driving his hips forward and locking both the extended and straightened arms of the defender.

There are countless ways to catch an opponent with Juji Gatame in any number of positions. Constantly look for new ways and different positions to get training partners and opponents in Juji Gatame. It's hoped that what's been presented in this chapter will give you a good basis to make your Juji Gatame work for you.

Now, let's turn our attention to the subject of defense and how to escape from Juji Gatame in the next chapter.

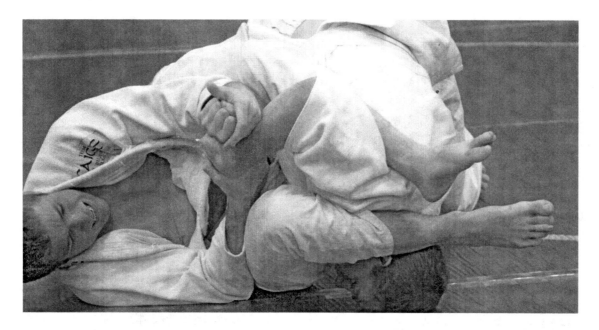

# DEFENSES AND ESCAPES FOR JUJI GATAME

**"ATTACK AND DEFENSE ARE ONE IN THE SAME THING, AND WHICH OF THE TWO RECEIVES PRIORITY DEPENDS ENTIRELY ON THE SITUATION." DONN DRAEGER**

This chapter examines two areas where most athletes are weakest, and for the most part, train for the least: the areas of defending against Juji Gatame and how to escape when caught in Juji Gatame.

Training in defensive skills isn't glamorous, and by our very nature, people who engage in combat sports are aggressive, and because of this we tend to relegate our efforts at working on our defensive skills to only once in a while. We all spend a lot more time figuring out, and then practicing, ways to get an opponent into Juji Gatame than in the ways necessary to defend and escape it. That being said, it's best to be objective about the whole subject and face the fact that the guy facing you on the mat has every intention of doing to you what you intend to do to him. It makes sense to spend some time during every workout drilling on defense and escapes.

The first part of this chapter will focus on defending against Juji Gatame and then transition into the skills of escaping from Juji Gatame. In many cases, the concepts of defense and escape will intermingle and as a result, an active defense leads to an escape, and ultimately to a counter attack.

## THE CONCEPT OF KOBO ICHI

The Japanese have an old concept called "kobo ichi" which translates into the idea of an "aggressive defense" or turning a defensive move into an aggressive counter move. Kobo ichi is a fluid concept of defense-offense with the athlete defending as necessary, and always looking for an opening to attack.

This concept can be applied to our study of Juji Gatame. It's recommended that whenever you defend against, or escape from, an opponent's Juji Gatame, immediately take the offense and attempt to secure your own Juji Gatame or other attack. If your mindset is to think of defense as a means of beating your opponent, then you have the right idea of what kobo ichi is about.

Realistically, in some cases, you will be happy to defend or escape and survive to fight another day, but whenever possible, make every effort in turning the situation around and taking the offense. In every situation presented in this chapter, keep kobo ichi in mind and look at how the skills presented in this chapter can be turned into an offensive move. (For a more comprehensive explanation and discussion about kobo ichi, refer to my book WINNING ON THE MAT, published by Turtle Press.)

## ▰▰▰▰ TECHNICAL TIP ▰▰▰▰

**When defending or escaping from Juji Gatame, think logically. Keep things simple and get out of trouble. Often, your defensive move will put you in position to better make your escape. Don't try some complicated technique or skill simply because some famous fighter or athlete has done it. It's your arm in jeopardy right now, not his.**

## AN OUNCE OF PREVENTION IS WORTH A POUND OF CURE

The old saying is true; an ounce of prevention is indeed worth a pound of cure. Obviously, the best defense is not getting caught in Juji Gatame. But that is easier said than done. However, if you develop a mindset that you will do everything possible to control the position and not allow your opponent to control the situation, you are a step ahead. As mentioned throughout this entire book, controlling the position is vital to securing the submission, and the reverse is true as well. If your opponent initiates an attack, work to get to a better position. It may take incremental movements to work to a better position so that you are not vulnerable to a submission technique. In a lot of cases, it may be best to engage in a scramble for position. A "scramble" takes place when neither grappler has the advantage in position. If your opponent has taken control, immediately do what is necessary to get out of his control. Often, a scramble is the best answer to getting you out of trouble. At least, in a scramble, the odds are more in your favor than if your opponent dominates the position.

Specifically, make sure to always keep your arms bent and close in to your body. Never reach too far or extend your arms out straight unless you are actively applying a technique on your opponent. Always work to get off of your back, and do everything possible to not be flat on your back. Instead, work off of your hips and buttocks. There will be times when you may have to be (temporarily) on your back, but the key word is temporary. Always work to get to a stable base and do everything possible to get behind your opponent and get his back so you will be able to launch your own attack.

## DEFENSE AND ESCAPE

If you get caught in Juji Gatame, there are some logical steps to take. First, "steal" your shoulder and arm back from his control. He stole your arm from you and it's your job to steal it back. Get out of trouble and pull your shoulder and arm back into you so that your elbow is no longer situated on the attacker's pubic bone area. It's best to position your arm so that it is below your opponent's crotch or public bone so he can't lever your arm against it. The defender can do this regardless of the position. The defender may be flat on his back with the attacker controlling him in a leg press or the defender may be on his knees with the attacker applying a spinning Juji Gatame. The concept is the same; steal your arm back so your opponent can't lock it.

Second, get to a stable base if at all possible. The odds are good that if you are in a defensive position with the attacker attempting a Juji Gatame, you are not situated in a stable position. An example is that if you are flat on your back, shrimp and bridge into your opponent so that you are better able to sit up and get to a position on your knees. As you get to a more stable position, continue to steal your arm and shoulder back away from the attacker.

Third, the odds are that if you are able to do steps one and two, you and your opponent are scrambling for the superior position at this time. This is the time to try to control the position and gain the advantage. By doing this, you can launch your counter-attack (remember kobo ichi).

## THE DEFENDER MUST PREVENT HIS OPPONENT FROM TRAPPING HIS ARM

The attacker wants to control the position, trap the defender's arm and then stretch it to apply Juji Gatame. Now, reverse the situation and put yourself in the role of the defender. As the defender, you want to get out of the bad position your opponent has put you in, and in the process, you must prevent your arm from being trapped and extract it so the attacker won't be able to extend and stretch it to apply Juji Gatame.

## A STRAIGHT ARM IS EASIER TO LOCK THAN A BENT ARM WITH JUJI GATAME

Maybe it sounds to obvious, but it's true. If you, as the defender, extend or straighten your arm it will be easier for your opponent to trap and stretch it. Always keep your hands and arms in close to your body and whenever possible, keep your elbows bent and at your side. There are times when you will have to extend your arm, but keep them to a minimum. A phrase that I like to tell my athletes is to "work close to your body." Keep your arms bent with your hands in front of you and don't extend your arms out straight. Don't extend your shoulders out too far ahead of your hips. If you do, you will be off balance and your opponent will take advantage of it. Don't get in a hurry to grab your opponent with your hands and arms. Be methodical; don't rush things.

## DO NOT EXTEND YOUR ARM OR ARMS: NEVER GIVE YOUR OPPONENT A STRAIGHT ARM

The grappler on his knees (in this photo) is making a fundamental mistake. He is reaching for his opponent and extending his arms. By doing this, the attacker (on the bottom) can more easily control the defender and apply Juji Gatame (or just about any technique). Do not get in a hurry or rush to grab your opponent. Take your time, keep your arms bent and in close to your body, and never reach for your opponent. If you reach, you generally extend your arms out straight, extend your shoulders too far out in front of your hips and become unbalanced.

## STAY SOUTH OF THE BORDER

In keeping with the fundamental skill of not extending your arm or arms, make sure to keep your arms bent as much as possible, in close to your body, and never reach too far to get to your opponent. The top grappler in this photo is using his hands and arms to control his opponent's knees and legs. By doing this, the top grappler is forcing his opponent on the bottom to extend his arms and reach out too far.

## GRASP YOUR HANDS TOGETHER AS QUICKLY AS POSSIBLE AND BEND YOUR ARMS IN AS CLOSE AS POSSIBLE TO YOUR BODY

As mentioned before, be realistic. If your opponent has the advantage and is rolling you into a Juji Gatame, start your defense immediately and grab your hands together. Do not wait until you've been rolled over and are on your back, looking up at the ceiling. By then, it's most often too late and your opponent has your arm stretched.

This photo shows what not to do. Look how the defender has his hands apart and is more vulnerable to having his arm stretched by his opponent. If you know you've been caught, clamp your hands in close together and close to your body.

The defender realizes he's in a bad situation and grabs his hands together in an effort to defend against the Juji Gatame. By grabbing his hands together and locking them, the defender can keep his arms bent. This is a start; at least the defender's arm has not been completely trapped and straightened.

IMPORTANT: The defender should do everything possible to prevent his opponent from trapping his arm, but if he can't, he should at least lock his hands together and bend his arms, pulling them in as close to his chest as possible to prevent the attacker from levering his arm loose.

## DEFENDER MUST BEND HIS ARM AND GET HIS ELBOW BELOW THE ATTACKER'S CROTCH

The attacker wants to straighten the defender's arm and stretch the defender's elbow across the attacker's pubic bone. This action places stress against the elbow of the defender, causing pain. To prevent this, the defender must withdraw his arm that is being attacked (in this

photo, the left arm of the defender) and bend his elbow so that his left forearm is jammed in the attacker's crotch.

This shows how the attacker bends his left elbow, pulling it loose from the attacker's trap and tucks it in to his body. Doing this enables the defender to jam his left elbow in the buttocks of the attacker as the defender jams his left forearm hard into the attacker's crotch. The defender, by making sure that his left elbow is below the attacker's pubic bone, has prevented the attacker from locking his arm with Juji Gatame.

### TECHNICAL TIP

No matter what position the defender may be in (lying on his back, kneeling, standing or in any position), he or she must extract and bend the arm that is being attacked and make sure that his elbow is below the attacker's pubic bone. The attacker's pubic bone is the fulcrum and the defender's arm is the lever. If that lever (the defender's arm) is stretched over the fulcrum (the attacker's pubic bone or crotch), the armlock is successful.

## DEFENDER MUST GET OFF OF HIS BACK

The defender must get off of his back as quickly as possible. If the attacker has the defender flat on his back and in the leg press, the defender is in real trouble. If you are on your back, you are more vulnerable. While it may seem obvious, it is vital that the defender gets off of his back and, if possible, gets to a stable base and position. This photo shows how the defender shrimps and turns into the attacker in order to get off of his back from the leg press position and initiate an escape.

### ▰▰▰ TECHNICAL TIP ▰▰▰

**Remember, defending and escaping from a bad position often happens in incremental steps. The defender doesn't jump up and escape from a leg press or other bad position in one big move. Be methodical, and realize that the only way you will get out of this predicament is to keep your cool and take care of things in order of importance.**

## DEFENSIVE ARM AND HAND GRABS

We've all been in this position on the back with the opponent using the leg press for control. And while we don't like it, it does happen, so it is important to know what to do. Often, before the defender can initiate an escape, he must prevent his opponent from stretching his arm. This is pure defense, plain and simple. Presented here are some of the many variations that the defender has when grabbing his hands and arms together to prevent the attacker from straightening his arm to apply Juji Gatame.

## DEFENDER SHOULD KEEP HIS ARMS AS CLOSE TO HIS CHEST AS POSSIBLE

The grappler on his back is in a bad position, so he must make sure to protect his arms (especially his right arm in this photo) so that his opponent won't trap and lever the arm and apply Juji Gatame. The defender must give a little space as possible to his opponent so he hugs his arms in tightly to his chest, making it harder for the attacker to lever his arms loose. The closer the defender holds his arms to his chest, the better chance he has of not getting them levered out straight.

## DEFENDER GRABS HIS UPPER ARMS OR ELBOWS

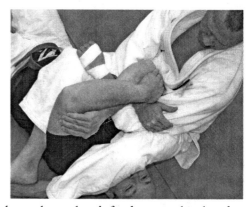

This shows how the defender uses his hands to grab onto his elbows in an effort to prevent the attacker from levering his arms loose. The attacker tucks his arms in tightly to his chest.

## DEFENDER GRABS HIS OWN SLEEVES TO LOCK HIS HANDS AND ARMS TOGETHER

The defender uses his hands to grab his sleeves. Often, the defender will grab his sleeves at the upper arm area, but anywhere on the sleeve will suffice if the defender is in trouble and needs something to hold onto to prevent the attacker from prying his arms loose and straight.

## DEFENDER GRABS HIS OWN LAPELS

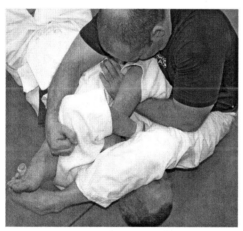

A strong defense from this position is for the defender to use his hands to grab his own lapels as shown here.

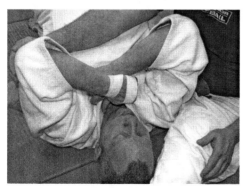

The attacker has withdrawn his left leg in this photo to allow you to see how the defender uses his hands to grab his lapels as a method of defense.

## DEFENDER GRABS ATTACKER'S LAPEL OR LAPELS

In some instances, the defender may grab his opponent's jacket, often grabbing the lapels. The attacker can use this grip to possibly pull his body upright but it mainly serves to negate the attacker's pulling action on the defender's arm.

## DEFENDER GRABS HIS OWN LEG

Sometimes, the defender may grab his own leg and then keylock his own wrist for additional support. This photo shows the defender (on the right) using his right hand to grab on his right thigh above his knee. As he does this, the defender uses his left hand to grab his right forearm or wrist forming a keylock to help anchor his grip.

## DEFENDER USES A SQUARE GRIP TO LOCK HIS HANDS AND ARMS TOGETHER

A defensive grip that is not as secure (but often done out of necessity) is when the defender grabs his hands together in a "square grip" where he clasps his hands together tightly. The defender's arms are elevated from his chest, making this a less than secure defensive grip. This can be a secure defensive grip if the defender is strong enough to hold out and attempt to escape further.

## DEFENDER GRABS HIS OWN WRISTS TO LOCK (LINK) HIS HANDS AND ARMS TOGETHER

Like the square grip, this defensive grip is not particularly strong, but often done as the only grip that may prevent the attacker from stretching the defender's arm. The defender uses his hands to grab his wrists as shown, resembling a link in a chain.

## THE "C-CLAMP" GRIP: DEFENDER HOOKS HIS FINGERS TOGETHER

This is often the "last ditch" attempt by the defender before the attacker levers his hands apart and straightens the arm. The defender grasps his fingers together in an effort to prevent the attacker from prying his hands and arms apart.

## DEFENDER GRABS HIS OWN WRIST TO PREVENT HIS ARM FROM BEING STRETCHED

The defender uses the hand that is not being levered to grab the arm that is being levered. Here, the defender uses his left hand to grab his right forearm or wrist to prevent the attacker from levering his right arm straight.

This defender is in a tough spot in this photo. The attacker has trapped and levered the defender's left arm and pulled the defender's hands arm, with the attacker starting to straighten the defender's left arm. The defender uses his right hand to grab his left forearm in a last-ditch attempt to prevent his left arm from being straightened and locked. While he uses his right hand to grab his left forearm, the attacker shrimps and turns into the defender in an effort to "steal" his left arm back from the attacker.

## HAND FIGHTING

When the attacker and defender use their hands and arms to gain control of each other, this is called "hand fighting." Often, there is a good amount of hand fighting taking place when an attacker attempts to pry the defender's hands apart so he can trap and straighten the arm. The opposite is true as well. The defender must do what is necessary to extract his arm and keep it from getting locked. This photo shows an intense hand-fighting episode where the defender was eventually able to escape this Juji Gatame attempt.

### ▪ TECHNICAL TIP ▪

**The defender must protect his arm. By grabbing his arms together and as close to his chest or torso as possible, the defender takes an initial step in preventing the attacker from effectively trapping and then levering the defender's arm out straight. It's a "stop gap" measure, but it is necessary for the defender to protect his arm. The defender must always keep his arms bent and do everything possible to prevent his opponent from pulling his hands or arms apart and straightening the defender's arm that is being attacked.**

## DEFENSIVE POSITIONS THAT DO NOT WORK WELL

Let's look at some often-used defensive postures and reactions people use in groundfighting that are not particularly effective. Three instinctive reactions and positions even experienced athletes may use are: 1) to ball up on all fours or be on all fours in parterre, 2) to lie

flat on the front or 3) go into a fetal position. None of these positions are very effective as a method of defense and are even less effective as a means of escape. By becoming aware of them, you can make sure to avoid them.

## BALL UP ON ALL FOURS

Getting into a tight ball on the elbows and knees may seem safe to a novice grappler, but it's one of the worst things he or she can do defensively. Getting balled up on all fours may give the illusion of hiding from the attacker, but it rarely works. In this photo, the bottom grappler is positioned on his elbows and knees, giving the top grappler a decided advantage. The bottom grappler is "giving up his back" by positioning himself on all fours. Look at how the top grappler is taking advantage of the situation and starting to sink his right leg in (get his hooks in) to assert more control with his legs. The top grappler is already starting to use his right arm to hook and control the bottom man's right arm in an attempt to trap it for his Juji Gatame. While all of us have been in this predicament on the bottom, it is important to do everything possible to avoid it. Sometimes, it may be the only option in an otherwise bad situation, or may be necessary to assume this position on the elbows and knees to get to a stable base. In these cases, getting to the elbows and knees quickly in order to establish a stronger position is the right thing to do, but do it quickly and move to a better position before your opponent gains further control of you and the position. The defender should stay on his elbows and knees only long enough to enable him or her to get to a more stable position and should avoid getting balled up at all costs.

### ▪ TECHNICAL TIP ▪

**A fundamental rule of groundfighting is to avoid giving up your back to your opponent. An athlete who gives his back to his opponent allows the opponent the opportunity to dig his feet and legs in, controlling the defender's hips and legs, breaking the defender down and setting him up for a submission hold or technique.**

## DEFENDER ON ALL FOURS IN PARTERRE

Another defensive position for the bottom grappler is to be on all fours with the arms and elbows straight, similar to the "parterre" position in wrestling. While this position is good for wrestling, it's not particularly good for submission grappling, judo, sambo, jujitsu or MMA. The bottom, defensive grappler not only gives up his back, he also provides a couple of straight arms for his opponent to attack. Additionally, this position has more "holes" in it. In other words, extending and straightening the arms allows more gaps that the attacker could use to get his hooks in with his legs or hook with his arms to get a better handle on the defender. This photo shows the bottom grappler in the parterre position with the top grappler starting his attack from a standing position.

The top grappler takes advantage of the extended arms of the bottom grappler by hooking the defender's left arm with his left leg and the defender's right arm with his right arm. The body gaps resulting from the parterre position have given the attacker more room to use the defender's arms as handles to hook, grab and manipulate. Additionally, by extending his arms in the parterre position, the defender is only using his hands and arms to support the weight of his body and is unable to use them to fend off an attack by his opponent.

## TECHNICAL TIP

Groundfighting consists of one position followed by another position and then onto another position. This is "chain wrestling" or "chain grappling." One thing leads to another. If you are stuck on the bottom, do not ball up or lay flat on your front and "hide" from your opponent. Do everything you can to get to a stable base and either behind your opponent in a ride, or on your buttocks in the guard. If you are in a bad position on the bottom, balling up or lying flat on your front won't do anything to improve your position and will give your opponent time and opportunity to break you down or turn you over. In practice, drill on a lot of switches and go behinds so if you are stuck on the bottom, you can (at the very least) get to a neutral position, or even to a better position so you can launch your counter-attack.

## DEFENDER LAYS FLAT ON HIS FRONT

There are some athletes who purposely lay on their front sides (as shown in this photo) in a misguided effort to defend themselves or avoid engaging with the opponent. As this photo shows, the attacker is quickly working to turn or work a breakdown on his vulnerable opponent on bottom. An athlete who lays on his front side in this way is extremely vulnerable to any attack made by his opponent. Years ago, in an effort to prevent my junior judo athletes from assuming this highly defensive (and useless) position, I named it "chicken judo." The name stuck and served its purpose. Lying on the mat and attempting to hide from an opponent does not place the defender 1) in a position to escape, 2) gain a better and more stable position, or 3) in a position to launch a counter-attack. Lying there and waiting for the referee to call a halt (or "matte" in judo) to the action is not a reliable defensive tactic (or position). A good way to think of it is to compare the rules of any of the combat sports to a real fight on the street or in a combat situation. Would the person lying on his front in a prone position be able to defend himself? The obvious answer is no, so why would any athlete in any combat sport assume this position unless he or she absolutely had to for a temporary (and very brief) period of time in order to get out of a bad situation and get into a more stable and effective position.

This photo shows the attacker using a "judo stack" to get the defender onto his side or back to set him up for a Juji Gatame or other scoring technique.

## DEFENDER GOES IN THE FETAL POSITION

While it happens more often with novice grapplers, even experienced athletes may "go fetal" when disoriented, surprised or if an opponent has put them in some kind of pain or in a very uncomfortable position. It is an instinctive behavior to assume the fetal position when threatened or in pain, and while it may be useful in some circumstances in life, it doesn't help when it comes to any of the combat sports. If you do find yourself reacting in this way, quickly do what is necessary (depending on the situation) to get to a more stable position in an effort to defend yourself and launch a counter-attack. This photo shows the bottom grappler in the fetal position, giving his opponent ample time and opportunity to secure his Juji Gatame.

## THE BASIC ESCAPES AND THEIR VARIATIONS

Over many years of competing, coaching and refereeing, I have observed that there are several basic methods of escaping from Juji Gatame. While there are almost as many escape variations as there are people doing them, these are the ones that I have seen most often used.

## DEFENDER TURNS IN AND STEALS HIS ARM BACK

The attacker controls his opponent with the leg press. As pointed out previously, the leg press is a strong controlling position for the top grappler. For the bottom grappler, it's a sure sign he is in trouble. Because of this, the bottom grappler must do everything possible to get off of his back and out of this predicament; but first, he must protect his arm and escape form the immediate threat, that of having his opponent trap, lever and stretch his arm. This photo shows the bottom grappler grasping his hands together in an initial effort to prevent the top grappler from levering his right arm loose and straight.

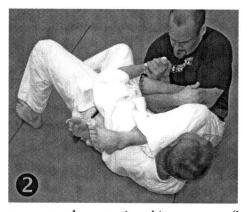

The bottom grappler turns into his opponent (here he turns onto his right side). By doing this, the bottom grappler starts to "steal" back his right arm and shoulder from his opponent. **IMPORTANT:** The defender (on bottom) must keep his arms bent and his hands grasped tightly together. It is vital that the defender does not allow his right arm to be straightened by his opponent.

The bottom grappler may bridge or shrimp into his opponent and use his feet to drive off the mat for stability as he turns into the top grappler. Look at how the bottom grappler continues to turn into his opponent (to the bottom grappler's right side). As he does this, the defender (the bottom grappler) pulls his right arm back toward his right ribcage in an effort to extract his right arm from his opponent's trap.

The defender continues to pull his right arm in tight to his body as he turns into his opponent as shown. (This is what "stealing your arm back" from your opponent means.) As he does this, the defender comes onto his knees to provide a stable base. The defender makes sure to have his right elbow placed above the attacker's pubic bone so that the defender's right arm cannot be straightened.

The defender continues to pull his right arm back and free as drives his left bent arm over in a motion that resembles an elbow strike. This ballistic action helps extract the defender's right arm free from the attacker's trap. The defender can now move to another position to escape further or launch a counter-attack.

## TURN IN AND BACK-STEP

The attacker controls the defender with the leg press. The defender grasps his arms together as tightly as possible as an initial defense.

The defender shrimps into his opponent, turning (here) onto his right hip and side. Look at how the defender starts to drive off of his feet and into his opponent.

The defender continues to turn into his opponent, driving off of his feet as shown. As he does this, the defender is better able to pull (or steal) his right arm back from the attacker's trap.

The defender drives his right foot back hard onto the mat as he turns into his opponent. This is a fast, whipping action. As he does this, the defender jerks his bent right arm back and away from the attacker.

---

---

The defender pulls back his right arm as he completes his fast turning action toward his opponent. The defender is now better able to escape further and launch his counter-attacker.

## SIT UP AND STACK ESCAPE

This is a common escape. It's common because it is simple and has a good ratio of success (especially considering the weak position that the defender is in initially). This photo shows the defender on his back with his opponent controlling him with the leg press. The defender grasps his arms together in an initial effort to defend his right arm. The defender immediately starts to swing his legs up into the air to create momentum.

The defender rocks back and onto his buttocks as he quickly turns into the attacker (in this photo, to the defender's right) as shown. The defender uses his head to assist driving upward and into the attacker's left leg.

This view shows how the defender sits up and into his opponent. Look at how the defender keeps his arms grasped together firmly. The defender is sitting up and onto his right hip as he positions his feet and legs under him for stability.

The defender sits up and off of his right hip and buttocks and onto his knees as shown. Look at how the defender starts to roll his opponent onto the opponent's right shoulder.

The defender comes up and onto both knees for stability as he rolls his opponent onto the opponent's upper back and shoulders, "stacking" him. The defender drives down hard on the bottom grappler at this point, weakening the bottom grappler's position substantially.

This view shows how the defender (on top) stacks his opponent. As he does this, the defender pulls his right arm (that is still bent) from his opponent's grasp.

The defender pulls his right arm free, emphasizing pulling with his right elbow (similar to hitting someone behind him with his elbow). By doing this, the defender starts to extract his right arm free. Look at how the defender continues to stack his opponent.

The defender yanks his arm free from his opponent's trap and is now in a position to launch a counter-attack.

## STACK OPPONENT HIGH ON HIS UPPER BACK AND SHOULDERS

The defender should "stack" or position his opponent as high as possible on the back of the opponent's shoulders as possible as shown in this photo. By stacking the bottom grappler, the defender can better stabilize his position and extract his arm free from the bottom grappler's hold.

### ▮ TECHNICAL TIP ▮

**"Stacking" is an important skill in defending against Juji Gatame. The defender must try to "stack and pull" when possible in his effort to pull his arm free from his opponent. Stack your opponent high on the back of his shoulders and on the back of his head to weaken his position and then pull your arm free.**

## SIT UP ESCAPE AND COUNTER WITH JUJI GATAME

The defender does the sit up escape as previously shown.

The defender stacks his opponent as shown. Look at how the defender is on both knees.

The top grappler launches his counter-attacker after stacking his opponent and pulling his right arm free. The top grappler quickly gets off of his knees into a squatting position. The top grappler uses his left arm to hook and trap his opponent's right arm as the top grappler swings his left foot and leg over his opponent's head. The top grappler also uses his right hand to grab his opponent's right upper leg to control it immediately after he has pulled it free.

The top grappler does a shoulder sit on his opponent as the top grappler quickly initiates his own Juji Gatame as a counter-attack.

The top grappler uses his left arm to trap his opponent's right arm and rolls back to apply Juji Gatame.

The attacker rolls back and secures his Juji Gatame.

## GRAB LEG AND SIT UP ESCAPE

The attacker is trying to lever the defender's right arm, but the defender uses his right hand to grab the inside of his upper leg (just above his knee) as shown. As he does this, the defender uses his left hand to grab his right forearm or wrist, forming a keylock, to stabilize his grip. As he does this, the defender turns into his opponent slightly to steal back his right arm as much as possible.

The defender rocks up and onto his right hip and buttocks as shown.

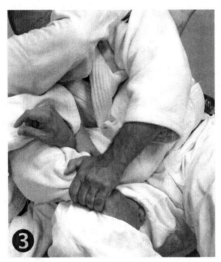

This view shows how the defender uses his right hand to grab his right inner thigh above his knee and how he uses his left hand to grab his right wrist for stability. This prevents the attacker from prying the defender's arms apart.

The defender continues to rock forward up onto his right hip. Look at how this action rolls the attacker over onto his right shoulder and side.

The defender comes up onto his knees or feet and is better able to extract his arm from his opponent's trap.

## SIT UP AND PUSH LEG ESCAPE

The defender rolls his opponent onto his right side and stacks him as shown. The defender makes sure to turn his head so that he looks toward his opponent's hip. Doing this prevents the attacker from controlling him with his left leg.

### ▰▰▰▰ TECHNICAL TIP ▰▰▰▰

**Look at how the defender turned his head so that his face is not on the inside of the attacker's knee. The defender turned his head so that he is looking down the leg and hip of his opponent. By doing this, the defender has better control of his head (where the head goes, so does the body) as well as being able to better see what is going on. The defender has taken control of his head away from his opponent who has been hooking it with his left leg. The defender can now better use his head as a "third arm" (as Rene Pommerelle called it) to help manipulate his opponent.**

As he stacks his opponent, the defender uses his left hand to push down (and away from the defender's body) on the attacker's left leg near the ankle. As he does this, the defender pulls his right arm (the trapped one) free.

## STACK AND STAND ESCAPE

The defender (on top) stacks his opponent high on the attacker's shoulders as shown. As he does this, the defender starts to stand. The defender has both arms bent and firmly grasped together in an initial defensive move.

The defender stands, and as he does, he uses both arms to pull his opponent up and off the mat high on the attacker's shoulders.

The attacker is committed to securing his Juji Gatame, so the defender must aggressively pull the attacker up and off the mat.

At the first opportunity, the defender yanks his left arm (that the attacker was trying to stretch) free from his opponent's grasp. This jerking action often causes the bottom grappler (the attacker) to fall back onto the mat.

The defender has extracted his arm and escaped the Juji Gatame.

## PICK UP DEFENSE AND ESCAPE

In the sport of judo, picking an opponent up off the mat as shown here stops the action. This is a good rule for the safety of the athletes as the bottom grappler is at risk of being slammed back (in a "pile drive") down hard on his head, neck or upper back. This also prevents injury to the standing athlete as the bottom grappler is still in a position to lock and possibly injure the top grappler's arm. Not all sports have this rule, and while aggressive groundfighting is desired, this old rule from judo is in the rulebook for the safety of the athletes. As a sambo referee, I saw an athlete almost have her neck broken when her opponent drove her back down to the mat. However, if you are not in a judo match, be fair warned that picking up an opponent will not stop the action. The bottom grappler can continue to arch his back and stretch his opponent's arm to secure his Juji Gatame from this position.

## BRIDGE AND TURN IN ESCAPE

This is a fundamental skill in your study of Juji Gatame. The defender is on his back with his opponent riding him in a leg press. The defender traps his arms together as his initial defense. The defender has both of his feet firmly planted on the mat with his knees bent as shown.

The defender arches up and bridges on the top of his head as shown. As he does this, he quickly turns into his opponent (in this photo, onto his right shoulder). The defender immediately starts to pull his right bent arm back, stealing his right arm back from this opponent.

The defender kicks his left foot over as he continues to roll onto his right shoulder as he steals his right arm back away from his opponent.

The defender kicks his left leg over so that the lands on his front in a kneeling position as shown. This is a good base for the defender to continue to pull his right arm away from his opponent. The defender can now launch his counter-attack.

## TECHNICAL TIP

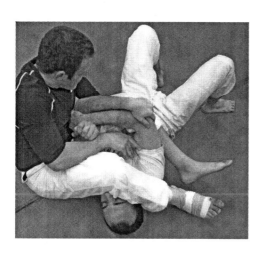

Here's a coaching tip that really pays off. As a coach, when teaching Juji Gatame, I make sure to teach beginners that when laying on their backs during practice, they always bend their knees and place their feet on the mat so that they are always in a position to drive off the mat and turn, shrimp or bridge. Doing this allows the bottom grappler more mobility. This photo shows how the bottom grappler should have his legs and feet: knees bent with the bottom of his feet on the mat. Do not get in the habit of lying on your back with your legs extended and feet not on the mat. This may seem like a small thing or not worthy of the effort, but it is worth the effort. No matter how good we are, all of us have been in this position and if we instinctively have our knees bent with the bottom of our feet on the mat, we can more quickly drive off our feet to bridge, shrimp, turn or escape.

## BRIDGE AND KICK OVER ESCAPE: AS IT HAPPENED IN A MATCH

The top grappler controls his opponent with the leg press. The bottom grappler has his feet firmly planted on the mat so that his heels are almost touching his buttocks. This will enable him to bridge more effectively.

The bottom grappler bridges up and off the mat as shown.

As he bridges, the defender quickly turns into his opponent and steals his left arm back. This action has forced the attacker onto his right side as shown. Look at how the defender is hand fighting with his opponent in an effort to pull his left arm free.

As the hand fighting continues, the defender kicks his right leg up and over his opponent.

The defender continues to kick his right leg over and now swings his left leg over as well to wrench out of the leg press. This upside down position enables the defender to better pull his left arm free and escape.

## BRIDGE AND KICK OVER ESCAPE: THE BASIC APPROACH

The defender is on his back with his opponent controlling him in the leg press.

The defender bridges up off of his back as shown.

The defender kicks his left leg up over his opponent as the defender turns on his right shoulder into his opponent.

The defender kicks his left leg over so that he is now "upside down" with his opponent. All the while, the defender is pulling his right arm loose from his opponent's trap.

The defender pulls his right arm loose and escapes the Juji Gatame.

## TURN IN AND HEAD HOOK ESCAPE

The defender is on his back but has been able to shrimp into the attacker and is on his right side. The defender is grasping both hands together and is stealing his right arm back from his opponent. As he does this, the defender kicks or swings his left foot and leg over the attacker's head as shown.

The defender continues to turn into his opponent and onto his right side. As he does this, the defender uses his left foot and leg to hook over the attacker's head. The defender uses his left leg to hook onto the defender's head making it easier for the defender to pull his right arm free.

The defender slides his right foot and leg under his opponent's right side and shoulder and is able to hook his ankles together as shown. This forms an upside down position. The defender applies as much pressure as possible with his leg scissors on his opponent's head and shoulders enabling the defender to pull his right arm free and escape the Juji Gatame.

## ANKLE AND LEG LOCK ESCAPE

The bottom grappler uses his left hand to grab his opponent's right ankle or foot as shown.

The bottom grappler uses his left hand to push his opponent's right foot and leg toward the bottom grappler's crotch. As he does this, the bottom grappler starts to swing his left leg upward.

The bottom grappler quickly swings his left leg over his opponent's right ankle and lower leg (trapping the ankle inside the bottom man's left knee joint).

The bottom man drives his left leg down to the mat, trapping the top grappler's extended right ankle and leg.

## LEG TRIANGLE ANKLE LOCK ESCAPE

The bottom grappler uses his left hand to push his opponent's right leg down toward the bottom grappler's crotch area. As he does this, the bottom grappler swings his right leg up.

As he swings his right leg upward, the bottom grappler places his left leg over his opponent's right lower leg

and forms a triangle with his legs, trapping the top grappler's right leg.

The bottom grappler has a tight triangle hold with his legs on his opponent's right leg and arches his hips to apply pressure against the top grappler's extended right leg.

## TURN IN AND KICK OVER ESCAPE TO STRAIGHT LEGLOCK (FROM SIDE) COUNTER

The bottom grappler has slid his left hand under his opponent's right leg and grasped his hands together.

The bottom grappler quickly turns into his opponent and onto the bottom grappler's right side and hip. As he does this, the bottom grappler swings his left leg over his opponent's head as shown.

As he continues to roll to his right side, the attacker uses both of his arms to hook and trap his opponent's right leg to the attacker's chest as shown.

The attacker continues to roll to his right, hooking onto his opponent's right leg firmly.

The attacker swings his left knee in, tucking it as he does. This traps his opponent's right leg with both the attacker's arms and legs, firmly controlling it.

The attacker rolls onto his right side, firmly trapping his opponent's straight right leg and locking the knee.

The attacker arches his hips, applying pressure on his opponent's straight right knee and leg.

## TURN IN AND KICK OVER ESCAPE AND SEATED STRAIGHT LEGLOCK COUTNER

The bottom grappler quickly lets go of his grip and starts to slide his left hand (the hand farthest from the top grappler) under the top grappler's right leg (the leg closest to the belt line of the bottom grappler).

The bottom grappler re-grasps his hands together as shown with his left forearm trapping the top grappler's right lower leg.

The bottom grappler quickly turns to his right and into his opponent and swings his left leg over his opponent's head as shown.

The bottom grappler continues to turn to his right side as he starts to pull his right arm free of his opponent's arms.

The bottom grappler continues to roll to his right, hooking his left foot and leg over his opponent's head. As he does this, the bottom grappler uses his left hand to grab his opponent's left leg at about the knee to assist him in his turn. The bottom grappler also uses his right hand and arm to trap his opponent's right leg.

The bottom grappler continues to turn to his right as he swings his left leg over his opponent. The top grappler continues to use his right arm to hook his opponent's right leg.

The attacker turns and rolls over on top of his opponent and sits on his chest. The attacker is starting to trap his opponent's right leg firmly to the attacker's chest.

The attacker uses both hands to hook and trap his opponent's right leg tightly to his chest as the top grappler sits on his opponent's chest.

The attacker firmly traps his opponent's right leg to his chest. The attacker helps to control his opponent's right leg even more by squeezing his knees and legs together as the attacker rolls backward. **IMPORTANT:** As the attacker rolls back, he must stay as round as possible to ensure that he controls the rolling action and cinches his opponent's leg as firmly as possible to his chest.

As the attacker rolls onto his back, he squeezes his knees together (trapping his opponent's right leg more tightly). The attacker arches his hips as he rolls back, stretching his opponent's right leg and locking (or barring) his opponent's right knee.

## KICK OVER ESCAPE AND COUNTER WITH TOEHOLD

The top grappler controls the position with the leg press.

The bottom grappler uses his left hand to grab his opponent's right foot. The bottom grappler uses his right hand to grab his opponent's left leg under his knee to prevent the top man from levering his arm straight.

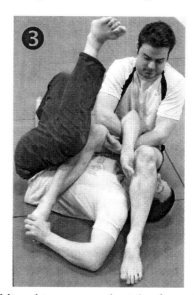

While holding his opponent's right foot, the bottom grappler starts to swing his left leg up and toward his opponent. As he does this, the bottom grappler turns into his opponent.

As he swings his left leg over and onto his opponent's right leg and hip, the bottom grappler pushes his opponent's right foot to the bottom man's left hip as shown. This often forces the top grappler to loosen his trap of the bottom man's right arm. As this happens, the bottom man pulls his right arm back toward him.

The bottom man quickly uses his hands to secure a toehold on his opponent's right foot.

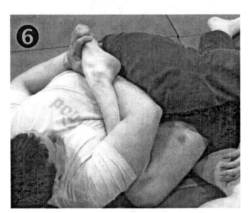

This shows how the toehold is formed. The bottom grappler applies pressure on the toehold and gets the tap out, not only escaping the Juji Gatame, but also countering it with a toehold.

### ▰▰▰ TECHNICAL TIP ▰▰▰

**Any time the bottom athlete's arms have been levered loose and his opponent has control of the arm, he's in trouble. By turning in or spinning out, rolling over a shoulder, the bottom grappler may escape from having his arm stretched and losing the fight. If you are caught on the bottom, keep trying to escape until you absolutely have to submit. Sometimes, the last-ditch attempt can save your arm.**

## SPIN OUT ESCAPE

This escape is used when the top grappler has levered the bottom grappler's arm straight and is rolling back to apply the Juji Gatame.

The top grappler has levered the bottom grappler's right arm loose.

The bottom grappler uses his left hand (the hand farthest from his opponent) to push the right leg downward toward the bottom man's left hip.

As he does this, the bottom grappler starts to spin toward his left shoulder (the shoulder farthest from his opponent).

The bottom grappler continues to spin to his left forcefully.

The bottom grappler spins to his left and onto his knees, escaping the Juji Gatame.

## SHUCK LEG AND TURN IN ESCAPE

If the bottom grappler is in real trouble and his opponent has levered his arm straight, this may be the last-ditch attempt at an escape from Juji Gatame. While it's not the ideal situation, this escape does work.

The top grappler controls his opponent with the leg press. The bottom grappler uses his left hand (the hand farthest from his opponent) to grab the top grappler's right foot (the foot closest to the bottom grappler's belt line).

As he uses his left hand to push up on the top grappler's right foot and leg, the bottom man starts to slide in the direction of his feet and slide his head from under his opponent's left leg.

The bottom grappler explosively turns into his opponent, driving off of his feet for extra power. As he does this, the bottom grappler pushes the top man's right leg up and off of the bottom grappler's torso as shown. As he does this, the bottom grappler turns in to his opponent and pulls his right arm away from his opponent.

The bottom grappler continues to turn into his opponent and uses his left arm to reach over his opponent's right leg to help turn his body into his opponent, loosening his opponent's hold on the bottom man's right arm. At this point, the defender gets to his knees and is at the right side of his opponent in a position to launch a counter-attack.

## PILLOW LEG AND TURN IN ESCAPE

The top grappler controls his opponent with the leg press.

The bottom grappler uses his left hand (the hand that is farthest from his opponent) to push the top grappler's left leg up and over his head.

The bottom grappler uses his left hand (the hand farthest from his opponent) to grab his opponent's left leg (the leg over the bottom grappler's head). The bottom grappler uses his hand to push or move his opponent's left leg over his head and as he does that, the bottom grappler drives his head up and over onto his opponent's left leg (in what looks like the bottom grappler is using his opponent's leg as a pillow).

The bottom grappler uses his head to push and drive off of his opponent's left leg.

The bottom grappler bridges and turns into his opponent as he continues to drive off of his head, which is placed on the top grappler's left leg.

The bottom grappler quickly turns into his opponent and comes up onto his knees as shown.

The defender has escaped and gets to a solid base on his knees. He is now able to pass his opponent's leg and launch his counter attack.

## REAR SOMERSAULT ESCAPE

While this is not an escape that has a high ratio of success, it may be the last ditch attempt in an effort to escape from Juji Gatame.

The top grappler controls his opponent with the leg press.

The bottom grappler drives off of his feet and whips his legs over in a somersault.

The bottom grappler continues to somersault over, and as he does, he rolls his opponent over as well.

The bottom grappler completes the somersault and pulls his arm free.

## DEFENDER DOES A LEG SHUCK TO ESCAPE FROM OPPONENT'S LEG HOOK

If the attacker hooks his leg over the defender's head to control it, the defender must get his head free.

The attacker is using the hip roll Juji Gatame in an attempt to roll the defender over and onto his back. The defender immediately tucks his head in and down as he uses his left hand to grab the attacker's left ankle or lower leg (the leg hooking the defender's head).

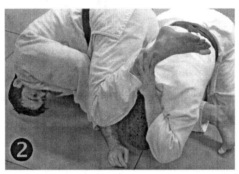

As the defender continues to tuck in his head, he also starts to move backward. The defender uses his left hand to continue to push the attacker's left leg from around his head as shown.

The attacker continues to back out of the situation and attempt to get to a more stable base as he pulls his right arm free from his opponent's trap. This may not be the best position for the defender, but at least he has freed his head from his opponent's leg hook.

A key rule in defending and escaping from Juji Gatame is for the defender to (first and foremost) protect his or her arm that is being attacked! After the defender is as sure as possible that his arm is safe, he must incrementally and methodically turn into his opponent so that the defender can steal or pull his arm back and away from his opponent's control. After that, the defender can work to improve his position so that he is more stable and can further escape the position and work to improve his own position.

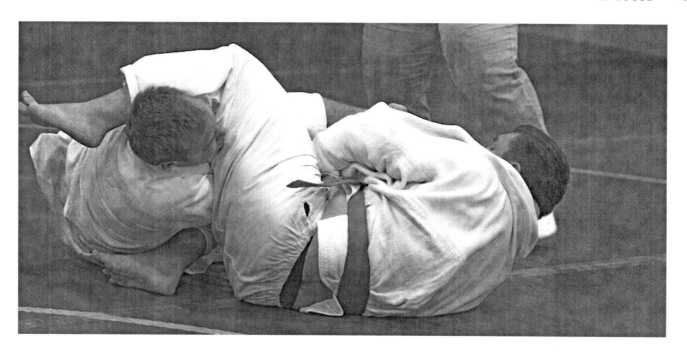

## EPILOGUE

"YOU FIGHT THE
WAY YOU TRAIN. IF
YOU DON'T TRAIN
HARD, YOU WON'T
FIGHT HARD
EITHER."
JOHN SAYLOR

## SOME FINAL THOUGHTS ON THE JUJI GATAME ENCYCLOPEDIA

The word "encyclopedia" refers, among other things to "a general course of instruction" and "a kind of dictionary of things, not words." It's adjective "encyclopedic" conveys "comprehensive," "inclusive" and "wide-ranging."

This is what I've tried to provide in this book and while this encyclopedia isn't the final word on the subject of Juji Gatame, it nonetheless serves its purpose as the first comprehensive book of great length published to focus directly on this unique armlock. And, as just mentioned, what has been presented on these pages isn't the final word on the subject of Juji Gatame. This book isn't complete. It's up to you to add more to it. Not every entry, set-up, breakdown or application for Juji Gatame could possibly be shown in this book. No single book, or author, is capable of doing that and no claims have been made to that effect.

This book's purpose has been threefold: 1) Present Juji Gatame in a logical and systematic way so that everyone will be better able to teach, and learn, this armlock. Up to this point, there have been few attempts at examining the fundamental skills that make up the various parts of Juji Gatame or analyzing the primary applications of this armlock. Further, there has not been a large-scale attempt at systematically teaching Juji Gatame from its basic skills to its more complex applications and variations. It is hoped that this book provides a framework for the systematic teaching and study of Juji Gatame. 2) Present Juji Gatame from a functional perspective, showing the many practical and effective variations that can be used in a variety of real-world situations. As shown on these pages, Juji Gatame is versatile, adaptable and can be used in a wide variety of positions and situations. 3) Present Juji Gatame without an agenda and in an unbiased way. When writing this book, it was my intention to provide a balanced and open-ended approach so that athletes, coaches and enthusiasts of all forms of sport combat or martial arts could find something useful. Good skill is good skill, no matter who does it or in what sport, activity or context it is used. A technique such as Juji Gatame is one of those versatile, adaptable and multi-faceted skills that is appealing to anyone who wants a winning edge over his or her opposition. In that sense, this book is not confined to one martial art or combat sport. Athletes, fighters, grapplers and martial arts enthusiasts, irrespective of each individual's area of expertise or interest, use Juji Gatame. In other words, Juji Gatame works, no matter who does it or where it's done.

Finally, as a coach and author, if you learned something from this book and are successful, then I am successful and that pleases me. It is my hope that you can refer to this book for many years to come as a reliable source of information and inspiration.

Steve Scott
Kansas City, Missouri

# REFERENCES

ALL ABOUT JUDO
By Geof Gleeson
EP Publishing, Ltd.

ARMLOCKS by Neil Adams
Published by Ippon Books, Ltd.

CONDITIONING FOR COMBAT SPORTS
By John Saylor and Steve Scott
Published by Turtle Press

GROUNDFIGHTING PINS AND BREAKDOWNS
By Steve Scott
Published by Turtle Press

JUDO GROUNDPLAY TO WIN
By P.M. Barnett
Published by U.S. Judo Association

MODERN BUJUTSU AND BUDO
By Donn Draeger
Published by Weatherhill, Inc.

NEWAZA OF JUDO
By Sumiyuki Kotani, Yoshimi Osawa and Yuichi Hirose
Published by Koyano Bussan Kaisha, Ltd.

RUSSIAN JUDO
By Alexander Iatskevich
Published by Ippon Books, Ld.

TAP OUT TEXTBOOK
By Steve Scott
Published by Turtle Press

WINNING ON THE MAT
By Steve Scott
Published by Turtle Press

# ABOUT THE AUTHOR

This is the thirteenth published book written by Steve Scott on the subject of combat sports and the tenth that Turtle Press has published.

Steve Scott holds advanced black belt rank in both Kodokan Judo and Shingitai Jujitsu and is a member of the U.S. Sombo Association's Hall of Fame. He first stepped onto a mat in 1965 as a 12-year-old boy and has been training, competing and coaching since that time. He is the head coach and founder of the Welcome Mat Judo, Jujitsu and Sambo Club in Kansas City, Missouri. Welcome Mat athletes have represented the United States in the Olympic Games, Pan American Games, World Judo Championships, World Sambo Championships, World University Games, International High School Judo Championships, Pan American Annual Championships in both judo and sambo, WOMAA World Martial Arts Games, the Pacific Rim Judo Championships, U.S. Open International Judo Championships and international events in over 30 different countries. Steve has personally coached 4 World Sambo Champions, a member of the 1996 Olympic Judo Team and over 350 athletes who have won national and international championships in judo, sambo, submission grappling, sport jujitsu and amateur MMA.

Steve also served as a national coach for United States Judo, Inc., the national governing body for the sport of judo as well as the U.S. Sombo Association and the Amateur Athletic Union in the sport of sambo. He also served as the coach education program director for many years with United States Judo, Inc.

Steve served as the national team coach and director of development for the under-21 national judo team and coached U.S. teams at several World Championships in both judo and sambo. He was the U.S. women's team head coach for the 1983 Pan American Games in Caracas, Venezuela where his team won 4 golds and 6 silvers and the team championship. He also coached numerous U.S. teams at many international judo and sambo events. Steve conducted numerous national training camps in judo at the U.S. Olympic Training Centers in Colorado Springs, Colorado, Marquette, Michigan and Lakes Placid, New York.

As an athlete, he competed in judo and sambo, winning 2 gold medals and a bronze medal in the National AAU Sambo Championships, as well as several other medals in smaller national sambo events and has won numerous state and regional medals in that sport. He was a state and regional champion in judo and competed in numerous national championships as well. He has trained, competed and coached in North America, South America, Europe and Japan and has had the opportunity to train with some of the top judo, jujitsu and sambo athletes and coaches in the world.

In 1994, Steve was one of the people responsible for the Amateur Athletic Union of the United States again recognizing judo as an AAU sport and re-established the National AAU Judo Championships in 1995. In 2008, Steve was the innovator of freestyle judo and with the help of John Saylor, Becky Scott, Ken Brink and Norm Miller, developed the rules for the sport of freestyle judo. Steve served as National AAU Judo Chairman from 1994-1998 and currently serves as National AAU Judo Vice-Chairman. He is a national AAU judo referee and accredited coach.

Steve is active in the Shingitai Jujitsu Association with his friend John Saylor (www.JohnSaylor-SJA.com) and has a strong Shingitai program at his Welcome Mat Judo, Jujitsu and Sambo Club. He has authored numerous other books published by Turtle Press. Steve is also active in training law enforcement professionals with Law Enforcement and Security Trainers, Inc. and is a member of ILEETA (International Law Enforcement Educators and Trainers Association).

Steve is a graduate of the University of Missouri-Kansas City and teaches jujitsu, judo and sambo full-time as well as CPR and First-aid. For over thirty years, he worked as a community center director and coached judo, jujitsu and sambo in various community centers in the Kansas City area. He has conducted over 300 clinics and seminars across the United States and can be reached by e-mailing him at stevescottjudo@yahoo.com or going to www.WelcomeMatJudoClub.com or www.FreestyleJudo.org. For many years, he was active as an athlete in the sport of Scottish Highland Games and was a national master's champion in that sport. He is married to Becky Scott, the first American woman to win a World Sambo Championship. Naturally, they met at a judo tournament in 1973 and have been together ever since.

Steve's first coach, Jerry Swett, told him as a teenager that he had a God-given gift for teaching and this impelled Steve to become a coach, and eventually, an author. Steve's second coach, Ken Regennitter, helped him start his judo club and loaned him the mat first mat ever used at the Welcome Mat Judo, Jujitsu and Sambo Club. Steve owes much to these kind men. His life's work and most satisfying accomplishment has been his effort as a coach to be a positive influence in the lives of many people.

CPSIA information can be obtained at www.ICGtesting.com
Printed in the USA
LVOW09*1115301113

363319LV00009B/362/P